# Teaching Yourself Social Theory

# Teaching Yourself Social Theory

David Harris

SAGE Publications
London • Thousand Oaks • New Delhi

SAGE Publications Ltd
6 Bonhill Street
London EC2A 4PU

SAGE Publications Inc
2455 Teller Road
Thousand Oaks, California 91320

SAGE Publications India Pvt Ltd
32, M-Block Market
Greater Kailash – I
New Delhi 110 048

**British Library Cataloguing in Publication data**

A catalogue record for this book is
available from the British Library

ISBN 0 7619 7687 9
ISBN 0 7619 7688 7 (pbk)

**Library of Congress Control Number: 2002108289**

Typeset by M Rules
Printed and bound in Great Britain by Athenaeum Press, Gateshead

For Maggie and Andy

# Contents

# List of Figures

# Acknowledgements

I would like to acknowledge the efforts of family and friends and the 'support staff'of the College of St Mark and St John (especially the librarians). Special thanks are due to Jan for keeping me going during some quite difficult times. Hilkka John has also been a thoughtful friend.

Thanks to Chris Rojek and Kay Bridger at Sage for their patience, advice and encouragement and for keeping faith with me when this book was much delayed. The production staff at Sage, including the excellent copyeditor, Justin Dyer, also deserves special thanks.

I was much encouraged in the early phases by some generous feedback from Prof. Anthony Synnott of Concordia.

I am very grateful to those colleagues at the College who supported me, and still unapologetic towards those who did not.

# Introduction

This Introduction outlines a rationale for writing this book, but it is not primarily addressed to student readers directly, unlike everything else that follows. I wanted to describe my intentions in more abstract terms, relating as much to colleagues as to student readers. I suggest that students might find it more profitable to proceed to Chapter 1 and return here afterwards if they are interested.

I hope colleagues will consider this rationale as a partial explanation at least for some of the things that they might find controversial in the body of the text. There are the usual sins of omission and commission, but I have tried particularly to avoid an excessively 'academic' style, for example, and this involves a clear risk: colleagues might come to think of my approach as simply an inferior version of a 'correct' or 'acceptable' style, whereas I have tried deliberately to develop it as an alternative. I do not want to seem too defensive about this, but it is worth stating my case, even if only to provoke debate.

I have tried to write a book that will introduce students to aspects of social theory in a different way. I have drawn on my experience in teaching to do this, but I have also kept in mind findings of some of the well-known work on student learning styles that has been so influential in recent discussions about course design (see, for example, Entwistle and Ramsden 1983, or Morgan 1993). It is unusual to use this work as a strategy to guide the writing of a book, rather than teaching as such, but I am interested to see if it brings positive outcomes, despite the risks.

I have some reservations about this work, which we will come to below, but many people know the main findings, which are that there are three basic learning styles widely found among students in the UK and elsewhere: the 'deep', 'surface' and 'strategic' approaches. There are several more recent alternative classifications and some subtypes, but the basic divisions will serve us for now. The research projects involved go on to suggest that the 'deep' approach pays off in terms of delivering a greater understanding of academic subjects. This is revealed in terms of gaining both good grades and a sense of involvement and pleasure. Those pursuing 'surface' approaches often spend a great deal of time engaged in unrewarding 'reproducing behaviour' – and still get poorer grades.

Some implications arise immediately. To be brief, it might be argued that it is essential to try to get my readers to adopt a 'deep' approach, not only because this approach seems to pay dividends, but also because social theory seems impossible to understand unless one can take an approach that looks beneath the surface of social life. It might be possible to 'reproduce' texts of social theory in assignments, but not to be able to 'locate oneself' in them, or use social theory to ask 'syllabus-independent' questions about the social world. I find many of my students attempting to manage social theory in this frustrating and infantilising manner, trying desperately to 'please teacher' by memorising favoured phrases or stock arguments, attempting to assemble little nuggets of facts and information, quotes and paraphrases which can be scrambled together with very little understanding. I have read too many essays over the years that can offer a seemingly sophisticated account of the intellectual origins of Durkheim's sociology, mentioning Fustel de Coulanges and Comte as if they were old friends, for example, yet which seem unable to distinguish between mechanical and organic solidarity.

I have even met colleagues drafted into teaching social theory courses, sometimes unwillingly it seems, who adopt the same approach, and for them it must be very discouraging indeed to experience teaching material in which they have never felt secure to students who react with open indifference and sometimes even hostility.

I am not condemning such students or colleagues. I am also aware that there are strong pressures, emanating from the system of higher education itself very often, which encourage a particular kind of 'surface' or 'strategic' approach in students (and in lecturing staff). I call this an 'instrumental' approach, drawing upon some slightly different and more sociological work on how students cope with academic life (such as Becker et al. 1995), and believe it can be clearly linked to more general work on the rationalisation or 'intensification' of work, or on cultural alienation.

It is tempting to ignore this uncomfortable area altogether, and to address only the ideal student (very often, an idealised juvenile version of oneself). Writing a book can offer this sort of sanctuary, in my view, where one is free to address readers in a spirit of detachment, and without the need to impose on them university regulations and assessment schemes (incidentally, I think that teaching on the Web offers even more potential for pleasures of this kind – see Harris 2002).

However, I want to be both more realistic and more ambitious, and to attempt to engage the instrumental student as well. I try to do this here by attempting to deliver summaries of well-known works, to organise arguments which are accessible, and to offer some asides and comments, all of which might 'add value' to a student attempting to assemble materials for an assignment.

This involves more than just attempting to use 'plain English', of course. We know the problems with such attempts from Derrida (see Kamuf 1991: xii) – 'Standard notions of clarity . . . must be seen as, themselves, obscurantist since they encourage a belief in the transparency of words to thoughts, and thus a "knowledge" constructed on this illusion') or from Bourdieu (1993: 21) – 'In order to break with the social philosophy that runs through everyday words and also in order to express things that ordinary language cannot express . . . the sociologist has to resort to invented words which are thereby protected . . . from the naïve projection of common sense'.

I want to show how an instrumental student might be able to develop a 'deeper' approach, involving a transition to specialist terms and concepts, if only for 'strategic' reasons at first. In teaching, an initial appeal to such a student might involve pointing out that a deeper approach does genuinely deliver better grades. In this sense the descriptions of the 'deep' student can be reread not as a description of an abstract 'learning style' but rather as a (rare) attempt to clarify the 'high aesthetic' of academic life, to borrow an argument from Bourdieu (1988).

The arguments about the pleasures that the deep approach also delivers might be left for a more gradual kind of revelation – involving me in what might be called a 'seduction strategy', although I am worried about the manipulative undertones in this term. I think these pleasures are genuine and important ones, and that the satisfaction of feeling relatively secure and 'at home' in social theory is a major benefit. I still think of it as a right, to which all students are entitled, regardless of the relatively humble nature of the institutions in which they might find themselves. However, it is also a matter of acquired taste, to be developed in conditions of 'optimal challenge' – too much challenge and 'hostility mixed with panic' (Bourdieu 1986) can result from the encounter; too little and one settles for a complacent and conservative cultural relativism that tamely agrees that social theory is only for an elite.

To turn to specifics, I try to 'deepen' students' approaches by drawing initially on the work of Ramsden and the others as an operational guide for action, an heuristic. Thus if the 'deep' approach involves an ability to connect current material with material that has been studied in the past, I attempt to encourage this both explicitly, with my own examples, and by trying to resist any suggestion that one can close off discussions, or put them into convenient categories. Again, if the 'deep' approach involves an ability to grasp the principles rather than to try to learn a lot of facts, it becomes important to write that way, to avoid excessive description (and excessive theoretical asides) and to try to focus on underlying issues and debates.

These two strategies can be brought together by a deliberate attempt to connect theoretical debates with much more mundane everyday and common-sense issues and concerns. It is not always easy to wean oneself away from the more familiar 'academic' context in which one operates, however. This often prioritises a rather esoteric 'scholastic' relevance to what one is discussing. There is more than ineffective teaching, boredom or irrelevance at stake, as Bourdieu (2000: 25) points out:

> . . . academic aristocratism draws [a line] between the thinker and the 'common man'. . . . This aristocratism owes its success to the fact that it offers to the inhabitants of scholastic universes a perfect 'theodicy of their privilege', an absolute justification of that form of forgetting of history, the forgetting of the social conditions of possibility of scholastic reason.

In summarising Bourdieu at an academic conference, for example, I have discussed with colleagues the connections between his work and that of Merleau-Ponty or Ricoeur in a fully 'scholastic' manner. Such discussions probably would be entirely redundant and exclusionary if addressing first-year students, however. They would probably not know yet who Ricoeur was, let alone be interested right away in any connection between his work and Bourdieu's. They would have enough difficulty in grasping the significance of Bourdieu, without having to locate him in a welter of other names and theories. We should not keep from them the need to develop this scholarly understanding eventually, but it seems wise to acknowledge their more mundane or even 'practical' interests initially. Students too, like the 'common man' in the quote above, simply can be fully 'absorbed by the trivial concerns of everyday existence' (Bourdieu 2002: 25).

In much of what follows in this book, I attempt to put my intended student audience very much in the foreground, for example by starting with the issues that are discussed in the press and on TV, and then trying to move fairly gently into more specialist theoretical arguments. The outstanding examples of such a technique are found in cultural studies, perhaps, as in the work stimulated by Ritzer (1993) and his discussion of 'McDonaldization'; as many colleagues agree, this work is an excellent and accessible route into more technical discussions of Weber, and rival accounts of modernity and postmodernism.

A special focus for this book is based on the observation that what does unite us all is that we are engaged in higher education. In referring to this context, risks are run once more, and one has to balance carefully the need to retain a 'professional' relationship with the perfectly valid interest in theorising even about intellectuals and their organisations.

I have always found it important to try to understand the cultural context of learning for current students as well. This is one of my objections to the focus on 'approaches' to study as discrete psychological matters. I have explored these reservations elsewhere (Harris 1993), but the main point is to suggest that there are strong value commitments and hints of social distancing in the discussion of 'deep' and 'surface' approaches as well. Thus the usual lists of characteristics contain an unmistakable moral objection to surface approaches, in my view, seen best, perhaps, in the remark that a surface approach views completion of the task 'as an external imposition' (Morgan 1993: 73). I think this remark requires us to investigate this attitude – why might this be so for so many students, and, equally, why might so many academics feel resentful, superior or insecure by discovering such a stance?

An answer might be found initially in reminding ourselves of some sociological banalities about the social role of the academy in necessarily disciplining students, or 'reproducing the social relations of' capital or patriarchy (according to choice). Assessment is at the sharp end of the tension between the desire to 'pursue arguments for their own sake', and these social functions, which are usually seen as far less honourable, although they are held by powerful stakeholders. We know from Bourdieu's work that these tensions are likely to be classically misrecognised, of course, as a clash between those possessing different degrees of some neutral 'expertise' – hence the unusual disdain for instrumental students as dangerous 'outsiders', who somehow challenge the whole ethos of university life.

However, more practical implications also arise. There are no clear guidelines in Bourdieu, alas, to suggest ways in which possessors of different 'aesthetics' might be able to communicate effectively with each other, although we have some idea of how the powerplay between them manifests itself in 'structures of judgement'. But there are some suggestions from a much earlier tradition in the sociology of education on how to manage an 'intercultural' classroom, where pedagogues attempt to build bridges between the cultures of their pupils and the academic culture which they represent. Pioneering work by Barnes et al. (1971) was supplemented here by more recent interest in 'critical pedagogies' of various kinds (see, for example, Giroux 1992). Many of the applications of this work have been developed in the context of dealing with students from different ethnic minorities, but my interest is in dealing with students with a range of different cultural habituses, possessing different amounts and mixes of cultural capital.

Some basic principles seem apparent at least. For one thing, it does not hurt to express a certain level of respect for and sympathy with the cultural values of such students, to engage in a little 'phatic' communication which 'maintains the contact between narrator and addressee' (Barthes 1977: 95) in order to build bridges for later, more challenging discussions, or to listen to and engage in common-sense argument before sliding into more technical forms. This sort of thing can be manipulative, and it can also go badly wrong, as when middle-aged teachers or writers head unerringly towards misusing the street jargon of a decade ago. What stifles initial communication altogether, though, is a perception of disapproval and hostility, or a thinly suppressed intention to disqualify, as student after student has reported, for example: 'The only time I can remember receiving a positive response to a piece of writing was on an occasion when I used the . . . book provided and strung together . . . [elements of a piece of work] . . . in a language I did not speak' (Plummer 2000: 166).

However, another form of phatic communication can sometimes be attempted with less immediate risk – an ability to see the cultural flaws and sometimes the symbolic violence in academic discourse 'from the inside'. It is important to encourage critical engagement with one's work by being open and critical about it oneself. Obviously, one welcomes sophisticated academic criticism, but I find that it is important to permit less sophisticated kinds too: sometimes these need to be structured, much as when a 'straight man' 'feeds' a comic. The occasional attempt to distance oneself as an academic from perceived orthodoxies can be helpful, which is the reverse of the more common tendency to pose as a perfect and natural representative of that orthodoxy. Any reader of Goffman will also recognise the manipulative and self-aggrandising elements in such 'role distance'. All of these techniques seem much easier to

practise in face-to-face communication, where one's performance can be moni-
tored and adjusted fairly rapidly, but, despite the risks, I have decided to attempt
some of them in this book as well.

This is not only a 'seductive' device for me, but also an expression of my own
sometimes deeply ambivalent and 'open' feelings about academic culture. I do
not see how we can expect students simply to attempt to adopt academic culture
as a way of life: as Bourdieu indicates, it is possible to do that only if one is finan-
cially and culturally secure in that milieu, and probably has been so from birth.
Few modern students would be willing to undertake the painful and life-long
labour of the self-surveilling autodidact devoted to the pursuit of academic
interests, which is Bourdieu's main alternative.

The reality for many students is that they must 'normalise' academic life,
and manage it alongside many other competing demands for their allegiance
and their time (see Hebdige's essay on the reactions of his students as he struggled to wean them off *The Face* and on to more 'academic' journals, in Hebdige
1988). It is partly that the predictions of some postmodernist thinkers (like
Lyotard 1984) are correct in suggesting that university discourses and their
claims to privilege and to emancipatory potential are very much in doubt.
Universities have also done much to dispel their own mystique by appearing so
frequently to the newcomer (and to their parents) as thoroughly modern profit-
seeking corporations. Scepticism can be lived out on a daily basis as students
manage families and working lives alongside the rather limited and sometimes
far more hostile and manipulative social relations on offer in the academy. I am
aware that making these points may induce an intention to disqualify me in any
colleagues who happen to read my work, but again, all genuine communication
carries risk.

There is a more direct sense in which the cultural preferences of possible
readers have also been borne in mind. I have developed some web-based materials, which offer a complementary level of analysis to that attempted in this
book. I have noticed that students often seem happier to browse websites than
to read books (it is usually the opposite for colleagues, however); approval or
disapproval of this practice seems irrelevant if you want to communicate with
modern students. There are also definite advantages offered by web-based materials in that a writer can offer 'levels' of hypertext to 'individualise' teaching,
attempting to solve the problem of different levels of difficulty, or different
motives for learning. There are drawbacks too, including a danger of adding to
the relativism and 'normalisation' I mentioned above: it is rare for students to
stay on task exclusively as they browse and surf, and confine their attentions
solely to 'serious' academic sites.

To take one obvious problem, there is so much material available on the Web
as it is. If you merely enter key terms or names into a search engine you will
encounter dozens of websites. I have done this recently with terms like 'ethnomethodology' and names like Elias, Becker and Bourdieu, and discovered
some rich materials. But you need to know what you are seeking; you need

some underlying principles to guide you to material that will be useful. It is this that separates out mere browsing from purposeful learning.

I have tried to provide the reader of this book with a list of 'reading guides' on my personal website (www.arasite.org/). These offer summaries of some of the key readings I have suggested in the book. Readers can gain a preliminary understanding of the principles of the arguments by reading the book, and then choose to pursue these arguments in more depth by locating the appropriate 'reading guide'. I hope that they will do so, if only from an initially instrumental interest in writing better assignments.

'Reading guides' also focus on underlying principles, with a minimum of scholastic detail. I have attempted an accurate if occasionally theoretically naïve summary and restricted my own comments to a minimum as well. These 'guides' are meant to be an additional step into academic culture, for the non-traditional and non-scholastic student, standing between textbooks and lecture notes and the original works themselves, and demonstrating ways in which one might indeed take notes from famous books and cope with some of the more challenging formulations and arguments. Some of the 'guides' contain hyperlinks to additional web-based material, either found on my own site, or on the sites of others. Students can follow these conveniently, and thus build up a set of electronic resources and files of their own. The important goal of 'syllabus independence', another key characteristic of the 'deep' approach, becomes achievable if students can be encouraged to search electronic materials autonomously: my initial guidance is meant to be extensively modified or abandoned as confidence grows. For the complete beginner especially, I think my easy-to-use and low-technology reading guides are a good way to establish confidence.

Finally, I want to encourage students to interact with the materials, both those in this book and those on my website. As usual, basic and simple forms of interaction are to be encouraged first, and it might be necessary for the more confident to skip those. I have not included extensive 'in text questions' or other familiar self-assessment items in this book, despite their recent popularity in conventional teaching (they have been around in distance education since 1970 at least). For one thing, there is evidence that they do not sufficiently engage readers, and many students simply ignore them altogether (Henderson and Nathenson 1984). There is a danger that they will be seen as heavy-handed, patronising or dominating. More technically, much will depend on the sort of reflexivity they are designed to encourage – reflexivity on the task as defined (or imposed) by the writer, or a 'deeper' reflexivity designed to broaden horizons, engage readers in reflection about their learning and its characteristic 'blocks' (engaging in 'metacognition' is a popular way to think of this). Then there is the whole issue of emancipatory reflexivity, so to speak, of the kind that invites students to 'look behind' the whole process of education, asking questions about the social context or role of assessment and the university, for example; the classic question here is one I raise below about how university education comes to

be provided in that form. I also offer further thoughts in the two online introductory essays on my website (Harris 2002).

Generally, mine is a more 'cultural' strategy, as I have indicated. The idea is to
provoke thought primarily in and by the text itself, so to speak, not only in
terms of its content but also through the openness of its form. More strategically,
I have devised an online tutorial on my website which begins with simple
forms of electronic interaction with files – altering fonts, backgrounds or margins, for example, going on to suggest more extensive forms of cutting, pasting
and inserting paragraphs (including paragraphs written by the user), and
ending with the suggestion that materials be structured in order to identify
'deep' principles and more 'surface' elements such as introductions, examples,
illustrations, and so on. In this way, I hope to move students from an initial
interest in developing more sophisticated forms of plagiarism to practical techniques for the critical reading of texts. If all goes well, they will be teaching
themselves social theory.

## Social theory and the university context

Waters' excellent book (Waters 1994) begins by warning the would-be student
that social theory characteristically takes quite a different unusual stance
towards the social world. Social theory is unusually abstract, 'technical and
arcane', general, systematic and formal, Waters reminds us, and there will be a
problem for anyone approaching this topic from the usual engaged, involved,
unsystematic stances of 'common-sense'. Theoretical statements 'must be independent. They must not be reducible to the explanations participants themselves
offer for their own behaviour' (Waters 1994: 3).

This is really quite a good description of the current state of play with social
theory courses, and it accurately describes the most fundamental problem in
learning to study them, which might be indicated by asking how social theory
courses got that way. Young (1971) once asked how the sort of education which
many people fail at came to be provided in the first place, and we might begin
with this as a suitable provocation too.

I should say that this is far too ambitious a question for me to answer seriously in this book, but I hope it is clear at least that a suitable answer would have
to involve a history of the university, as well as a history of social theory. There
happen to be some interesting specific histories which show how the development of the university, its faculty structure and the precise shape of the academic
subjects that emerge are interwoven: (see for example, Bourdieu 1988; Collins
1994; and Gouldner 1979).

My task in this book is far more modest. I hope to show how an analysis of
the institutional dimension is required in order to understand particular developments in apparently abstract theoretical arguments. I outline some of the
general examples in the next chapter, but the importance of the university

context arises quite frequently during discussions in other chapters as well. To take some quick examples, it seems clear to me that particular 'perspectives', notoriously those of British A-Level Sociology, only make sense by considering how professional academics actually go about their work. We know, for example, that they have to synthesise various approaches, and distinguish them from rivals, in order to organise and pursue coherent 'research programmes' (this is the term originally introduced by Lakatos (1979) to explain some characteristics of theory development in natural sciences).

I think traces of these rather interesting but also arbitrary attempts to group things together into some coherent programme can be detected in the emergence of 'action sociology' in Britain in the 1970s, which joined together work that originally belonged to very different traditions – American interactionism and Weberian sociology, for example. Something similar happened in radical sociologies of youth culture, media studies and education in the 1970s, where a looser cluster of different radical traditions was collected at first; it took some time, and an agreed turn towards Gramsci, to sort and systematise these traditions. Doubtless there are other examples too, but what happened in those cases is that a number of quite diverse and different theoretical elements were synthesised, weighed, evaluated and considered, and then eventually homogenised into a more coherent programme for much more 'practical' reasons than might appear to be the case. It need not have been like this at all. It must be quite puzzling to people coming recently to those traditions, and looking only for logical or theoretical reasons for their coherence.

I think that the requirements of designing and running high-quality university teaching also have definite effects on the ways in which theoretical elements are grouped together. Courses become 'teaching objects', in Bennett's (1980) very interesting account of the emergence of a famous and definitive Open University course in cultural studies. I explore this in more detail in Chapter 6, but what I want to argue here is that the institutional background of theoretical work is crucial. It provides us with an explanation of some of the twists and turns and emphases found in social theory.

To take another example, we shall encounter feminist criticism, like that launched by Fraser (1989; and see the online reading guide) against some prominent male theorists such as Foucault and Habermas, on the grounds that they have ignored gender politics in their development of critical social theory. It is easy to see this as a classic omission by remote and smugly secure university professionals who do not need to worry about the politics of gaining access to welfare or housing benefits. It is tempting to think of Gellner (1968; and see the online reading guide) teasing linguistic philosophers of the day by suggesting that their interest in the detailed unravelling of language games is a philosophy suitable for gentlemen ensconced in the cosy and protected environment of Oxford University. However, it might also be possible to see particular theoretical analyses as the results of very powerful political interests, albeit those of university professionals and not 'ordinary people'. University professionals have their struggles to win space for their own views, to attract resources to them, and to attempt to beat off rivals, including a rather specialist attempt to incorporate rival theories into more suitable conceptual schemes.

I think that another prominent development of social theory can also be traced to the university contexts in which theorising takes place and the peculiar politics that go on inside them. This is the tendency for theory to become more abstract and self-referential as it has proceeded. Ritzer (2001) has described this as the tendency to develop 'metatheory'. Feminists such as Humm (1992; and see the online reading guide) refer to a 'first' and 'second wave' feminism, which seems to sketch the same kind of trajectory. To simplify, feminism first concerned itself with the struggle to establish women's rights, but then subsequently found itself forced to engage in theoretical struggle against rival theories themselves.

Gellner (1968) has also offered us an account of how theory evolves like this. As thought develops, it begins with 'preoccupation with objective issues . . . its centre of gravity . . . still lies outside the universities'. When philosophy gets professionalised, more formal themes emerge at the expense of 'mere "content"'. Such philosophy can still be critical, undermining orthodoxies. The final stage in the 'emasculation of thought' requires a rejection of this whole tradition, in the name of an accommodation with the 'reality of the objective world' (Gellner 1968: 291). This accords nicely with 'what the more comfortable Dons had always been inclined to believe . . . that the world was much as it seemed to them' (Gellner 1968: 291). Teasing aside, and generalising away from just Oxford philosophy, I think this evolution is impossible to understand without looking for the role of specific university-employed intellectuals whose job becomes one of developing social theory in a particular professional and scholastic direction, inevitably losing connections with the everyday concerns of those outside the university as their specific agenda comes to dominate their deliberations.

It might be seen as if I am accusing my fellow academics of some moral flaw here, but this is not my interest. The kind of advanced division of labour that produces the modern university will almost certainly produce a separation in culture, segmentation between politically motivated theorists and theoretically motivated theorists (taking politics here to mean a very general interest in engaging with the world). The point really is to try to explain why social theory often appears in the form that Waters has described.

It might be worth explaining to students that it may not be their fault if they find social theory difficult to grasp. Probably it was not written for them in the first place, but either addressed to some quite different 'public' in the past, or constructed with rather specialist professional and intellectual constraints in mind in the present. I have discussed these points, and some implications arising from them, in the two introductory files on my website, and offered some suggestions for those students interested in investigating the specific history and context of academic social theory and their effects.

I have tried to pursue a definite pedagogic intent in this book. First of all, I have tried to focus on the sort of social theory that is still recognisably connected to the 'issues outside the university' that Gellner describes. Thinking of these issues, the bedrock of practical concerns with freedom, constraints, emancipation, struggles for recognition of minorities, and so on, does not entirely cede the ground to the more specialist intellectual theoreticians. It gives relative newcomers a chance to find a way into theory. To this end, I have chosen examples that can be useful for pedagogic purposes from a number of fields, including sociology, media studies and cultural studies, rather than keeping to the usual academic subject boundaries. I hope readers will see how arguments in one 'applied' area can be linked to arguments in another, perhaps via 'deeper' principles – if this happens, readers can experience teaching themselves social theory.

Secondly, I have organised my book into sections based on broad themes in social theory and then into short chapters around common writers or approaches. This cannot be comprehensive, of course. I have spread critical debates over two chapters, in many cases, so as to keep the length of each one down and to give the reader time for a pause. I have found students like to stop to consolidate their thoughts before being rushed on breathlessly to rival approaches or critiques. I have not always assumed it is necessary to 'balance' contributions immediately, and in the usual ways.

Thirdly, I have tried to avoid the usual kinds of university textbook summaries of theoretical issues, which proceed in a classically specialist, and sometimes rather scholastic, fashion. I admire these texts, such as Waters (1994), May (1996), Turner (1996) or Ritzer (1996) – the last-mentioned is the most accessible introduction of all, in my view — and I suggest that you read them together with this one. But I also think, in line with lots of other teachers, that you might need some other kind of access to works of social theory, again to give you the chance to impose some sort of agenda of your own.

Hence the book itself is one component of a double strategy to encourage 'syllabus independence', the other component being the online material, with its 'individualising' potentials that should be seen as a necessary component as well. No book can offer a self-sufficient and exhaustive coverage of social theory, of course; mine tries to lead outwards, to other books, to websites, to a whole network waiting to be explored. This network structure, with the opportunity for guided exploration, is a prerequisite, a necessary but not sufficient condition, for any strategy aimed at permitting students to teach themselves.

# PART I

# 1 Economic Constraints: Marxism and the Mode of Production

In this chapter, I am going to discuss some themes that will lead us into marxist modes of analysis. Marx's work is a real challenge right at the start. In social theory his work has produced a long tradition of analysis that until quite recently had been almost an orthodoxy. This only adds to the problems for students in 'the West', who are likely to think of marxism as a pretty unpleasant political creed associated with repressive regimes in 'the East' that have now been overthrown.

Winnowing out the academic concepts from this unfortunate public image is not easy, and when we first encounter some of the work it can look alien and odd. Incidentally, I am going to follow one of the rather mysterious scholarly conventions we mentioned earlier in referring to marxism, with a small 'm' throughout, even though my spellchecker does not like it. This is simply in order to acknowledge the work of other writers, as well as Marx himself, in the construction and development of a substantial body of work; it is a kind of political correctness, if you will, that reserves its position in the huge debate about the role of named individual authors in developing theory.

Teaching about marxism can be difficult since students often perceive the work of Marx and Engels as both 'difficult' and 'political'. If students encounter any marxists these days, they are likely to appear as rather quaintly old-fashioned, far too 'serious', too 'committed', and with a capacity to make listeners feel guilty about the inequalities in society while offering deceptively simplistic solutions. Other problems can arise when lecturers specifically seem to be committed to marxist work – marxist sociology can look and sound like moralising or 'preaching'.

These are problems that need to be acknowledged in any teaching. Marxism is not a neutral approach to social life. It has always been woven through with political commitments: 'Philosophers have always sought to understand the world. . . . The point, however, is to change it' (Marx 1968: 367). Marx's style is not always calm and dispassionate, he writes scathing critiques of his opponents (with apparently devastating effects on their self-esteem), and there is seldom doubt as to whose side he is on.

Further, the entanglement of analysis and politics is not seen as a problem in marxism; indeed it is a sign that we are on the right track. There is an explicit rejection of the rather convenient way in which other analysts have tried to separate the worlds of economics and politics (and the world of social life for that matter). Such separations lead to misunderstandings that have political consequences, where apparently abstract theory ends up justifying the way things are (one version of what Marx meant by 'ideology'). Seeing the connections between these areas is also one of the main reasons Marx thought that he had developed a full social theory, a 'science' with a broad scope and with considerable power to explain a range of events. As with other sciences, the ability actually to do something, to cause or at least to predict social change, was another key factor in knowing you were on the right lines. First, though, you had to criticise those 'ideological' understandings held by others.

Of course, we do not have to share personally those political or academic commitments in order to grasp what marxism wants to say about modern societies like ours. Part of the challenge of doing sociology is to try to grasp arguments that might seem quite alien to our personal beliefs and experiences, although we noted (in the online introductory essays on the website – Harris 2002) that this is a stance which is not always easily acquired.

In what follows, I am going to try to be an advocate for marxism (and for other approaches in subsequent chapters, of course). I should confess that I am going to try to play down the political commitments in favour of the more technical approaches to understanding social life. Marx himself would probably not have approved of this rather 'distanced' approach. As a pedagogic strategy it has risks as well as advantages – I might be able to play down some of the unfashionable politics only at the expense of playing up some of the other problems of technical difficulty.

## The economy as external reality

Let me begin the discussion by returning to the 'root metaphor' that features in this section – society as 'external reality'. This is an abiding theme in Marx's work and one of his most successful and relevant. In his day (1818–83), changes in the economic system were making a clear impact upon the whole of social life. There was the development of factories and mass production, the growth of towns and cities, the development of what might be called these days the 'infrastructure' – all the transport, trading, financial and banking systems needed by the new companies and enterprises – and the changes in the political system to manage the new requirements. Tremendous social changes ensued, in work, leisure, living patterns, family life, education, and health and welfare. The substantial growth of this new system, seemingly under its own steam(!), must have appeared as an external force to many of the people alive at that time, altering their lives dramatically and raising all sorts of problems about how to regulate or control it. This vision of industrial society operating apparently 'on its own', regardless of anyone's wishes, is common to Durkheim and to Weber too.

I am sure it is quite a common image of society today, probably more common than it was in my youth. When I first studied economics in the 1960s, there was a rather smug view that the economy was under full control, that we (or our governments) knew how to run the system to avoid booms and slumps, to maintain a steady growth of prosperity. The 'bad old days' of economic depression, grinding poverty, slums, homelessness and unemployment seemed far away, a nightmare our parents had once lived through.

We can all appreciate much more readily today that the economic system has not been domesticated so easily, of course, and that all those social ills are still around. Unemployment is probably not too unlikely a fate for many students, and poverty, indebtedness or homelessness seem still to disturb the sleep even of those in employment. Even the relatively well-off have seen recent substantial fluctuations in the value of their wages, houses, savings and investments, and have felt the cold winds of job insecurity once more.

Most of us have felt the anxiety and insecurity of having to depend in these matters on remote and abstract institutions like stock exchanges, governments (both our own and overseas), multinational corporations, obscure aspects of international finance and banking (exchange rates, common currencies). Our lives can be affected deeply by what can look like mere whims of powerful individual entrepreneurs like Rupert Murdoch or Bill Gates or by the schemes of once little-known multinationals like Enron. These strange bodies and individuals are remote from our experience most of the time, and they operate in ways in which we take little interest – but a decision taken elsewhere can undo all our careful efforts to save, take away our work, close down our local hospital, uproot the woodland we have known for decades or expose us to new risks of disease or injury.

Of course, it is worth stressing the nice surprises that the economic system delivers periodically too. There are the great technological breakthroughs from moon landings to microchips, medical advances, the enormously increased flow of consumer goods and services, and the real growth in incomes for the richer segments of the richer countries.

A number of commentators, including marxists, want to suggest that both the nice and nasty aspects of the system owe a lot to the existence of a key institution in our society – 'private property'. Marxists have done much to analyse the phenomenon of private property, to explain its importance and to insist upon its rather strange social nature. This is still an important analytic task – the institution is so widespread and common that we tend to think it quite natural to own things, to possess the power to dispose of them as we please. But it is not a natural institution at all, for marxists, but a rather recent one, historically speaking, and one which has involved real political struggle.

To clear the ground a little I should make it clear that by 'property' I do not mean the personal trinkets and possessions that we all cherish. These items are 'private property' too, and they do have an important role in helping us retain a sense of our own identities. For marxists at least, however, the more important

kind of private property centres on the ownership of productive assets – factories, land, machinery, industrial wealth – owned directly or indirectly as shares
in companies. It is a common practice in 'bourgeois' social science to confuse
things by giving them the same generalised name, Marx tells us on several occasions, and this kind of private property often gets lumped together with the
nicer, more agreeable kind mentioned above. In this way, personal private property helps dignify and legitimate the industrial kind of private property –
'private property' is 'natural'; it is a universal good; it is an essential aspect of
personal freedom; evil communists or terrorists want to take away even people's
personal possessions; and so on.

Ownership of this latter important kind of private property gives tremendous
potential for controlling key aspects of social life. Owners of industrial property
have legal rights to benefit from that ownership and to dispose of their property
if they cease to gain a benefit. The negative impact, on others who might not
own factories but who work in them, for example, is not a sufficient reason to
prevent the legal owner of an asset disposing of it, nor is any long-term adverse
impact on the environment. There is a legal framework to regulate the ownership and use of assets, but it is a very loose one on the whole, as recent scandals
about 'tax loopholes' in the UK reveal. To take more specific examples, it is possible to acquire assets with borrowed money, or to take control of an enterprise
if one owns merely a working majority of shares. A number of notorious individuals in Britain in the 1980s benefited considerably by taking advantage of
these favourable conditions to borrow enough money to acquire majority share-
holdings in famous British companies (at a time when the price of shares was
low) and then promptly to close them down and sell off the productive assets
(worth more than the value of the shares at the time). People who had worked
in those factories all their lives, customers who wanted to continue to buy the
goods, small shareholders who had invested their savings in the company, were
powerless to prevent this perfectly legal form of 'asset stripping'.

There have been many examples of this kind of procedure in the UK in recent
years. The *Guardian* newspaper (2 August 1996) reported how one entrepreneur
stood to make a personal profit of some £40 million by selling off a transport
company which he had bought as a result of the British government's policy of
privatising formerly state-owned assets. The political party elected to government at the time (by a minority of all voters in fact) was able to use its legal
ownership of state assets to sell them at a price they thought suitable, and then
the market promptly revalued those assets at a much higher figure, to the great
delight of the new owners. Some private individuals were able to borrow
enough money to set up a company to acquire some of the assets; the British
government helped them secure a substantial loan partly by guaranteeing a
high level of the company's income for the first eight years. During their short
period of ownership of the company (seven months), the directors simply sat on
their assets and waited for the market value to rise; certainly they showed little
interest in investing in the actual business of the company, the *Guardian*

reported. This kind of short-term approach, with companies being operated to provide maximum returns to current shareholders, even if this means little investment in the actual business, has been identified as a chronic problem for the British economy (Hutton 1995).

Revelations of misleading accounting practices offer another example. What seems to have happened in the companies affected is that senior managers engaged firms of consultants to advise them on maximising the figures showing company growth. One strategy involved estimating future returns on investment and including these estimates as actual revenue in any one year. The same firms, appearing in the guise of accountants this time, often audited company books and thus legitimated these rather controversial financial practices. Senior company management benefited directly from the increase in share values since they were major shareholders themselves, and they often received special bonuses linked to share prices. The scale of this sort of exercise is revealed in a report in the *Guardian* newspaper (9 July 2002): Enron paid out 'almost $750 million (£517 million) in bonuses in a year when net income was $975 million (£672 million)'. The eventual public disclosure of these practices and arrangements led to a loss of confidence, the financial near-collapse of global companies such as Enron and WorldCom, and one of the worst falls in the stockmarket in recent memory. Apart from these substantial real economic consequences, which had a personal effect since one of my own insurance policies matured during the crisis at a very low value, it is interesting that the scandal revealed that the apparently fixed, natural and objective categories used by auditors to calculate income, growth and other matters, and the apparently clear division of labour between consultants and accountants were open to strategic reinterpretation after all.

There are many international examples too, some of which reveal even more bizarre notions of ownership. In simple terms, some banking scandals have uncovered the strange world of foreign currency dealing, for example. Banks began by acquiring some foreign currency to help their industrial clients trade with foreign countries, but they soon realised that the rates of exchange of those currencies were likely to change from month to month – one month a single British pound would cost $1.56, and the next month $1.60, say. Clearly it made sense to buy in some sterling when it was cheap and keep it in stock. From here it is but a short step to more adventurous types of speculation – if you can buy sterling while it is cheap, you can supply your own customers and make lots of money selling any surplus stocks to others when the price of sterling rises again. If I have understood this correctly, what the banks then began to do was to buy foreign currency 'futures', where you reserve the right to buy certain amounts of money at some time in the future, gambling, in effect, on the price being higher when you actually come to own the currency and can sell it. If one deal loses money, there are deals stretching into the future that might pay off overall. Banks only get into difficulties when a series of gambles fail to pay off, and debts mount. Creditors can panic and demand payment immediately, instead of waiting for future deals to mature. We now know that very considerable sums of money – hundreds of millions of pounds – have been 'lost' in this way.

Here, we have left far behind the simple world of trading companies asking the banks to acquire currency for them – we are in an abstract world of a kind of 'second-level' ownership of the rights to buy, a world where 'credit-worthiness' and promises to pay in the future, and confidence that these promises will be kept, are equally crucial dimensions of ownership as is actual possession of the goods in the present.

One interesting aspect of the situation these days is that such forms of ownership have progressed beyond the terms and definitions of the legal frameworks which permitted them, and 'the market' now seems to be beyond current legal or political control. In 1992 currency speculators showed themselves able to manipulate exchange rates more effectively than the British government at the time, for example by forcing it to exhaust its reserves trying to maintain the price of the pound during a 'run'. Briefly, the government hoped to stabilise exchange rates by buying all the available sterling at the set rate, thus restoring confidence to holders of sterling. But market operators were able to lay their hands on so many cheap pounds and offer them for sale again that the government was forced to back down in the end (but only after handing over huge sums to the dealers). The government was forced into this position after having made a promise to maintain the pound at a rate determined by the Exchange Rate Mechanism (an agreement on margins of fluctuation in national currencies by the European Union). After giving in, the UK government was forced to leave the ERM, and a number of other economic policies had to be changed; the market seemed to be able to force a change of policy on the British government in a few days of trading. Had the government not given in, the British reserves (stocks of money and other assets held by the government, running into the value of billions of pounds) would have been exhausted in a few days.

Even the mighty US government faces a similar potential threat, incidentally, since so many dollars are now owned privately, and thus can be used for private purposes (including speculation). As did the UK government before them, the US government is sometimes forced to support rather unpleasant regimes which hold large dollar balances for fear of a 'run' on the dollar, for example – a further example of the complex intertwining of economic and political factors.

Some additional examples make this point slightly more explicitly and 'politically'. An article on the plight of Native Americans shows some interesting possibilities. It describes how a piece of legislation in 1971 – the Alaska Native Claims Settlement Act – offered a chance to local people fully to own their land in a modern capitalist sense. Before, they had 'traditionally held property in common and [had not believed] that land [could] ever be "owned"' (Walker 1997: 44). Properly constituted native-owned corporations were to own 44 million acres of land, and were given some funds to develop the natural wealth of the region 'all in order to sustain the traditional cultures'. However, once firmly in the capitalist system of ownership, the rules of the game become familiar ones: '. . . being capitalist entities, they were subject to the laws of the market . . . They became targets for hostile takeovers from companies who could make shareholders offers they would find hard to refuse . . . as long as it remains a corporate asset, their land will be vulnerable' (Walker 1997: 42).

Another paradox appears in a similar example. Two 'tribes' are now in conflict because the land traditionally hunted by one group has been found to contain 'the last big undiscovered oil reserves on US soil' (Walker 1997: 42). This has immediately put them at odds with their traditional neighbours, who do not live off this land and who wish to exploit the mineral resources beneath it. A spokesperson for this latter group 'does not . . . want to return to the days when the long winter nights were kept at bay only by lamps that burned whale blubber'. In this way, capitalist forms of ownership have created two new 'tribes – 'the briefcase Indians and the headband Indians'.

The same piece reveals another bizarre and highly 'unnatural' form of ownership, to set alongside the strange examples of futures trading and so on discussed above. Apparently, it is possible in the USA to sell tax losses:

> The corporations valued the timber on . . . ['tribal'] . . . lands at the high 1970s prices when they acquired these assets. They then felled trees at a furious rate and sold the timber at depressed 1980s prices. They pocketed the money and between them claimed a total tax loss of more than $1 billion. They then sold these losses to giant American corporations such as Ford Motor Company, Pillsbury, Hilton Hotels and Quaker Oats, who used them to reduce their own tax bills. (Walker 1997: 44).

Such strange and advanced forms of ownership have developed since Marx's classic work, and we shall have to review these cases when we consider whether marxist analysis can deal with these abstract and globalised forms. Yet for marxists, the right to benefit from the rather generously defined legal ownership of a factory operates on more familiar and routine daily basis as well as in these spectacular cases: private property lies at the heart of one of the key analyses in marxist work, known technically as the issue of 'surplus value' (see the online reading guide). As always, there is a level at which we can grasp this discussion before getting into the technicalities too deeply. To begin, let us attempt a thought experiment.

### How to run a successful business

Let us imagine that you are about to launch a small business, say in the manufacture of confectionery. Before you approach the bank for a loan to start up, you will have to draw up a business plan. There are several templates to help you to do this, these days, but what they all have in common is a need to demonstrate an ability to make money from your enterprise. How can this be done? In many ways, there is surely no mystery – you just have to ensure that your costs are lower than your revenues. In a business plan, you would have to try to specify all your costs (which is not all that easy at first). You would note the costs of raw materials (sugar, cocoa beans and flavourings are easy ones, but you need also to assess the rent for office premises, charges for telephones, replacement costs for machines, and so on). Labour costs would clearly be an important element – wages for the actual factory hands and for the people who handled sales, publicity or buying, and, of course, your own wage as a manager.

Having totalled the costs, as fully as possible, you can now turn to the revenues side. How much do you have to earn to break even (cover your costs), or perhaps even to make the minimum profit acceptable to the bank? This sum in turn has implications for the price you should charge, or, if this is already established, the amount of confectionery you should attempt to produce. You aim to receive a certain amount each week, say through sales of either a small number of expensive luxury items, or a large number of cheaper mass sales items. It takes quite a bit of experience and market research to know which alternatives to back, of course.

What if the sums do not balance? Perhaps we can do more business and increase revenues, but this would not be easy in a competitive market where everyone else is trying to do the same. One obvious solution is to reduce costs, and, of course, one way to do that is to address the costs of labour. You can keep wages low, or you can make your labour more productive so you get a better return (or both, but they sometimes contradict each other). Making labour more productive can involve making the working day (or week, or year) longer, or using 'labour-saving devices' like machinery to increase productivity, to speed up the work, or to make it more intensive. These are familiar boss-type activities, and, because they are likely to be unpopular with the workforce, you can start to see why, for marxists, work in capitalism must involve at least a local conflict of interest between owners and labourers. Bosses can claim to be doing this unwillingly – the system sets the rules, and costs must not exceed revenue or no-one will lend them the money even to begin. Bosses can comfort themselves by saying they are therefore offering 'a fair day's work for a fair day's pay'.

There are subtler considerations here too. Note that the qualities of labour are rather special – it is the only 'raw material' that can be 'stretched' by being made more productive. Of course you can make your chocolate bars thinner, or whatever, and save on cocoa essence, but only up to a point. Labour seems much more flexible than that, and it is uniquely *productive*. It is the only 'raw material' or 'factor of production' that adds value, for classical marxism. If the sums are done correctly, and the business organised properly, the value of the goods produced at the end of the day will contain the value of all the raw materials contained in them, including the value of the hired labour; but only labour can produce such combinations of raw materials in the first place. Only human labour can take sugar, vanilla essence and chocolate and turn them into a finished tray of confectionery. Labour uniquely adds value.

Even if the value of the goods sold is sufficient only to get back the value invested (the 'break-even point' in business plan terms), labour is still being exploited by this sort of system, for marxists. It is not that labourers must necessarily receive an 'unfair wage' – even bosses must pay them what 'the market' says is the going rate (although such a rate can be driven down or kept pretty low by concerted economic or political action, such as banning trades unions). There is a more technical point – it is that labour has been bought and sold as though it were just like any other raw material, even though it is a special and unique raw material. In more technical terms still, human labour is bought and sold on the labour market just like any other commodity. The market determines its 'exchange value' (which is ultimately reflected in its price, for Marx). But labour has a unique 'use value' (another kind of value revealed only when commodities are put to use, a matter far too complex to be represented adequately in market terms). The unique use value of labour is to add value to all the other commodities, as we have argued.

Labour cannot be rewarded adequately, because the economic system could not grow if it were. No-one could produce any surpluses. In the long term, goods would simply be exchanged at the appropriate exchange value: one value would merely be exchanged for its equivalent, because no-one would willingly and knowingly trade their goods for goods of a lower value (except in very exceptional circumstances). The astounding capacity of capitalism to deliver sustained, structured economic growth depends entirely upon one primary lack of equivalence, one basic and fundamental inequality affecting labour – labour is not the simple equivalent of any other commodity but one with a unique use value, although it is universally treated as if it were not unique at all.

There is no real reason to treat labour in this way, of course. It might be perfectly possible to conceive of a system where labour was rewarded for its unique qualities, separately from all the other raw materials. But the system we have – capitalism – does not do this, for a number of reasons. The most obvious one is that it is not in the interests of the powerful groups in capitalism who benefit from the existing arrangements. On the contrary, they would be advised to try to enshrine the current system in law as well as in custom and practice, to defend existing notions of wages and labour markets, labourers' rights and duties, owners' rights and duties, and so on. If they could persuade people to see these arrangements as 'natural', inevitable, universally beneficial or even as sanctified by tradition or by God, all to the good. Of course, the enormous productivity of the system has brought a substantial rise in the standard of living to an increasing number of people (but by no means to everyone), so there are real benefits and gains to point to as well.

More charitably, another reason for preserving the existing system is that it is peculiarly hard to understand what actually is going on. It took Marx years of hard intellectual labour to puzzle out the secret of surplus value, which included long struggles to examine and reject some apparently plausible rival theories. Much of the misunderstanding is due to the search for simple explanations, tidy categories that fit everything, lazy theories that fail to penetrate too deeply into things but which stick with what seems to be the case on the surface (sometimes because it is in our short-term interests to do this). Marx referred to this search for simple explanations as an aspect of 'commodity fetishism' (see the online reading guide), a deliberate reference to the ways in which some religious systems invest objects (fetishes – little carved idols or stones) with magical powers, because they do not understand how the natural world really works.

Thus labour appears to be a simple commodity or 'factor of production' just like all the others, and to make an exception of it threatens the ambition to develop a simple science of economics. Few economists of the time (or since) would have had much time for dubious 'philosophical' categories like 'use value', or for the idea that 'the same' commodity can contain two kinds of value. Indeed, the very idea of 'value' seemed imprecise compared to the nicely quantified balance sheets of costs, prices and revenues rendered in terms of money – all categories that simply reflect what happens 'on the surface'. I have argued above that the simple category can be 'ideological' when discussing the notion of 'private property' itself, so it should be no surprise that a limited notion of (economic) science is perfectly at home with more explicitly 'political' interests in defending the existing system.

In a rather intuitive way, many entrepreneurs seem to know that they depend on being able to exploit labour. In a famous section in *Capital*, Marx describes how the daily hire of labour (as it was in many jobs in those days) begins with a nice egalitarian moment as owner and worker meet as fellow human beings and agree a price for the day's labour that both can accept. This is a moment in the cycle, says Marx (1977d: 172), that becomes a 'very Eden of the innate rights of Man', which 'furnishes . . . [those believing in the perfection of the system] . . . with [their] views and ideas and with the standard by which [they] judge a society based on capital and wages'.

As soon as that contract is agreed though,

> we think we can perceive a change in the physiognomy of our dramatis personae. He who before was the money-owner, now strides in front as a capitalist; the possessor of labour-power follows as his labourer. The one with an air of importance, smirking, intent on business; the other timid and holding back, like one who has brought his hide to market and has nothing to expect but – a hiding. (Marx 1977d: 172)

Leaving aside for a moment the personal abuse (and the exclusive use of the male pronoun) in this argument, the owner really has no choice but to get the maximum productivity from the hired hands who have to work to produce goods of enough value to repay the owner for their hire, and cover the costs of all the other raw materials (including the owner's wage as manager), just to let the business break even.

Of course, if the owner can squeeze even more work out of his hands, not necessarily with cruelty, there is the prospect of even more surplus value (what is usually called 'profit', an excess, even after all the costs, including managers' wages, investment to replace machinery and a reasonable return for capital invested, have been met). Similarly, if for a short while prices for finished goods happen to be favourable (for various reasons), the owner can still receive a substantial revenue from charging an unusually high price, benefiting from the market, so to speak. This can be pocketed, or distributed to customers or to workers. The peculiar institution of private property in capitalism permits the owners to decide how to respond and to act within the system in so far as any individual can decide. None of this affects the main, long-term source of growth, the systematic exploitation of the unique qualities of labour to add value. Some people, however, are probably content with short-term gains, as we shall suggest below.

## The threats to the system

Overall, and in the long term, there is instability built into capitalism. Competition is mutually destructive, for example, as firms vie with each other to beat the market or to put each other out of business. Social upheaval is chronic as the restless search for opportunities to develop capitalist enterprise forces change on more and more aspects of 'traditional' life – families, communities, townships and neighbourhoods are destroyed, natural resources exploited, rivers canalised, the countryside 'developed'. (Marx and Engels were by no means completely unhappy about these trends, by the way – at least they stripped away the 'sentimental veil' that concealed the harsh realities of social life for so many.)

According to Marx and Engels' *Manifesto of the Communist Party* (1977) inequalities grow between the classes as small capitalists are put out of business by their larger competitors and forced to join the swelling ranks of the labourers: the system becomes so obviously polarised that a radical political consciousness easily takes hold and people see that their collective future lies in the abolition of a system that benefits only a few. This instability seemed built in in 1848, when the *Manifesto* was published, but in the calmer periods that ensued (in Europe) Marx was able to devote more time to examine the ways in which the system could be stabilised politically – albeit only temporarily, he hoped.

Despite all the changes in the economic system (already becoming apparent in the 1880s – company ownership, the growth of a sector of 'unproductive labour' and of some sort of 'middle classes'), the economic system still tended towards long-term crisis, as even labour eventually becomes exhausted as a source of surplus. Even the dominant groups seem to sense impending disaster, although they think about it in an odd and typically 'ideological' way, in terms of 'natural' threats or catastrophes. Malthusian accounts of overpopulation were one fashionable anxiety in Marx's day, and perhaps we could extend the analysis to include some recent 'millennial' fears (ecological instability, asteroids striking the Earth, uncontrollable epidemics caused by antibiotic-resistant organisms, and so on). In these fears, a nervous acknowledgement of the externality and uncontrollability of the system is manifest.

At the end of it all, capitalism remains as the most innovative, dynamic, productive – and harmful and exploitative – system we have known. The more it develops, the more out of control and 'external' to the vast majority of us it becomes, until, Marx hoped, everyone can finally see that it is holding back social development, and that it becomes crucial for all of us to work toward an alternative.

Marx remains as a splendid social critic, and as a towering intellectual force. I have not even mentioned so far his influential 'early works' (see Colletti/*New Left Review* 1975) , which offer a famous analysis of 'alienation' in modern societies (where human beings increasingly develop powerless, artificial and abstract ways of life). Those pieces also contain important philosophical critiques of various writings, like Hegel's. Colletti (1975) claims that such critiques operate with the same sort of analysis as the arguments offered against 'scientific' economics – briefly, that philosophy operates with categories that fail to grasp the real mechanisms of the material world and thus often end by sanctifying existing political arrangements. There was once a tremendous controversy among marxist scholars about the relative importance of these and other works, whether or not there were continuous threads of 'method' in Marx's work, how we should 'read' different fragments of his vast (and originally unpublished and unsystematised output), and so on. These rather specialist and technical debates (which sometimes turned on which version of Marx, in which European language, we should read) will have to be left for further study, of course, although there is an online reading guide on the concept of 'value' in Marx for reference. Sayer (1991) has an excellent discussion too.

## A summary

Let us review the marxist work so far. We have seen that the economic system is the dominant feature of our society, especially its potential to offer sustained economic growth. Yet the development of this system is far from natural, or simply 'evolutionary'. On the contrary, in order to get where we are now, we have had to undertake a drastic social programme of reform, and this has emerged from a colossal political and ideological struggle. Marx's splendid and very readable Part viii of *Capital*, Volume 1 (Marx 1977d), details some of the processes required to develop a 'free' labour market, for example – old agricultural communities were destroyed by practices like land clearances (which had a considerable effect on emigration from Britain and subsequent European colonisation of the USA and Australia), leaving labourers with no alternative but to sell their labour in the booming urban centres. Clearances were pursued by the small group of existing owners of the land, in search of maximising their revenues (and, more charitably, in pursuit of their own beliefs in modernisation). This group had long pursued an exploitative relation towards their social inferiors and the natural world. Later we saw struggles to limit the length of the working day, to gain the right to form trades unions, and a welter of social welfare legislation to regulate the lives of urban dwellers. We are far from the innocent and still common 'primitive accumulation' account, where the whole system begins by thrifty and hard-working Protestants saving their money, reinvesting it in new enterprises and thus gradually building great capitalist companies.

Early social upheavals were followed by even greater ones, as capitalist industry organised itself more and more pervasively. Nation-states emerged, and, as trade and markets expanded under the pressure of competition, colonial expeditions and wars with other peoples developed – such as the civil war in the Australian State of Victoria in the 1840s between settlers and 'Aboriginal' Koorie peoples, much of which turned on ownership of the land. These episodes show links between economic, political and ideological 'levels' again – for example, people have to develop suitable belief systems (belief in 'progress', in 'civilisation', in racial superiority, in national, religious or racial 'missions') for colonialism to be acceptable).

## Problems and debates

The main criticisms that usually occur first concern Marx's prophecies of capitalist instability, which we mentioned above. Why has none of this long-term decline happened? Why has marxism as a political creed failed so spectacularly in Eastern Europe? Answers to these sorts of question can lead to more technical issues about the validity of marxist theory, as we shall see. Of course, there are more obvious answers which you might like to think about and debate:

1   Marx has got it right, but he just got the time-scale wrong. Capitalism has proved itself able to prolong its life by expanding into even more remote parts of the world, for example, finding new sources of labour in the 'developing world', or exploiting existing ones ever more efficiently by using advanced science and technology. The whole notion of polarisation and eventual revolutionary struggle is still there, but this time on a world scale instead of a national one. Moreover, there will be a limit to expansion eventually – perhaps this is appearing in the guise of an ecological crisis, as the planet's raw materials are threatened? Incidentally, the idea that Britain, the USA or Australia are somehow 'naturally conservative' is also a myth: those countries had powerful working-class radical movements that have challenged the system, although it is sometimes hard to get to hear about them.

2   The political system in Eastern Europe was not really a marxist one. In many ways, the political situation in Russia (or China) did not follow a 'classic' marxist route. There was no substantial industrial expansion and subsequent polarisation, with its creation of an experienced and active industrial working class to lead the struggle, for example. The Bolsheviks

and the Chinese Communist Party (and others, notably the Cubans) had to improvise, and, inevitably, compromise as well. Since then, communist regimes have been the subject of sustained campaigns against them by powerful capitalist countries using weapons ranging from trade boycotts to the attempted assassination of leaders. Inevitably, this state of war (actual or undeclared) has distorted the social development of those countries.

For the specialists, the debates take a different turn, however. Doubt has been expressed about the explanations of economic growth as inherently exploitative of labour, for example. I hope we have signalled some of these problems in our account. Can growth take place without the exploitation of labour? What about those banking scandals we discussed, where it seemed possible to make large amounts of money from trading in currency futures? A whole range of operations simply involving the transfer of money seem to be able to deliver profit. This system – some call it 'finance capitalism', others 'casino capitalism' — seems to have escaped marxist analysis and provided growth without systematic exploitation (and thus growth without contributing to class conflict). It is worth saying immediately that these developments seem to have escaped the grasp of the main alternative forms of analysis (conventional micro- and macro-economics) as well, as the following points by billionaire financier George Soros (1997) make clear:

1    Older markets worked within a system of social constraints and values (a point which we will make when discussing Durkheim later), but those values are too weak to restrain activity in the international finance market, which is indifferent to any regional values. A common interest prevails simply in making money.

2    The old markets worked on a huge scale with many participants, and this gave them a rather abstract and 'objective' quality, apparently with 'laws' of their own, and with their own long-term trends towards equilibrium and relative stability. These 'laws' (of supply and demand) are the ones at the heart of modern (post-marxist) micro-economics, of course. The new financial markets are much more small-scale, so that different individuals know they can influence matters like the price of money. As we saw above, national governments are not the biggest influences any more (which poses problems for modern macro-economics too).

3    As a result of these two changes, money markets are much more influenced by the subjective actions of the participants rather than the long-term interests of the whole system. Prices reflect the ever-changing wishes, desires, hopes and experience of a relatively small number of buyers and sellers. A considerable built-in instability results as these players try to move from one temporary equilibrium to another, to jump on one of the ever-present bandwagons to buy or sell this or that currency, to both predict and influence its future price.

## Marxist responses

Marxists could reply to this sort of analysis in several ways. One way is to point out that the transfer of funds is still a secondary activity, playing with surpluses still generated by the exploitation of labour. A rather obscure example discussing revenues and their sources (Marx 1977c) traces this argument through by examining the origin of apparent monetary surpluses like 'interest'. Briefly, when you put money in a bank account you 'earn interest' on it, without seeming to have to do anything at all: saving money seems to be sufficient in itself to generate more money. For marxists, examples like this have led to all sorts of misunderstandings among social commentators, such as those economists who thought that the development of the money system itself was the secret of growth in the economy, or socialist critics who wanted to single out such sources of 'unearned income' for particularly heavy taxation or moral condemnation.

For Marx, there is no real mystery in the category of interest: the money you deposit gets used by the bank to engage in standard capitalist enterprise. It is invested, perhaps overseas or in companies of which you know little. It is turned into productive capital (plant or machinery), and then used to extract surplus value from labour in the usual way. Some of the surplus generated is turned back into money and paid back into the bank as a 'return on investment', and you receive a share of this surplus as your 'interest'. It is not too difficult to proceed to a more general point from this example – to put it in terms which you can hear used every day, even the finance economy has to be connected somewhere with the real economy, although you have to use terms like 'ultimately', 'in the long term' or even 'in the last instance'. Finance on its own does not generate long-term, sustainable wealth, jobs or products.

If we had more time, we could illustrate how agriculture was also examined in this way. Here again, there is a misleading surface appearance to agricultural surpluses, which appear to be generated by 'Nature' alone – seed is planted, and after a suitable interval it grows all on its own into more valuable mature crops which are harvested and sold for a profit. You might like to think out a possible marxist argument here: in essence, it would turn on having to show how natural process must still be connected to an organised wage-labour system and system of exchange – an agricultural industry, with a key role played, as always, by the unique qualities of labour in adding value to seed, fertilisers and soil. At this point, you might like to construct for yourselves a marxist analysis of other relations between humans and 'Nature' – can the *structured* exploitation of natural resources, or of animals, be considered separately from a consideration of massively organised industrial development, the continuing, dynamic, globalised extension of a system designed to produce commodities for exchange?

Another obvious objection can be dealt with in a similar way – the role of machines. They seem to produce value 'on their own' (perhaps the best example is the automated car industry, where, apparently, robots make vehicles in eerily deserted factories). In those circumstances, capitalism seems to work without any labour, a point developed by analysts critical of capitalism as well as enthusiasts for the system: 'Capital has liberated itself from labour' (Sivanandan 1990; and see the online reading guide), or, in a slightly different formulation, we are heading for a 'workless' society (Beck 2000). The usual marxist view is that such machinery embodies the skills and productivity of the labour coded into the machine, and that isolated examples of robotic production are possible once more only against a background of more familiar labour-intensive production which produces everything else (the tyres, the steel, the wiring harnesses, the buildings, and so on) – so the analysis can be rescued once more, even if a little more ground has had to be conceded.

## The debate about social class

In a final example, there are clearly much more complex social relations these days than in the polarised class model of 1848. We return to this issue in Chapter 5, but some initial points can be made here too. What about 'middle classes', 'new classes', 'service sector jobs', and the rest? Again, it would take a long time to pursue these developments in detail, but marxist analysis can still deal with them using the same basic strategy as in the other examples. Thus Poulantzas (1975; and see the online reading guide) has used a basic model of the social formation developed first in Althusser's work (see Figure 1.1) to suggest that modern social classes are shaped by influences at the different 'levels' of the social formation. The 'middle classes' are the most confused and unstable: 'determinations' from the economic level tend to lead them to identify with the working classes, but determinations from the other levels give them quite different models of the class system. Thus, ideological forces might persuade them that society is best understood as a meritocracy, political ones persuade them to think in terms of interest groups, and so on.

'Service sector' jobs can be grasped as 'unproductive labour', in Marx's own phrase, still funded out of the general surpluses generated by the exploitation of labour, even though such jobs themselves do not produce surplus value (a technical angle on the rather abusive term 'unproductive').

Apparently complex new middle classes can still be explained as surface features of the traditional class system. Some 'middle-class' jobs turn out to be pretty much like 'working-class' ones on closer inspection, for example, requiring little skill in practice, and offering little more control over the job than that experienced by a factory hand. Indeed, some commentators have identified a major trend, 'deskilling' (Braverman 1974), which has affected a large range of office jobs (and even some semi-professions like teaching – see Lawn and Ozga 1988) precisely in this 'proletarianising' manner.

On another tack, it is possible to see the old system still apparent under such surface features as the alleged extension of share ownership to the new classes

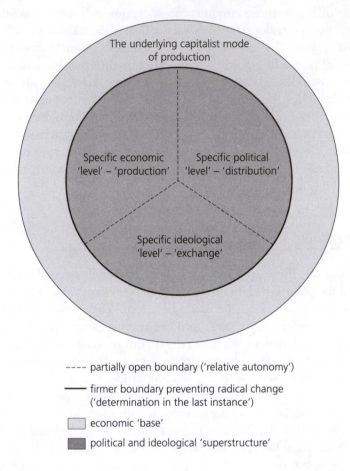

The underlying capitalist mode
of production

Specific economic
'level' – 'production'

Specific political
'level' – 'distribution'

Specific ideological
'level' – 'exchange'

---- partially open boundary ('relative autonomy')

——— firmer boundary preventing radical change
('determination in the last instance')

□ economic 'base'

■ political and ideological 'superstructure'

**Figure 1.1 The model of the social formation (after Poulantzas 1975)**

of managers or small investors. It is clear to the most casual observer that the powerful individual capitalist is still with us, for example, with people like Bill Gates, Rupert Murdoch or the Sultan of Brunei personally owning a considerable amount of the world's wealth, and enjoying the same social and political influence as the big Victorian capitalists of Marx's day, if not more so.

There are some startling data revealing that international inequalities are as large as ever. The same analysis points to the enormous power and influence of the World Bank, following the decline of the old Soviet Union, which is able to insist that many smaller countries follow monetarist policies (cuts in welfare spending, low direct taxation, privatisation, financial deregulation, and so on).

Of course, there is a major controversy over the existence of social class analysis specifically as a concept to explain such empirical inequalities, which I shall postpone to Chapter 5 (but see , for example Pakulski and Waters 1996, and see the online reading guide). The issue is still being contested, as a number of papers at the British Sociological Association Annual Conference 2001 revealed (for example, Bottero and Prandy 2001; see the online reading guide).

Once more, this is a technical matter, developed in a sociological specialism. One aspect of it concerns the debate about the usual empirical (factual) indicators of social class such as data on ownership, on occupational mobility or on voting or consumption patterns. As always, these data are ambiguous – for Pakulski and Waters (1996), sociologists have to strain increasingly to make them fit theories of social class (including marxist ones), and it is likely that this effort is driven by political commitment as much as by dispassionate inquiry. But the reverse can also be claimed: the apparent picture of the decomposition of classes into a range of other more diverse groups, for example, results from a refusal to pursue any marxist themes which might discover 'deeper' structures that unite the fragments after all.

## Foundationalism: privileged beginnings in marxism?

I hope it is clear from these short examples that marxist analysis is not that easy to dispose of, even though it is not very fashionable at present. Of course, I have had to simplify a good deal, and I should confess that I have also grouped these examples in such a way that you might be able to see a general problem with all of them, a problem which 'post-structuralist' and postmodernist analysis has done much to clarify. All the examples above make marxism look rather oddly 'philosophical' these days, somewhat dated and rather partisan. For example, of all the possible characteristics of modern machinery, why focus on its origins, so to speak, on the beginnings of the story, on that fundamental first moment when a human being programmed the robot and modelled it on a human expert, when labour was 'coded' into a machine?

It is an important political or 'philosophical' point to make to remind us that human labour was involved, but is it strictly a necessary one, essential to grasping the purely technical aspects of machinery and its contribution to productive work? Think back to the example which we discussed above – for Marx himself, liberal thinkers wrongly assumed that one original moment of equality in the day's work can be used to explain the whole system as egalitarian. That little moment of 'free' negotiation between worker and boss, at the start of the day, acts as a 'very Eden of the rights of man', Marx sarcastically argues. Marxists seem close to repeating the error themselves, however, in insisting that one primary moment of exploitation, when human workers had their skills extracted from them and built into a machine, serves to explain all the rest of the cycle. The primary moments privileged by marxist analysis seem more and more remote, especially as we develop specialist knowledge about the detailed workings of our society; the growth of sociological knowledge leads to more and more uncertainty that we can fit it all back together under one over-arching theory (which is one version of a more general thesis about the effects of the 'delegitimation' of knowledge to which we shall turn when we discuss postmodernism in Chapter 13 – if you want to skip ahead, try the online reading guide on Lyotard).

Similar questions arise with all the other examples. I am sure you can try them out in each case for yourselves. Here are some initial questions to think about:

1   Is it still *necessary* for understanding, or even just profitable, to trace the connections between the money economy and the real economy in every case? What would be added to our discussion of the banking scandals (above) by trying to trace those connections? Does it really matter how the money was actually invested at some point, or can we see enough of what happened just by looking at the flows of money within the money economy?

2   What is actually gained by wanting to translate all the complex social differences in a modern stratification system back to some fundamental underlying class structure? No doubt it can be done, but a lot of important detail will be lost. Can we really understand the dynamics of a class system, the important social and ideological differences between 'white collar' and 'blue collar', say, or between male and female workers, skilled and unskilled, those on permanent contracts and those on short-term ones, older and younger generations of workers – the list is a long one – in terms of the one original underlying thing that they have in common (their formal position in a production system)?

3   Questions 1 and 2 cast doubt upon the use of a surface/depth metaphor, of course, and the marxist habit of reducing 'surface' features to 'deeper' determinants without asking permission, so to speak. There are questions too about the connections between the economic analysis and the political implications that follow. Is it still politically useful to trace back specific abuses of people's (or animals') rights to one fundamental inequality at the heart of the system? And is it still politically useful to see the exploitation of labour as the real, fundamental form of exploitation explaining the origins of, or fundamentally structuring the shape of, other forms (like the exploitation of women or of animals)? Is the marxist political promise still valid – that class exploitation is the only really fundamental one, essential in capitalism, so that ending it would disestablish, destabilise or uproot all the other types?

4   As with the other examples, the issue turns partly on what counts as 'short term' in these cases (to challenge another characteristic aspect of marxist argument). Even if capitalism as a system does underpin all the other forms of political or social divisions, can we ignore the 'short term', and wait until the system finally crashes in some huge and irrecoverable political crisis, or should we be intervening now? The same considerations play back to the economics: if, in the short term, companies can make a fortune by shrewd market operations alone, why should they (or we, or any professional

economists) bother with any other kind of analysis of some abstract 'whole system', operating 'beneath the surface', and in the 'long term'?

These sorts of critical question can also be met, of course. Marxist analysis can still use forms of rhetoric or persuasion to convince us that it is plausible and worthwhile. However, social analysts of a different generation can admire the power of marxist work, but then move on in some liberal way to explore and manage other systems as well. This is also a feature of modern technical sociology, to offer new syntheses, new ways of combining the insights of the different traditions. Indeed, as suggested earlier, the organisational context of a modern university and its assessment system encourage exactly this kind of relativism rather than devotion to one approach. However, marxism also attracts commitment outside the academy, and has inspired many political movements and regimes. Let us explore this notion for a while: what grounds are there for such commitment?

## Marxism: what remains of the project?

We could be urged to commit ourselves to marxism on the same sort of grounds as we might commit ourselves to any other organised philosophical, religious or political system. There might be a combination of perceptions of personal advantage ('workers' rights' in this case) and belief in more abstract systems of values ('social progress', an 'end to exploitation', or a system which operates on the principle of 'from each according to his abilities, to each according to his needs'). Of course, adherents know they must take their place in a competitive public market for ideas. They will meet equally committed opponents, and they will meet also large numbers of people who do not seem to be that interested in getting committed to anything. One development, once common in some European Communist Parties, has been to accept this situation, and to operate just like any other organised movement seeking power and influence through the existing political system with policies of conventional kinds.

For other marxists, this route is a mistaken one. For them, marxism is not just another political belief system, not just another option alongside Christian Democracy, Liberalism or Fascism, but a better, more scientific account of social life than those rivals. There is an intellectual commitment here, a belief that marxism is more valid, offering a scientific backing for proper politics, whereas other approaches have mere beliefs or other irrational underpinnings. This gets us back on to more technical grounds again, as a result: what exactly is the difference between (marxist) science and its 'ideological' rivals?

Perhaps you have already encountered this question in a slightly different guise. It turns partly on the issue of 'economic determinism', a familiar problem in marxism, dealt with in most basic textbooks. In the specific context of debates about science and ideology, the problem appears in terms of Marx's attempts to explain the political beliefs and commitments of rival approaches (like liberalism specifically, or Christianity or Idealist philosophy more generally). Marx's general strategy here is to suggest not that these rival views are simply 'wrong', but that they are limited in some sense by the underlying economic system. In a way, this is an even more devastating tactic to dispose of rivals than simple condemnation, of course: if it works, such an approach helps us give rival approaches some sort of acknowledgement, only to go on to give calm, solid, 'scientific' reasons why they must be inadequate. We have already hinted at this with our discussion of economics above: rival economists have simply failed to grasp the deep complexities of the system; the strange double nature of the commodity with its combination of use and exchange value; the exceptional nature of labour as a commodity, despite its apparent similarities to all the others; and so on.

The same sorts of points can be made against other systems of belief. For example, liberals have over-reacted to the wonderful single moment of democracy when we go into the polling booth and vote for our political representatives (or delegates). That moment, in one specific day every four or five years, is another 'very Eden', just as is the first five minutes of the working day when master and hand agree the day's rate. But also, just as in economic life, the moment of democracy in politics is followed by a much longer period of fundamental inequality, when our elected representatives act in ways which are largely unaccountable and which often produce results against the interests of the very people who once elected them. Of course, we all know these days that there are also many powerful groups and individuals who are not even elected, and who are quite capable of resisting bodies who are. It is an analytic error, and a kind of justification of the system, to use the one moment of formal equality in the voting booth to describe the whole system as 'democratic'. In Marx's own work, this sort of point is made to criticise those who think that political emancipation (for Jews in his example) can be delivered simply by a right to vote for politicians every four years or so (in Marx 1977a).

A similar point can be made against a liberal over-reaction to the dynamics and freedoms offered by aspects of market systems. In a famous section in *Grundrisse*, Marx (1977b) wants to separate social life into different spheres or 'levels': production, distribution and exchange (to alter the terminology slightly). In more recent marxist theory, as we have seen in Figure 1.1, these three sectors also stand for 'the economic', 'the political' and 'the ideological' levels, respectively. The social conditions can look quite different in these different sectors. In terms of distribution, for example, capitalism can seem progressive and dynamic, extending more and more opportunities to more and more sections of the population, extending human rights, improving living standards, and so on. In the sector of exchange, there is a genuine kind of democracy of the marketplace: markets are indifferent to the gender, age, racial groupings or sexual preferences of the individual consumer (or producer), and they tend to regard the uses to which goods are put as none of their concern, enshrining an important area of individualism, personal freedom and choice.

It is easy to see why some political theorists thought that their main task as reformers would be to operate in the non-economic sectors, to improve access to markets, and to promote a social market system to break down the old traditional patterns of privilege and social control. Why should people be forced to follow the same occupations and lifestyles as their parents, for example, or to let gender determine their choice of leisure pursuits? Are the traditional elites the best ones to be left in charge of the dominant institutions, or should fresh young entrepreneurs be given a chance in a market regardless of their social origins? We shall be returning to some of these ideas when we discuss functionalism in Chapter 2 (which is politically akin to liberal social theories).

## Base and superstructure

I hope it is already possible to see where a marxist critique would start to apply to the above questions: we have omitted production again. In the production sector, for marxists we would still have structured exploitation, regardless of the possibilities in the other two sectors. How important is this sector for the others? For liberals, the progressive elements of the other two sectors outweigh the inequalities of the production sector and even offer a kind of reforming mechanism: production will become more progressive in the wake of changes happening in distribution and exchange, as a kind of contamination effect.

For marxists, it is, of course, just the opposite way around: whatever the progressive tendencies of the other two, the production system sets the limits of change, deep down, 'in the final instance', as a kind of 'base' (to use one of Marx's famous formulations – see the online material on Marx's methods, or try the online reading guide on Althusser to explore some of the implications here). Specific forms of production can change – the system is continually in flux as new technologies replace older ones, and as factories close in some areas only to reopen in others – yet overall, the capitalist framework must remain. Any changes which threaten the system as a whole will not be developed, they will not 'make sense' in market terms, or will seem unnatural or inappropriate, and they will not be supported by the capitalist institutions. That still leaves a large area for change and development, of course, since capitalism can operate very flexibly with a wide range of distribution or exchange systems (from full 'market forces' to liberal 'welfare' to centrally directed wartime economies with rationing).

I hope it is also clear where marxism would stand in relation to the rival claims of the other sociological perspectives and approaches we are considering in later chapters. They also make the mistake of over-specialising, so to speak, focusing exclusively on one sector of the overall system, and, crucially, ignoring the over-arching influence of the whole capitalist system. Thus the impact of 'industrialisation' is described in functionalist sociology, but it is inadequately theorised as a kind of background variable (and the politics are softened).

Functionalists also operate too much in the realm of cultural adjustment without ever clarifying what it is exactly that drives the whole process of social change. Marxist critiques of Weber can also fit here: Weber described well enough the advance of bureaucracy (for example), but saw these developments as the result of some abstract process ('rationalisation' or 'disenchantment') instead of tracing the economic pressures from a capitalist system (see Marcuse 1972 and the online reading guide for a slightly unusual example of marxist critique of Weber).

Even interactionist sociology can be rebuked easily enough for its uncritical analysis of just the one sector (personal life) of the overall system; more specifically, the fascinating analyses of the flexible actors who negotiate their way through the complexities of social life fail to realise that they are describing human action in advanced capitalist society and not 'action' as such. At their best, such analyses can be critical (of the manipulations of image in 'professional' behaviour, say), and help us sympathise with the victims of our society (as in the famous studies of deviants) – but there is no proper analysis of the origins or social contexts of these behaviours. (I have several online reading guides which pursue this argument – try Gouldner 1971 for a general one, and Taylor et al. 1975 for a more 'applied' discussion of the limits of conventional approaches in deviancy theory.)

Finally, Jameson (1991) offers a well-known argument for recapturing the ground staked out for 'postmodernism' for marxist analysis of 'late capitalism' (and see his Foreword in the online reading guide on Lyotard 1984).

It is in these senses that the 'economic base' 'determines' the 'superstructures' of legal and political institutions which regulate distribution and exchange – rather like the foundation of a house (to borrow Althusser's analogy [1977]). The foundation does not determine fully and precisely the shape of the floors above, whether there is one large bedroom or two smaller ones, say, let alone the colour of the wallpaper or the type of heating system; yet it does hold up everything else, as a first requirement, and houses fall down without one. I personally think that many introductory texts suggest some ridiculously detailed mechanisms for economic determinism, as if marxists were claiming that every particular aspect of life could be explained in some simple and direct sense as a matter of social class membership, or whatever. Figure 1.1 depicts one possible way to grasp the point that subtler forms might be involved.

In the figure, 'the economic' appears twice: once as a specific 'level' within the social formation, and once as a more general system of production underpinning the whole superstructure of 'levels'. Each level has a degree of autonomy, has its own momentum and dynamics, with only weak interconnections between them. It is quite possible for developments in the 'ideological level' to take place without tight reference to the economic level. For the overall mode of production, it is different, however. Here, any developments are controlled and restrained: any radical, threatening changes are turned back inside the circle, so to speak. How exactly does this happen?

There are two sorts of mechanisms, usually expressed in terms of some of the famous (but hard to understand) quotes from the works of Marx and Engels: I have offered a slightly longer debate in my online material on Marx's methods, but to summarise:

1   We are told that 'The ideas of the ruling class are in every epoch the ruling ideas' (Marx and Engels 1970: 64). This is not surprising, of course, since those with wealth and power are likely to be able to develop their ideas much more easily than those whose lives are dominated by a more brutal struggle for existence. Institutions that disseminate ideas – publishers, churches and scholarly institutions – are funded and patronised by elite groups, and there are many studies which have attempted to show the ways in which the values of ruling-class or elite groups get coded into the very conventions of academic life itself. This is 'vulgar ideology', to borrow a marxist phrase.

2   In a less specific sense, existing arrangements provide people with the raw materials for their ideas, so to speak, and these raw materials are incorporated into systems of ideas without proper analysis. We have all assumed at some stage that what exists around us is somehow natural, proper or universal, that it is simply 'normal' to live in the families we know, to live in certain ways, or to pursue careers in particular areas. It is not so common to inquire carefully into the origins of these practices or systematically to consider alternatives, even where we are aware they exist. Even the professional thinkers of Marx's time were insufficiently curious about what they took as 'natural' forms of social life or mechanisms of social change: this is clearest of all, these days, perhaps, in their common views of 'progress' that saw nineteenth-century Europe as some kind of world vanguard of human evolution. These assumptions persist even in 'scientific ideologies', which do try to develop some sort of conceptual penetrations of the existing system. For Idealist philosophers, including those holding religious conceptions of the spiritual nature of 'Man', it is necessary to point out the social origins of the raw materials of ideas in general – thus the idea of an all-powerful God is the result of a misplaced ('inverted') conception of the tremendous powers of human beings to transform their world, while attempts to demonstrate that Reason is at work in human history offer obviously selective readings of past events from the present, and quietly privilege current systems as some sort of culmination of a divine purpose. For political economists, it is necessary to point to their assumptions more specifically about the economy, as we have tried to demonstrate above.

These are powerful and convincing arguments, and it is easy to see why the intellectual potency of marxism is a crucial element in its appeal. However, there is a problem again. If all the rival ideas have been contaminated by unclarified assumptions emanating from existing social arrangements, how exactly has marxism managed to escape into science? More technically, where exactly should marxist science be located in the model of sectors or levels? Marxism might have avoided the precise mistakes of its rivals, but can we be sure that there are no additional assumptions lurking there in the analysis, where marxists have been taking things for granted? Several candidates appear immediately: Marx happened to be alive at a particularly revolutionary period in European history, for example, and it is possible that he assumed that this was normal (we are not so sure these days, perhaps). The model in Figure 1.1 above might represent another historical phase of capitalism rather than its essential nature: perhaps in our current society, distribution and exchange really have made our social arrangements far more independent of the requirements of the production system than Marx thought possible. Terms with the prefix 'post-' start to appear again here – perhaps we live in a post-capitalist society, or a post-cultural one, where the various 'superstructural' elements have finally broken free of their anchorings in an economic base and really do exert an independent effect. As we saw above, people like Soros argue that even the financial subsections of the economic sector have broken free like this.

## Marxism in the present

It is fair to say that most of those wanting to preserve marxist insights have been forced to backtrack considerably on the issue of economic determinism in the tightest sense. We shall be examining some examples in later chapters. In one case, for example, one set of marxists (gramscians – see Chapter 6) have had to accept a much greater autonomy for the political levels of activity, and there is an interesting story to tell of early attempts to preserve orthodox economic roots, followed by a gradual drift towards theorising political activity as an independent 'discursive' activity. Other theorists in this tradition have recast marxism as an early and specific model of nineteenth-century European politics, and have fitted it into a more general account of politics, just as we have outlined above.

As another possible example, writers such as Habermas have tried to preserve the critical insights offered by marxist analysis but not as a monolithic and self-sufficient system. The insights offered by alternative modern social sciences and philosophies cannot be neglected, and Habermas has undertaken several synthetic activities in his career, beginning with an early denial of economic determinism. At one stage (see Habermas 1972; and the online reading guide) he was working with three separate 'quasi-transcendental human interests' to ground the areas of 'work', 'communication' and 'emancipation' (still graspable, perhaps, as a contribution to the debate about the links between the three levels). Marxism was to play a small part in such a system, though – conventional (American) interactionist sociology was more fruitful in analysing the 'communication' interest, for example, and later even Parsons found a place in the system. Habermas, along with many other theorists, regarded language as the root of social life, as we shall see in Chapter 12, and thinking of different modes of communication led him to develop, among other things, a model of society as a combination of 'system and lifeworld', a step which takes him far from marxism.

It is clear that for most current social theorists, marxism has finally lost its monopoly. Of course, it is easy to connect this rejection with the political unpopularity of marxism among western intellectuals too. For such people, there can be no more apologising for the political excesses of the communist system as somehow justified (however thinly) by a prestigious social science. As Adorno (1976) once put it, there is a definite connection between scientific systems that want to dominate concepts in the name of intellectual debate, and tendencies towards real political domination (although this connection is not confined to marxism, of course).

Perhaps the last attempt to rescue marxism's claims was offered by Althusser in the 1970s, and we have considered some of his work already (the rethinking of the remarks about 'economic determinism', for example). Even for him the usual claims to scientificity had to be rethought. Marxism was a science in a rather different sense: it offered a technically more appropriate grasp of reality than rivals, by no means a perfectly elaborated system, but an approach that avoids the limits of others. We start to see arguments about the ability of marxist work to generate new knowledge, for example, to avoid the circularity and 'closure' of other approaches. This new knowledge could be delivered because Marx had begun to develop genuinely new concepts (like 'mode of production'), which were consistent and capable of development. In the course of this argument, Althusser was led into some rather strange directions (denying that it was conventional empirical knowledge that marxism generated, for example), but, for a while, it looked as if the initiative was back with marxism.

Of course, these new criteria led to further criticism. Some writers who began as followers of the Althusserian readings of marxism (see Crook 1991; and see the online reading guide on Hindess 1977) undertook a project to test out the new claims – and became considerably disillusioned. Even marxism, it seemed, was no better than any of the other social sciences in achieving internal consistency. To be brief, apparently 'foundational' concepts were used in highly inconsistent ways, and these inconsistencies were often glossed over by sudden switches into rhetoric or appeals to commitment. This kind of analysis runs parallel to the whole 'post-structuralist' form of critical reading, and we shall discuss it below. For many sociologists in Britain at least, the episode was the route into full-blown postmodernist scepticism about 'foundationalism', where general theories claimed to explain everything in terms of a few privileged concepts. Others might have come to this critique through Lyotard (1984; and see the online reading guide).

It is hard to say whether this sort of specialist intellectual critique was the most important element in the gradual abandonment of marxism as a natural framework for analysis. It is a peculiarly technical and scholarly reason for rejecting a whole system, and one which only arose with such force when marxists (like Althusser) began to defend marxism on such specialist 'scientific' grounds. Specialists can be relied upon to find flaws in every and any position, of course, including their own. Nevertheless, marxists have been rather caught out by making strong claims themselves about the scientific status of their approach – I hope I have been able to demonstrate how this came about.

We have already discussed other elements, which included the feeling that the complexity and variety of modern life could not be easily reduced to marxist terms, especially in terms of modern politics. Of course, political commitments might still produce an allegiance to marxism, and, technically, it has proved itself able to maintain plausibly that modern culture, for all its diversity and variety, still remains closely linked to a capitalist system of accumulation. We now have to proceed to try to see how the other main approaches deal with similar sorts of criticism.

# 2 Moral Constraints: Functionalism

The previous chapter considered ways in which the economic system of a social formation can come to take on a momentum and dynamic of its own, in such a way as to dominate social life, but there is another famous sociological variant of this story. It is fairly easy to get to the heart of the arguments, again, before becoming too technical. Perhaps I should remind the reader that I intend to present a sympathetic account of the sociological approaches we shall encounter here, as with all the approaches we discuss. To put this in terms that are recognisable to the relatively experienced student, I am going to argue that even 'functionalism' has its useful and critical side. In the company of radical colleagues, this is an unforgivable heresy, but let us proceed.

It is easy to demonstrate that there is a sense in which everyday life is experienced as external to our lives as individuals. Common terms to describe this sort of experience include 'social pressures', 'social forces' or 'social contexts' to describe the limits and foundations of our individual actions as soon as we consider the reactions of other people (which is, after all, the basis of *social* action itself – action which is 'oriented to the actions of others'). Clearly, other people react back to us, and their responses lead to problems like how we can co-operate with each other, how we can come to agreements and how we can harmonise our interactions in an orderly way.

In addition, it is soon clear that there is a history to these problems of co-operation and coexistence (the 'problem of social order' as it is usually termed): when we grow up, we enter an existing society with its traditions, customs and habits. It is the custom in university seminars, for example, to argue about things in particular ways, and not to settle matters by a fist fight, for example (although I have been in some seminars which came close to one). More generally, there is a whole network of social institutions – markets, banks, local government agencies, schools and families – which have a history of managing things in an orderly manner. We just 'know' how to behave when we enter into contact with those institutions, and if we falter, they have ways of reminding us.

More informally, everyone will have felt the force of social pressures to behave in particular ways at particular times. It is a common experience to feel some sort of local group pressure to dress in a particular style, for example. I find it common for students to deny that these pressures are acute these days, but broad patterns of dress, speech and behaviour can be noticed among the very people who are denying their existence. Sometimes the pressures have the force of tradition, so that it is considered important to attend both the Leavers' Dinner and the Graduation Ceremony at my college, for example, and most people dress conventionally at the latter at least. These social pressures operate informally and just 'get around', so that somehow 'everyone knows' what to do.

If this sounds a bit vague or metaphysical, there are more mundane and identifiable factors too. In practice, people often attend these occasions as observers first and so learn what participants do (and then tell their friends), and participants themselves help each other to achieve some common standards. Sometimes there are clues provided by the very layout of the building or furniture, in modern societies as much as in the famous examples of household layout and the ways in which it controls social interaction among the Kabilyia, as described in Bourdieu (1977). Bourdieu is also famous for offering an account of how these insights into how to behave become internalised and unconsciously held as an 'habitus'. That is not to say that people behave entirely automatically thereafter, though – even something as implicit and unconscious as an habitus constantly has to be creatively 'applied' in practice, Bourdieu suggests (see the online reading guides to Bourdieu for some very important implications of this position).

There need be little at stake in these examples if people deviate, but in other areas sometimes a social reaction can be pronounced, and a strong sense of shame or embarrassment can arise in those who defy convention (or who are present when conventions are broken by others – I can still remember the ripple of deep embarrassment among the guests at a social gaffe, committed by the host, at an official opening ceremony attended by members of the British royal family). We all know of some cases of severe shaming (mortification) experienced by some individuals who are of an unconventional shape or physical appearance, for example, and this can lead to dangerous behaviour (such as eating disorders), depression or suicide. Social pressures can also be positive too, of course, as when coaches 'psych up' players before an important game by reminding them of the high expectations of their families, friends, fellow players or even their country.

These examples offer accounts of local groupings or gatherings where terms like 'social pressures' are easily understood, and the sources of those pressures can be located and identified – actual individuals or groups are embarrassed, or identifiable people are the ones who express the values or beliefs of the group. Things get a little more obscure if we try to apply this sort of insight more generally, to social life in the abstract, as it were. Sometimes, of course, social forces have the backing of the law and can be seen concretely embedded in the agencies of the law – there are strong social and legal pressures to drive on the same side of the road as everyone else, for example, and definite mechanisms to exert these pressures come into play if you decide not to conform. For some analysts in the functionalist tradition, laws largely express earlier social pressures concerned with 'survival value', that is with avoiding harmful and anti-social behaviour (such as homicide, theft or incest). More generally, social pressures support and reinforce laws, providing a kind of social context for law. Motoring laws or laws of contract would probably break down if they were not reinforced by a strong sense of social obligation to act properly: it is that sense of social obligation that really keeps most of us from driving recklessly or from cheating on our debts.

Durkheim's work can be seen as building upon simple insights like these to make them more systematic and technical. What we have called social patterns in behaviour (such as conforming to dress codes) he would call 'social facts': '. . . *every way of acting, fixed or not, capable of exercising on the individual an external constraint*; or again, *every way of acting which is general throughout a given society, while at the same time existing in its own right independent of its individual manifestation*' (Durkheim 1964: 13, original emphasis; and see the online reading guide for Durkheim's important Author's Preface to the Second Edition) .

These remarks have been the subject of a great deal of secondary commentary, and it might be possible to see immediately that two sorts of 'externality' may be already implied in the double-headed definition (see Lukes 1975 – there is an online reading guide to Lukes' work with extracts relating to the more 'applied' work in Durkheim – or some of the more recent textbooks, like May 1996; Ritzer 1996; or Waters 1994). As for social contexts, Durkheim was to use an argument like this against those who thought of social life as simply made up of personal contracts between people: the bonding that this sort of personal exchange provided was really an expression of a deeper social solidarity, a more general way of organising social life. No-one would keep contracts unless there was this notion of social solidarity, we have already argued, but, more than that, no-one would think of using legal personal contracts to buttress personal deals unless this were an acceptable form of social solidarity already, one fully compatible with the form of society in which we were living at the moment.

The experiences of social change going on in Europe at, and immediately before, the time of Durkheim's writing (the 1880s through to his death in 1917) would point to the crucial role in personal and economic behaviour played by social traditions in the classic way – as traditions change and new ones arise, everyone can see the part played in social life by social contexts. Earlier models (including those of some of Durkheim's immediate predecessors like Comte – see May 1996) had tried to formalise these experiences of social change in terms of some sort of evolutionary theory in which societies passed through definite stages – from primarily religious to primarily scientific stages, for example.

In the USA, or in Australia or Canada, there were different factors. In those 'new' countries ('new' for the European immigrants and colonists), social traditions had to be invented, blending different national cultures and devising new ones to suit the new traditions. The popular term for this kind of situation is the 'melting pot'. New arrivals would experience the melting away of some of their old ways of life in the new social conditions. Their children would take the new conditions as 'natural', however. In fact, the 'melting pot' probably does not describe modern conditions very well – existing cultural traditions seem to have persisted in a complex 'organic' mixture rather than a new homogeneous 'mechanical' blend.

With developments like these, we can start to see a role for a special academic discipline that studies these social forces and pressures – sociology. Naturally, such a special academic subject would require its own concepts (such as 'social facts'), its own procedures (only using social facts to explain other social facts) and its own methodologies (special ways to uncover the dimensions, extent and functioning of social facts). Other academic approaches, such as psychology or economics, would be operating at different levels and so would not be able to grasp events at the social level. Of course, they still had their place in explaining aspects of life in society, but sociology threatened to become the most general and powerful of all. Let us sketch out some implications before proceeding in detail.

Explaining social facts by other social facts leads to two possibilities at least. Perhaps some social facts, or changes in them, cause other social facts to happen, for example. Types of social solidarity might change as a result of the impact of industrialisation and the (practically simultaneous) experience of encountering different societies (to take a major theme in Durkheim). Here we would need some sort of methodology to isolate and identify causes and consequences, some causal chain to explain alterations in social life that we could perceive on the surface as effects of some underlying social causes. The prime causes would not necessarily need to be located in the economic system, of course; to insist on always looking there would be to risk economic determinism. Economic factors might be important on occasion, as when changes in the organisation of work (the division of labour) have obvious social consequences in producing social divisions. Cultural factors in the broadest sense – ways of looking at the world, including ways of classifying it – could be the main focus as well, however. To cut a long story short, we shall see that for Durkheim, types of social solidarity, which are themselves a product of various mechanisms of social regulation and social attachment, are a crucial causal variable uniting cultural and material factors: as they change, so do specific patterns of social life.

In his actual work, however, Durkheim varies his analytic methods, from rather specific causal analyses to more general interpretations of trends from selected examples. The study of suicide is an example of the former sort of analysis (Durkheim 1951). This famous work has been ably summarised in a number of commentaries (one of the best, in my view, is Ritzer 1996), and it serves as a demonstration of the power of social forces over even such an apparently individual act as killing yourself. To be brief, for those who do not know this study, Durkheim showed how the rates of suicide in different areas of France varied, and he went on to demonstrate that these variations corresponded to variations in certain measures of the strength of the communities concerned. By mapping patterns of suicide to patterns of such factors as religious belief, marital status or occupation, Durkheim was able to eliminate some explanations (that alcohol consumption was a major factor, for example) and work towards his own. He relied upon some earlier research too (see the chapter on the 'suicide problem' in Giddens 1996). Finally, Durkheim argued that suicides could be classified into four major divisions according to the type of social solidarity that produces high suicide rates, as Giddens (1996) puts it. (NB: Giddens and several other writers refer to three main types, ignoring 'fatalism'.) Following Lockwood (1992: and see the online reading guide), I have reorganised them, for the purposes of a brief summary, into two main sections, reflecting those arising from the absence of social restraints, and those at the other extreme, where people are so dominated by social forces that they willingly kill themselves:

1    Anomic and egoistic types of suicide reflect the breakdown of social values and more tangible attachments (respectively), and are found among people who are only weakly linked to the community (through shared beliefs, marriage ties or work-based social networks). A number of social changes can weaken social attachment and regulation and leave individuals dangerously detached from their fellows. As a result they are prone to 'social currents' of depression.
2    Altruistic and fatalistic types are at the opposite end and indicate over-attachment to social values and beliefs, or over-regulation by the community. Altruistic suicides kill themselves for their strong beliefs in country or honour (such as members of religious cults who kill themselves as a sign of their belief in salvation or Palestinian suicide bombers, perhaps). Fatalists (and these are not so well discussed) are so well regulated by the social groups to which they belong that they see little value in their own lives (inmates in concentration camps or long-term prisons). 'The classic example is the slave who takes his own life because of the hopelessness associated with the oppressive regulation of his every action. Too much regulation – oppression – unleashes currents of melancholy' (Ritzer 1996: 91).

This has always been a controversial study, of course, but the principles seem familiar enough – we take a social pattern and try to explain it in terms of other social forces which are assumed to cause variations. Durkheim did not pursue this sort of detailed analysis when it came to religious belief, however, Lockwood (1992) points out. Instead he chose a rather more abstract approach, trying to illustrate certain basic types or 'elementary forms'. These could be found in societies that were assumed to be somehow 'primitive' or fundamental human societies, uncomplicated by industrial life or social change. Fashion and opportunity led him to select Australian 'Aboriginal' societies as examples that somehow expressed best these elementary forms. Engels, incidentally, was impressed by some early anthropological work on Native American societies too, which allegedly showed rather similar 'primitive' types of kinship and community; it was clearly an accepted technique in the early days. Having arrived at 'elementary' universal forms, we can trace through amendments and changes in modern complex societies.

This is an approach which is easily criticised today, of course, for its ethno-centrism and connections with colonialism, but again the method of abstraction can still make sense if we abandon the dubious notions of hierarchy and 'progress' involved – are there any fundamental forms or functions which can be identified as common to all human societies, underneath the specific variations of actual societies? This kind of approach is systematised in modern American functionalism, in the classic attempt by Aberle (Lockwood 1992) to specify cer-tain 'functional prerequisites' that all societies must achieve: a system to socialise the young, regulate the deviant, manage relations between the sexes and the generations, and so on. In the case of religion, there are fundamental functions, for Durkheim, as we shall see. Religious beliefs express, and religious rituals reinforce or even develop, certain core beliefs about societies.

Indeed, more generally, religious systems, which are found in all human soci-eties, tell us something about how human beings think, how the actual groupings or categories ('classifications') they use grow out of their ways of life. This is an intriguing point, one explored by a number of other thinkers, including marxists, as we saw in the previous chapter. (Lukes (1975) explores some of the implications; and see the online reading guide to his work.)

Some fascinating explorations of categories of social thought and their con-nections with social solidarities have been pursued in the work of people like Bernstein (Atkinson 1985) or Bourdieu (1977) (Collins in Alexander (1988) has a useful summary). To summarise one common theme in this work, these writers have drawn attention to a way of life that supports concepts and categories (organised into 'codes' or 'aesthetics') which are closely tied to the original social context, shared by the members of that community, symbolising the under-standings of that community, but not really generalisable to other contexts or other communities. Such a coded way of life produces habitual ways of thinking about culture, or expressing meaning, which are 'restricted' to members. Other ways of life are far more cosmopolitan and negotiable, much more like 'organic solidarity', and they lead to a much more 'elaborated' speech code or a more technical and abstract 'aesthetic'. Such approaches have led to interesting work in explaining the very different stances towards culture generally, and formal education specifically, involved in these two groups.

## Functional relations

Let us return to an earlier stage to focus on the non-causal relations between social facts – functional relations. To summarise, the argument is that one set of social facts exists in order to maintain social order itself, for example. We might begin by thinking of society as if it were an organism (a common enough metaphor in the earliest stages of analysing the social, in use long before sociol-ogy as such). Each complex organism has a number of specialised organs which contribute to the maintenance of the whole creature – hearts pump blood, lungs oxygenate that blood, muscles work the limbs, and so on. The activities of each organ only make sense by thinking of their function for the larger organism. Indeed, such organs would not develop if they were not meeting some functional need. Further, the organs are linked to the wider organism in a dynamic relationship: they contribute to the overall health of the organism and help respond to threats to overall health. As the organism places demands on the muscles (as in reacting to a threat, for example), so the heart has to pump harder to maintain healthy activity.

Thinking of another useful metaphor makes a similar point: in a complex technical system, each component makes sense only in the wider context – the processor on this PC has a definite function in handling electronic data, the hard disk and the RAM chips store memory required in different forms, and so on. I shall stop discussing this example before my technical inadequacies are revealed too clearly, and revert to a simpler mechanical device – a central heating system. This consists of a boiler to heat water, radiators to transmit the heat in the water to the air in the room, and a controlling mechanism, a thermostat, to regulate the system. When the temperature falls in the room to a certain level, the thermostat triggers a switch which lights the boiler and pumps the ensuing hot water – the system becomes a self-regulating or self-adjusting one, moving from one state to another within a range as the outside temperature changes.

This is a more dynamic form of functioning, involving constant adjustments and changes in response to the environment, and it is one developed by American functionalism especially, as we shall see when we discuss the work of Parsons below. At its most abstract, thinking of elements related together as systems provides a number of benefits for the analyst. It helps us to see things 'as a whole', for example, and to trace the implications of changes in one element for changes in others that may be related. To take two contemporary practical examples of its use:

1   It helps to think in terms of systems when planning complex organisations (such as a new university). The UK Open University, for example, insisted that course teams consider the easily overlooked implications of each element in terms of its relations with other elements instead of planning each on its own – how should the design of course materials relate to the need to assess students (which usually takes place much later), or to the requirements of the efficient production of printed texts and television programmes?
2   Concepts like an 'eco-system' help draw attention to world consequences of more local decisions like the use of fossil fuels or powerful pesticides: small changes in one area can have large and unwanted changes in others or, indeed, globally.

Systems thinking like this can be said to permeate a good deal of modern management too. The approach became the subject of some famous debates between Habermas, Luhmann and Lyotard (see the online reading guides to Habermas 1976 and Lyotard 1984 for a glimpse).

The first step to help us grasp functionalist analysis is to apply these metaphors to social life. Clearly, there is a sense in which patterns of behaviour can be considered as organs or as components in a wider system. As usual, we cannot proceed without a caution, of course: metaphors or analogies are helpful in some ways, but limiting if taken too literally. We ought to beware of those accounts which take money as directly equivalent to blood, for example, or which see the factory system as the muscles of society. The same problems arise with seeing societies as abstract machine-like systems with laws of their own. Both models minimise the specific qualities of human societies – our ability to become aware of the workings of our society and to intervene to change them, perhaps. A major political problem also arises with trying to define the overall health or technically efficient working range of a society.

However, with those cautions in mind, we can think of possible social functions of patterns of behaviour such as those found in families of various kinds: it will help a society to reproduce itself if adults raise children in a stable way and pass on necessary social knowledge to prepare them for independent lives as adults in turn, and so on. Family structures might be expected to adapt if there are factors which impact upon this process of social reproduction (for example, changes in working practices which affect matters like the 'necessary social knowledge' required to live in new settings, or the skills required to lead 'independent lives'). One famous debate concerned trying to explain an apparent shift from 'extended' to 'nuclear' families in terms of adaptations to changing functional requirements in industrialising societies, for example. As other institutions took over some of the 'traditional' functions of families (such as education), so families adapted to focus on their 'core functions' of providing emotional and personal development (see Fletcher 1966). This adaptation took the form of developing smaller, more emotionally intense units – the 'nuclear family'. Much subsequent debate has questioned the rather cosy interpretations of the activities in modern families here, as you might expect.

Religious behaviour can have a function too, in that it helps to reinforce a set of common values that develop group solidarity and cohesion. In Durkheim's famous analysis, mentioned briefly above, religious rituals focus on 'sacred' values, which, by definition, are not supposed to be debated, doubted or modified to suit individuals. The 'sacred' realm offers an area of social agreement, and therefore of social bonding. This realm too has been adjusted following industrialisation and social change – organised religions might have declined, and relatively simple and 'elementary' forms might have become much more complex and diverse, but are there any traces of religious functions in secular substitutes which might offer an equivalent? How about nationalism, a belief in the holy fatherland, or even, rather paradoxically, the sacred right to be an individual?

A market system is functional for societies like ours, it could be suggested, because it helps our economic system adjust quickly and flexibly: the market could act like the thermostat in the heating system analogy above, helping supply and demand to adjust to the right level within the range.

We are already starting to introduce a certain controversy here, of course, and marxists would want to start pointing to the ideological nature of a formulation of market forces as some sort of neutral subsystem ((re)turn to the previous chapter for more details). They would want to raise questions about religion, nationalism or individualism too, no doubt. Other examples are equally contro-versial. Can a stratification system (a system of unequally rewarded occupations) be seen as functional, for example? Can criminal behaviour be seen as functional?

Actually, it is possible to see both in these terms: the function of a stratification system is to reward jobs of different importance in order to persuade talented people to take on the most important jobs. It is 'an unconsciously evolved device by which societies insure that the most important positions are conscientiously filled by the most qualified persons' (Davis and Moore 1967: 48; and there is an online reading guide to their work for those interested in more detail). This view has some force, of course – clearly it would be in the interests of everyone, long term, that the best people got the most important jobs, since the whole soci-ety would become better-run. No-one would really benefit from having incompetents run industry, government or the courts (except possibly those incompetent individuals themselves, in the short term at least).

Davis and Moore's classic work actually seems rather contemporary. In my view, this sort of functionalist argument can be detected pretty easily lurking in many contemporary discussions of social and educational policy. The desire to achieve 'equal opportunities' or to head for some sort of 'meritocracy' implies a functionalist view of social stratification. If for no other reason than that, let us pursue a few common criticisms of functionalist analysis.

## Conservatism

It is often said that functionalist analysis is conservative, in that it justifies the existing system (stratification in the example above) as 'functional', as somehow grounded in fundamental social prerequisites or basic social categories inherent in a way of life, as the product of evolution, or as underpinned by some mecha-nism working in the background to ensure stability. Anthropologists like Radcliffe-Brown (see Giddens 1996; and the online reading guide to Giddens' essay on functionalism) suggested that this is a useful way to proceed, partly to overcome initial biases about pre-industrial societies. Instead of seeing these societies as 'primitive' or as 'backward' in evolutionary terms, one could begin to grasp them as perfectly well adjusted and functioning adequately in their own terms, despite their differences with our own society.

That said, there is still a tendency towards a conservative assumption that no politics have been involved, so to speak, in the construction of the current arrangements, that some sort of consensus produced the existing institutions. This often makes sense to a naïve observer of the social order, of course. To cite an example of my own naïvety in this matter, I have visited African countries and noticed various communities trying to scratch a living on arid land. My initial assumption was that this was some sort of 'traditional way of life', assuming that the people in those communities had adapted their social arrangements (farming patterns, divisions of labour and the like) to survive in that challenging environment. Not a bit of that was accurate, though – those people had been driven off more fertile land by their political rivals in the fairly recent past, and were still not being permitted to do much more than just survive, using the most basic techniques.

Davis and Moore's model can be seen in this way, as an apology for the American stratification system with its patterns of winners and losers. More generally, the themes of social integration, the importance of shared values, the necessity of social discipline, the anxieties over unregulated individualism, all look pretty uncongenial to some radicals. Yet it is equally possible to make functionalist analysis into a critical technique, by asking whether the existing system is the most functional.

On stratification, for example, questions like the following can arise:

1   Does the current system in the USA or the UK ensure that the most talented people get the most important jobs, or are there clear signs that relatively untalented people are still managing to gain positions of influence?
2   Can the large differences in rewards between the top and bottom jobs be explained simply in functionalist terms? Are the differences so large only because talented individuals have to be motivated to train? Can this sort of argument be used to justify large pay increases for those already in post, like the UK 'fat cats' who benefited from having their state-run enterprises privatised? What about the wealth provided by 'casino capitalism', or the large pay-offs for those who have spectacularly failed to ensure safety on the railways, or guarantee accurate book-keeping?
3   Are there mechanisms that help the stratification system become functional, and are there some which prevent it? Clearly, a meritocratic universal education system might help, for example, while a system of heredity which permits the transmission of substantial advantages from one generation to the next might stand in the way of a properly functioning system. If parental money can buy a good education, independently of merit, can the education system still be functional overall? These insights have led functionalist writers (notably Durkheim) to want to modify the present system of education and hereditary wealth severely to expand opportunities and restrict inheritance in ways that actually look rather 'socialist' or 'liberal'. There are also criticisms of meritocracy in Durkheim (see Gane 1992), although these are put in a context of general concern for the divisive effects of any stratification system.

4    Conversely, an influential British socialist tract from the 1960s (Crosland 1980) operated with clearly functionalist assumptions about stratification and the role to be played by functionally adjusted education systems. Indeed, it is possible to see the search for a functional education system as one element in the great political struggles over types of secondary education in Britain and in other countries in the 1970s and 1980s, and as still present in the stream of initiatives since about 'standards' or about 'vocational relevance'. I have also suggested that the development of Britain's Open University in the 1970s can be seen to involve similar arguments (Harris 1987). Of course, policies at this level involve far more than theories about education; they involve calculations of political and financial advantage as well.

These examples indicate an important point about the radical potential of social sciences to question existing patterns and beliefs, and to demand justification for them. Even where this is not clearly focused on recognisably 'political' issues or explicitly tied to political parties, it lies implicit in the very claims of the discipline to be 'objective' or 'scientific'. The rather abstract project we hinted at above – to explain the links between ideas or cultures and social life – implies a willingness to become detached from those ideas and beliefs and to analyse and criticise them. Functionalists are just as interested in this project as any other sociological tradition (including marxism).

Indeed, a careful reading of Durkheim's famous remarks about treating social facts as things (see, for example, the Author's Preface mentioned above) reveals that this is really a plea for objectivity, a way of avoiding dogmatism or prejudices, and a call for careful research (and not at all a rigid belief in the brute facticity or the remote nature of the social world, as it is sometimes rendered). Similarly, with American sociology, there are dominant trends towards system-building in Parsons, but also an empirical interest in exploring actual aspects of life (such as religious belief, the professions, the education system, social stratification), while Merton is also keen to explore problems 'in the middle range', to borrow one of his famous sayings, and to try out concepts from other disciplines (there are even marxist influences).

In many introductory texts, this common critical mission is forgotten. Indeed, in some, a particular kind of political activism (often a version of a marxist or individual-libertarian activism) is taken as 'normal', and functionalism is defined as hopelessly conservative by comparison. Functionalist writing offers challenges to both elements, it is true. Marxists are criticised for 'economic reductionism' in describing social solidarity (see Chapter 1). Gane's Introduction (Gane 1992) says that, for Durkheim, abolishing classes and letting the state 'wither away' would not by itself create a social system based on a new morality of mutual obligation.

Individualist libertarians are also rebuked for not seeing that a certain level of social discipline and restraint is necessary to individual freedom. On a social and political scale, a number of revolutionary episodes in different European societies have ended in terror and chaos, with the revolutionaries themselves ending as victims, to the disappointment of some initial supporters. It is not clear that it is necessarily 'conservative' to point this out, perhaps to marxists and libertarians especially; this insight could also lead to a better-planned revolution.

The point about social discipline is harder for younger students to grasp, perhaps, since it seems to contradict cherished principles of freedom and independence, but the removal of restraint on a more personal, cultural or local scale can lead to social chaos and harm, functionalists might insist – even to suicide, as we saw. Pointing out this unpopular finding can lead to functionalism being located in the same camp as all those parental obsessions about rules and limits to behaviour. Yet there is a need to step out of immediate understandings and to try to get detached or 'objective' about two matters. First, is there still a necessary level of social discipline somewhere, in any activity or group, or can people live outside of all social obligation and restraint? Second, do the current specific restraints, taboos and traditions express only that necessary level or some additional and unnecessary levels introduced by specific groups for their own benefit in the past?

To help focus this rather abstract issue, consider some applied examples. Most schools have rules governing matters like behaviour and attendance, and perhaps even a dress code. How many of these are really socially necessary for the smooth functioning of the organisation (which is the usual reason given for them), and how many simply reflect the tastes of the school administrators? Even asking this question might well be seen as radical in some institutions of my acquaintance. Proposing a cool, scientific investigation of the issue, involving research on the social effects of relaxing the dress codes, say, could be seen as a dangerous challenge to the 'natural' authority of the present leaders (which, indeed, it might well prove to be). Many conservatives have perceived the threat offered by even functionalist social sciences in opening up for debate what they would rather leave in the background, as a compelling 'tradition'.

On a more general tack, and in the reverse direction, what exactly is the balance between constraint and individual freedom in youth cultures these days? From the outside, it might seem that 'anything goes' in terms of clothing or musical tastes, and spokespersons from the inside often confirm this view that nothing really matters any more as long as people just express themselves. Yet is this the case, or is it that the constraints are just as powerful but different? Are the fine distinctions between good and bad (however the current argot expresses these terms) simply invisible to the non-participant? Let us not take the views of participants or their spokespersons at face value (as so many 'postmodernist' commentators seem to do), but conduct a calm scientific investigation again. Let us do some research on the actual processes of coming to choose an item of clothing for a night out in a club, perhaps. My own suspicion is that if we did so, we might find that the apparent general air of tolerance and 'cool' towards these matters would probably reveal deeper patterns of intolerance and conformity – but I could be wrong.

The promise of functionalist social science is that it might be possible to answer questions like these in a far more 'objective' and systematic way than is customary in contemporary social commentary, to get genuine answers to them, and perhaps even to generate a new social consensus as a result. There is no need to assume that the new consensus would be a narrowly conservative or repressive one. We might be able to demonstrate that dress codes really are irrelevant to social solidarity in schools, or that anxieties about being seen in the wrong gear at nightclubs are misplaced and irrational. It might be appropriate to make a more general and technical point about small-scale interaction too. As we shall see, a focus on such interactionism, as in sociological 'action theory', is by no means incompatible with functionalist views about the wider social structure.

On a larger social scale, we could really try to pin down issues such as whether single-parent families were threatening the basis of social order, or whether immigration really was weakening our sense of national identity. To raise an issue now that reappears later, we might begin to think out problems like the social divisions based on gender: do these arise out of 'natural' social divisions between men and women which are somehow integral to social life itself, or might they be investigated and reassessed in terms of their apparent functioning in contemporary societies?

We shall return to the issue of conservatism in some of the other sections below. Merton's more concrete and specific work on deviancy, for example (Merton 1968), attempts to analyse the phenomenon more systematically, to consider as deviant acts that are quite 'respectable' and fully legal (such as 'ritualism' – the wasteful 'going through the motions' that is characteristic of much white-collar work), not just those banned under current laws. He also wants to locate part of the cause in the structured contradictions of American society – which is hardly likely to endear him to some current American or British conservatives.

I hope I have shown in this section that functionalist analysis need not necessarily be conservative in celebrating the existing arrangements of society as the only functional ones. There are clear critical options in functionalism, at the most obvious level in the work of Durkheim (Gane [1992] points out that Durkheim can be linked directly with the support for the soviet system in revolutionary Russia, for example). Yet there are also conservative functionalist thinkers – or perhaps conservative tendencies in individual thinkers like Parsons – who do come close to an uncritical celebration of American capitalism. That is a pretty popular and widespread perspective more generally at present, of course.

The real issue is a technical one again – must the conceptual structure of functionalism lead more often to conservatism? Or, to put it slightly differently, can functionalism only become critical and analytic by borrowing more critical concepts from other traditions and somehow 'adding them on' to functionalism itself (which is one way of reading Merton's or Parsons' work)? In general, critical options might exist in a social science, but these might not be exercised unless a number of assumptions are carefully identified and thought out. The critical power of a perspective can be directed towards a number of targets, after all, while other possibilities are omitted: classically, social class divisions dominate the agenda but not gender divisions, for example. Why should this be? Is this an innocent omission, or one which reflects some deeper flaw in the project?

## Summary

There seem to be assumptions in functionalist work that social order is normal and revolutionary upheaval abnormal. This point is hard to illustrate in a short discussion, but it is sometimes shown best by specific arguments. In his discussion of role conflict, for example, Merton (1968) thinks that such conflict simply must be resolved in the end, even though the actual forces leading to role conflict seem strong and permanent – somehow, the brute fact of social order justifies this faith in order as an outcome. More generally, Parsons seems to believe that the USA represents some sort of well-adjusted and functional adaptation, compared to its Cold War rivals at least, even though his actual theoretical position (and some of his more concrete analysis) keeps open more critical options. This kind of point invoking some social drive or goal towards stability will be discussed below, and you might like to think out some possible problems with it now – is this sort of argument that order *must* be present based on empirical evidence, on some prior assumptions, or on some confusing mixture of the two? Shrewd readers will note that we raised a similar sceptical question (in Chapter 1) about the marxist claim that struggle *must* be present in current societies.

It could be possible to argue that this assumption of order is going to predispose functionalists to get 'lazy' about actual societies, again just as marxists can do, to assume (in this case) that stable ones simply must be functional for some deep reason. Tendencies towards trying to systematise and build general models of abstract social mechanisms (as in Parsons' work) can also draw attention away from specifics. On the other hand, there is also a scientific curiosity about functionalism, we have argued, that can lead it into a critical stance and an interest in specifics (including specific strains and contradictions) almost despite its founding assumptions. This is certainly detectable in the work of all three of the main spokespersons we have cited here (according to their more sympathetic critics). Even so there is not enough of a scientific drive to grasp the 'real' sources of strain and contradiction for marxists or feminists, though. To identify those would require placing them at the very heart of the project.

## Formalism

Functionalist analysis, like many general theories, is accused of operating with abstract models of the social system that are too general to grasp much of the concrete detail of its workings. We have seen something of this criticism in the asides on Bourdieu on the role of social practice; we have also seen this critique applied to marxism, and we will consider it again when we look at models which stress concrete political mechanisms as the main integrating forces in social life (in later chapters). The argument is parallel to the one we have seen in the previous chapter – how can we move from a general model to analyse much more complex specific cases, without just applying the same old concepts to everything? Parsons' work is usually held up to be the worst example of this tendency (see a number of commentaries, including Craib 1992 or Rocher 1974).

In the most abstract and theoretically systematised version of this work, Parsons suggests that the same structures or mechanisms underpin all aspects of social life. There are common 'pattern variables' to explain all possible options: for example, all institutions display a tendency to value either (essentially) personal or impersonal behaviour, or 'affective' (emotional) or 'affective-neutral' relationships, to reward 'ascribed' or 'achieved' statuses, and so on. There is also a model operating at more general levels – the AGIL model (see Figure 2.1).

This model clearly relates back to the idea of universal functions we discussed above, and suggests that any system needs specialised subsystems to achieve adaptation, goal-setting, integration and 'latency' (meaning the symbolic representation of functional mechanisms in cultural systems – this explains how individuals actually get to become motivated to act in the interests of the system). Rocher says that Parsons uses this model at a number of levels, to describe social systems, also the workings of small groups, and, indeed, even individual personalities. The pattern variables can be connected to the AGIL model, since particular activities require particular types of behaviour (adaptation favours specificity and performance, while latency favours quality and diffuseness – see Rocher 1974; there is an online reading guide to aspects of Rocher's work too).

Parsons' model seems to offer a very high level of explanatory power, and you can see the appeal for those interested in a general social theory of everything. Parsons seems to have integrated a number of levels of analysis and a number of trends in social theory for that matter: he thought he had integrated (and corrected) the main insights of Weber on rational action, and Freud on the personality, and linked functionalist sociology and biology (Rocher 1974). We might be able to illustrate the power of the approach, and get to the point of this section, by giving a few more concrete examples.

To cite a very brief example, Parsons (1961) applied the pattern variables approach to explain the relations between American families and schools. The child learns to experience all the nice, warm, person-centred, emotional types of relationship in families, but he or she also needs experience of the impersonal, rational, achievement-oriented relationships of the wider society. Families cannot supply this experience, so schools exist to fill the gap and to prepare the child to take part in the values and relationships of work.

This brief and simplified example may have helped to illustrate the power of the approach. The regime and culture of schools become explicable as following

**The AGIL model**

| A  (adaptation) | G  (goal-setting) |
|---|---|
| L  (latency) | I  (integration) |

**The pattern variables**

| Affective neutrality | Affectivity |
|---|---|
| Universalism | Particularism |
| Specificity | Diffuseness |
| Performance | Quality |
| Achievement-orientation | Ascription-orientation |
| Self-orientation | Collectivity-orientation |

NB: the last two pairs were dropped in later versions.

**The models combined (Rocher 1974: 44)**

|  | universalism (O) neutrality (M) | affective (O) particularism (M) |  |
|---|---|---|---|
| specificity (O) performance (M) | A | G | performance (O) specificity (M) |
| quality (O) diffuseness (M) | L | I | diffuseness (O) quality (M) |
|  | neutrality (O) universalism (M) | particularism (O) affectivity (M) |  |

(O) refers to pattern variables (PVs) that relate to 'attitude or orientation to the object'; (M) refers to pattern variables 'of object modality'. Rocher (1974: 39) explains that the PVs marked (O) refer to the 'actor and define his attitude towards the object and the type of relationship he has with it'. Those marked (M) refer to 'the object to which the actor relates, to the meaning the object has for the actor and the kind of judgement which is called for from the actor'. This reflects the action–situation duality, Rocher assures us, but he later confesses that he finds the word 'modality' 'impenetrably vague', and seeks another definition – 'a modality is a property of an object; it is one of the aspects of an object in terms of which the object may be significant to the actor' (Rocher 1974: 32 n. 9).

**Figure 2.1 Parsons and the social system (Rocher 1974)**

a deeper social purpose, rather than being designed simply to achieve the technical tasks of education. The social aspects of schooling are stressed and made much clearer than is usual in the continual discussions on them: we have here a powerful vocabulary to analyse the issue, to explain certain of the tensions between homes and schools, and almost to serve as a checklist to evaluate the extent to which actual schools really do function as they should.

You might already wish to note down some assumptions in this analysis too. Politically, it is uncritical of the actual values schools perpetuate, and it might be worth comparing it to a famous marxist approach to the social role of school values (Bowles and Gintis 1976, 2002; and the accompanying online reading guides). There are notions of 'ideal' families and schools, of course. More generally, concrete examples must fit these models and, in skilled hands, they always do, but in a suspiciously 'easy' way. Either people like Parsons really have discovered genuinely universal structures of functional integration, or there is a tendency to massage the concrete examples to make them fit, by overlooking details, perhaps, or by deciding in advance that schools must have the functions that theory suggests.

However, functionalist analysis can be developed in a more concrete direction. Rocher (1974) suggests that Parsons was alert to this problem and conceived the pattern variables as representing dilemmas for action, choices rather than universal trends heading in some inevitable direction (towards 'performance', for example). The social system might drive towards stability in the long term, but there are always disruptions and tensions to manage, introduced by the actions of people such as politicians or entrepreneurs.

Hopper (1971) has taken this reading and analysed the 'functionalist dilemmas' embodied in different forms of social mobility, for example. Social mobility is an important aspect of debates about social stratification, we have suggested already, since it (usually) refers to the ways in which people move up or down the system of stratification compared to their parents. Since 'merit' is probably not easily transmitted from parents to offspring, we should expect to find rather a lot of social movement between the generations, and mechanisms designed to ensure that such movement takes place efficiently. In Hopper's work, which draws on earlier models developed by Turner (see Hopper 1971), there are two main types of social mobility.

Firstly, 'sponsored' forms, as in Britain of the 1970s (and still today?), identified a future elite early and gave them a special education separated from the others, to fit them to their future role as leaders. Those who were not selected reconciled themselves to a modest status: the system produced little social unrest but also a great waste of potential talent. In Britain, the selection used to take place at the age of 11, for example, when most children took a national examination that determined their chances of entering prestigious schools. As many critics at the time pointed out, the tests were likely to reward the children of elite families anyway, and, more obviously, the system gave little comfort to 'late developers'. As an aside, the system persists in some parts of the UK – such as in my current home town – but as a voluntary form of selection. Debates about the 'fairness' of the test still occur (but without much research to support it these days). A recent finding was that the test rewards girls, for example, who mature much more rapidly than do boys at the age of 11. Many teachers still find the idea of selection at 11 to be morally repulsive but there are three points to make in response:

1   The selective system delivered a substantial number of 'working-class' males to university-level education, about the same proportion as the new 'comprehensive' systems did (in the 1980s when they were compared by Halsey et al. 1980 – an online reading guide summarises the main findings of this and its companion study).

2   Selection is still an important issue in the provision of schooling in Britain, despite the abolition of the formal examination at 11. It is just that selection now takes place through the housing market, as parents vie with each other to buy houses in areas where their offspring can attend 'good' schools. Middle-class parents are also increasingly turning to private tutoring for their offspring to confer an advantage, it seems.

3   Children did not cease to be tested at the early age of 11 with the formal abolition of selective secondary schooling – indeed they are now tested nationally at 11 years, and at 7, 14, 16 and 18 years as well.

To use Hopper's terms, given that we seem inevitably to use our education system to select children for subsequent occupations, what is the most functional (and fair?) way to do so?

The second type of social mobility involved more open 'contest' systems, as in the USA, which offered different possibilities. Here, the selection of the future elite was delayed, and was to be delivered after a long period of open contest or competition in schools that children from all social groups attended. This system arguably delivered a more efficient use of talent, by 'warming up' able members of non-elite groups (although there was unlikely ever to be a fully open contest). Such 'first-generation' scholars would come to mix with more ambitious teachers and colleagues, and would raise their own ambitions. This is precisely what was supposed to happen with 'social mixing' in British neighbourhood comprehensive schools, and advocates like Crosland (1980) also hoped that equal respect for members of different groups would develop too.

The 'contest' system also posed problems of potential social unrest, however, as many people came to realise they were not going to succeed fully after all, even after a long period of delay and hope. It might be expected that the toughest cases included those students from elite families who unfortunately lacked talent themselves, although these are not well researched. Such people had to be 'cooled out', to learn to adjust their hopes and ambitions to their actual merits and abilities. At one level, individual teachers had this cooling-out role, which was discharged through activities like assessment and counselling. More generally, the USA went on to develop an elaborate 'cooling-out' system which included the development of special 'junior colleges', (to use the terms in the classic analysis by Clark 1960) where people could still feel they had made it to college, while being steered gradually towards the less prestigious courses and options, and the lower levels of the occupational structure.

Reading this classic work over again reminds me of how important it still seems to be, setting aside its purely theoretical merits for a moment, in discussing both policy matters and professional practice. The UK government is struggling at the moment to reconcile an expansion of higher education with signs of social tension arising from the 'over-production' of university graduates. There is also a strain between granting nearly all institutions of higher education the title of 'university' (since 1992), and maintaining differential funding to protect the elite universities. Given the government's intention to increase to 50 per cent the proportion of the age group attending university, suspicions have been raised again that this will be achieved largely by granting more institutions the title but not the substance of 'university' as the equivalent of 'junior colleges'.

There is talk of a new division emerging between those elite universities (the Russell Group as they are sometimes known) and the rest, or between the 'new' and the 'traditional' universities. There is even explicit talk of developing a 'junior college' stratum. Underneath these discussions, conducted in the peculiar codes of British politicians and academics, it is possible to see the issues of 'the regulation of ambition' and 'cooling out' identified far more clearly by Hopper and Clark. Few of the politicians involved seem to have realised the importance of the professional teacher in regulating ambition, however, although many individual colleagues will see the significance immediately.

Before we leave the substance of the work, perhaps you will be aware of episodes in your own educational careers where you have been 'warmed up' or 'cooled out' by individuals or educational systems? Normally, these matters are discussed in terms of the actions of dedicated individual teachers, who, classically, take you aside for personal pep talks, but do you think it possible to analyse these episodes in terms of well or poorly functioning *systems*? Do some educational systems encourage these encounters with ambition-regulators rather than others? What aspects of the system (such as the assessment system) support these regulatory activities?

## An inability to explain change and conflict

This critique is usually connected with the others discussed above, but we can isolate it slightly artificially here. To summarise, the objection is that functionalism is not very good at explaining social change, or, indeed, social conflict. If most of the social mechanisms tend towards functional adjustment, as a general principle, how can societies change? For that matter, how can functionalism explain the persistence of what looks very much like structured social and political conflict around irreconcilable values – 'schisms', as Lockwood (1992) calls them? To take some obvious examples, the apparently functional and integrative mechanism we have mentioned already – families, religion, stratification systems – can also generate sustained factional conflict.

Functionalism can explain change, although, as before, the issue then becomes more technical – how *adequately* does functionalism explain change? To expand on the first point, functionalist writings, in the different forms of

Durkheimian or American functionalism, are concerned with social change, as we have seen, especially the changes introduced by pressures of economic growth and what might be called the forced social mixing of different social groups with their different moralities (in the general sense). These changes are seen as somehow external to the existing social arrangements, and require some sort of adaptive response – new forms of family life or of religion, or new meritocratic forms of stratification, for example.

This adaptation can even be thought of in terms of a kind of evolution, to pursue the biological metaphor: just as species adapt to new conditions in the environment, so societies adapt and 'evolve' to meet the new conditions. Other formulations use the other main metaphor (the systems approach), and describe more rapid adjustments, detectable in special adaptive mechanisms or special sectors, as we can see in Parsons' AGIL model.

Of course, there are bound to be areas caught in transition between the old and the new ways of life. Such 'functional lags' can produce social conflict between leading and trailing sectors. Given that no mechanisms of adaptation, integration or latency can be perfect, there will also be social deviants who are weakly socialised into the dominant norms for one reason or another (perhaps because they live in 'lagging' areas). Such deviance can take a number of forms, from a reluctance to move with the times and to seize the new opportunities, to more open expressions of discontent such as criminal activity and suicide, or 'norm-lessness' – 'anomie'. We will return to functionalist accounts of deviancy below, but as an aside, it might be worth noting that such deviance or social conflict can be 'functional' in the longer term, since, in a way, it assists eventual social adaptation. Deviance draws attention to social problems, focuses efforts to restore solidarity, and even helps 'normal' folk strengthen their own values by contrast.

Is this an adequate account of the sort of changes introduced by industrialisation and modernism? Clearly, rival accounts such as marxism would want to conceive of the dynamic force of industrialisation rather differently. As we saw in the previous chapter, the system has an ingenious form of exploitation at its heart, rather than some neutral evolutionary process, and class interests drive it. Of course, those class interests have long ago attempted to pass themselves off as representing 'society', or 'progress', and to label their political opponents as 'deviants' needing to move with the times. Marxist predictions of the future of capitalist societies were also rather different – not adaptation but a revolutionary break lay in wait, and, until that happened, conflict would be structured around the fundamental opposition of interests between exploiters and exploited, not a temporary problem of adjustment.

Marxism has its problems too, though. If you wanted to, you could choose between these alternative general models, with their technical and political implications. Which one seems best at explaining recent history to you, for example? Which one would serve us best in guiding social policy to alleviate some of the inequalities our systems seem to generate, or to help underprivileged groups adjust to social changes like the apparent 'collapse of work'?

Perhaps some sort of compromise might be possible. Modern marxists have had to acknowledge the persistence of mechanisms of social stability and the impact of conservative values, we have argued. Where functionalist analysis seems to be especially weak is in explaining those occasions where localised conflicts turn out to be not functional at all for the existing order. Such conflicts can escalate into serious disorder (as in civil war) or into substantial social change (such as successful independence movements for former colonies). Here, there is something more at stake than just a normal level of deviance – somehow, this sort of deviance gets patterned, structured and organised around a conception of an altogther alternative society with different shared values. Perhaps, from the perspective of functionalist theory, there is an equal need to address the issue of these structured conflicts, generated internally, so to speak, as a persistent possibility, as a result of some permanent mechanism in social life itself. There are at least two alternatives here.

Merton (1968; and see Sztompka 1986) has pointed to a permanent source of functional strain in contemporary US society between the value system and the social structure. To expand this famous account slightly, the common value system of the USA stresses individual achievement with no official regulation of ambition (to cite terms we used above). All citizens are encouraged to achieve, to dream the American Dream of going from rags to riches, from log cabin to White House. Yet the social structure offers its citizens very unequal chances of making that journey. In the most spectacular cases, some people are far more likely to be excluded from various higher circles because of their ethnic origins or their social background (and we might want to add gender). This is a permanent source of strain which is unlikely to go away; indeed it might well deepen as the belief in equal opportunity and limitless attainment spreads to groups who had been willing to exclude themselves before (Merton's original account mentions women and black people as just about to participate in the American Dream, and thus just about to experience serious social strain as a result).

Merton (1968) went on to classify possible responses to such strain in a famous and influential piece. Basically, people could restore some sort of equilibrium between dreams and opportunities in only a few ways (see Figure 2.2). People could both accept official values and try to take advantage of official opportunities ('conformists'), or, in an interesting option, radically reject both and engage on a career of political rebellion as permanent and dedicated opponents of the system. Other options depend on different combinations, as Figure 2.2 indicates. The 'innovator' is an interesting category, much debated as providing an explanation for professional crime, such as the criminal rackets in Chicago in the 1920s. It is interesting to note that 'ritualists' are still deviants for Merton: even though they are doing nothing illegal, they are engaged in activities that are, arguably, just as damaging to social life as criminal activities.

This model has been developed in various ways to explain crime and delinquency and, for that matter, 'youth culture' as a kind of symbolic protest (see Downes and Rock 1988), or solutions to the tensions produced by various

| Modes of adaptation | Culture/ goals | Institutionalised means |
|:---:|:---:|:---:|
| Conformity | + | + |
| Innovation | + | − |
| Ritualism | − | + |
| Retreatism | − | − |
| Rebellion | +/− | +/− |

Plus signs indicate acceptance, minuses rejection.

**Figure 2.2 Adaptation to Social Strain. (Adapted with the permission of The Free Press, a Division of Simon and Schuster, Inc., from Social Theory and Social Structure, revised and enlarged edition by Robert K. Merton. Copyright © 1967, 1968 by Robert K. Merton.)**

routes in social mobility (Hopper 1981). I hope it is also clear that it offers quite a check to those who want to argue that functionalism must be conservative or unable to generate concrete research – Merton's work, arguably, modifies, modernises and develops functionalism much as Althusser's did for marxism.

Of course, as with Althusser, not all the critics are satisfied by these modifications. The concept of what might be called 'functionalism in the last instance' is as problematic as is 'economic determinism in the last instance' for marxism: can functionalist concepts still be smuggled in at the end without some loss of detail? All the tensions and strains must be seen as ultimately traceable to some functioning social formation if the analysis is still to be called 'functionalist' in any real sense. But do we actually need this final level of explanation, and, if so, can this final level really be connected essentially to all the concrete variations, or is it something more like an optional extra? (See the essay in Giddens 1996 here, and the online reading guide.)

This sort of argument reappears in the next chapter when we consider what are often classified in British introductory texts as 'action' approaches. As is well known, these focus on the detailed interactions of individuals as they construct some kind of temporary social order. Other approaches also propose we abandon the functionalist final level of explanation, as we shall see. The main question to consider at this stage is still the original one of social order, however – why do social patterns arise and persist, and why is disorder not more common?

## Social goals?

I have left this type of criticism until last, as probably the most technical one. Functionalism is quite a normal and routine mode of analysis for concrete organisations or groups, as we have suggested with some of our examples above.

Politicians and administrators seem to think in functionalist terms quite 'spon-
taneously' when considering matters like how to plan an effective organisation.
Something like Parsons' AGIL model reappears quite frequently in management discussions (in educational management anyway), perhaps in a slightly
different order. Classically, we make our goals nice and specific, and perhaps
talk about matters of adaptation in the process, then we consider problems of
implementation and evaluation of our efforts.

If we have been on a course recently, we might talk more specifically about
the 'culture' of our organisations, and how to change or consolidate it (that is,
make it latent in Parsons' terms). We will be thinking generally in terms of isolating what is functional for the attainment of these goals, and we will often be
specifically discussing managing 'human resources' in functional terms – what
system of promotion (local social mobility) to install, and how to build a committed team (local social solidarity). Individuals too think in functionalist
terms – they pursue 'what works for them'.

Yet it is a different matter to think out more general social processes in functionalist terms, because there is no identifiable manager, person or agent to
calculate what works and what does not. No individual has actually designed a
stratification system, yet the system tends towards a functional state at a deeper
level, an 'unconscious' level for Davis and Moore, as we saw. If we have no individual designer, we cannot use a classic type of explanation in social science – to
refer to the motive of an actual person and then to see the result as an expression
of that motive. We seem to be left instead with some group – society itself —
with a motive. This can seem rather mystical: how can it lead to a social science?

Perhaps it need not be so strange an idea to think of some sort of separate
social level, even though it might offend our currently fashionable individu-
alised sensibilities to have to admit to such a thing. Durkheim and others did
flirt with the idea of a mysterious 'group mind', probably to help make the case
for sociology as a special science of the social (see Lukes 1975). An obvious
immediate candidate for an institution that represents the social level is the
modern state, of course. After all, officially, democratic states represent all of us,
some universal interest, 'the nation' or 'the people'.

It is not surprising to find a strong connection between functionalist conceptions of the social and liberal-democratic conceptions of the state: more than one
analyst has seen a major role for sociology in helping politicians decide what
really is in the national interest (by carrying out research on social patterns or
currents, or on the effectiveness on social solidarity of social reforms, for example). Of course, in western democratic societies, the state alone would never be
allowed to stand for the social – we are accustomed to a strong 'civil society' of
institutions outside the state, serving more specialised functions (integration or
latency in Parsons' terms), and helping to maintain 'balance' or to explore inno-
vations.

Back at the theoretical level there are other conceptions, in biology or ecology
(as we saw above) and in linguistics especially, which help us grasp the idea of

a collective social unconscious. Before we get there, though, let us consider another problem.

We also seem to have to abandon another type of explanation and thus to depart from the 'scientific' programme we discussed earlier, since classic science seems to operate with causal models. Causes of events have to happen first, but we only know about the functional trends in society after the event: looking back, we can see that the current social order is the result of past evolutionary or systems adjustments. But there is a dilemma here – should we see these past events as causes in the classic sense, or is a functional relation something else?

Those opting for functionalism as different from causal analysis encounter additional problems. Technically, functionalist models are different because they seem to run in the opposite direction to causal models, so to speak, and this can provide a logical difficulty. The flow of time helps us differentiate causes from effects (causes come first), and we can use this temporal dimension to test out causes (by asking 'Did X actually come before Y?' 'Does X always come before Y?', and so on). But there is no easy way to test out a functionalist account like this – all the elements of a system interact with each other. With social systems, we cannot unplug one component at a time and test the effects (although we can study deviants to see if any of the components are 'missing', so to speak). As a result, there is an inevitable element of circularity in functionalist analysis for some critics (see Hindess 1977 on Parsons; and the online reading guide to Hindess). We only know that elements interact to form a system by deciding to study them as a system in the first place. Once we have defined them as a system, it makes sense to see each element as functional, but only because we have been working backwards, so to speak. This is the problem of tautology.

This form of backwards working is open to all sorts of subjective influences and biases. It is suspiciously easy to introduce the conclusions you want to find. Persisting institutions must be functional, universal institutions must be functional, institutions which seem to have died out or faded must be dysfunctional, and any institutions which have lasted a long time despite being unpopular must be functional at the 'latent' level but not at the 'manifest' level. The problem arises when we come to consider just what we mean by 'persistent' or 'universal' (or, come to that, what counts as an 'institution'). What is it that defines a 'family', for example, so that we can use the same term to describe a number of different practices over time – the arrangements we have now as well as the arrangements our remote ancestors had? If we are not careful, we find ourselves defining concepts like 'family' in terms of their functions – organisations that raise children, offer regulated sex to adults, and so on. Now the circle is complete, however: we have defined all the terms so that they must support each other. The persistence of the family shows that social systems are best analysed as functionally organised, but then a 'family' is defined as an institution that has the same basic functions despite superficial changes!

I always think of this problem when watching wildlife programmes on television. The earnest off-screen commentary tries to explain to us all the wonders of Nature's functioning. The bright plumage of a bird of paradise is functional (in attracting mates), we are told, as is the poison secreted by tree frogs (deterring predators), and the social organisation of the termite colony. After a while, you suspect that anything and everything can be explained in this way, with little further effort – since birds, frogs and termites have patently managed to survive, any of their characteristics could be seen as having some in-built survival value, but only because we know that they have survived!

Biology (not necessarily the version which informs television programmes) has supported the idea of functionalism in sociology. In biology, for example, it is not uncommon to encounter notions of evolution or change at levels other than that of the individual animal. The species itself evolves, for example, or, more recently, genetic material (DNA) or 'memes' evolve. In both cases this evolutionary pressure goes on behind the backs of the individual members of the species, or individual carriers of the genes. In a similar way, it might be possible to think of human societies as an equivalent to a species, with goals of survival and adaptation that are not fully realised in individuals. These notions are not normally seen as 'mystical' in biology – indeed, they are probably essential, at least as 'heuristics' (explanatory devices), although it seems there are certain controversies about how the processes of 'adaptation' to 'environments' actually are to be conceived.

Of course, analogies between human and animal or mechanical systems are always debatable. Incidentally, I think the recent controversies about naïve versions of evolutionary theory in biology offer another point of contact for discussions of functionalism.

Would more sophisticated versions of evolutionary theory help to rescue functionalism from this problem? I have only access to popular accounts, but it seems that work like Gould (1990) or Gee (2000) seems to promise to develop an evolutionary theory that is not dependent on tautology. Nor is it dependent on teleology, that is, the assumption that there is some goal-seeking behaviour in evolution, some notion of progress towards more and more advanced forms. Instead, endless and unmotivated biological variety is both stimulated and 'selected' by much more complex and frequent changes in environments than had been assumed before. The concept of 'cladistics' also contains powerful methodological arguments against the usual narratives of progress, which, Gee (2000) argues, cannot be sustained over 'deep time'.

Finally, to revert to the other analogy we tried out earlier, even if components of a system had the ability to reflect on their own individual role, they would probably not realise at first that there was a deeper system role as well – it would be an 'underspecified goal' for them (Pask 1976). This notion too offers certain dilemmas when considering human societies specifically. On the one hand, it evokes some mysterious deeper purpose behind social life, but, on the other, it might be helping us to see that individuals do have a limited impact on systems. As an example, when the actions of many individuals get combined together, consequences arise that none of them was able to predict as an individual. In this sense, social systems really are more than just the sum of their individual parts.

## The linguistic variant of the *collective consciousness*

It is obvious that a language is a system which 'has a life of its own' – the words, and the rules to combine them, predate any current individual speaker, and also constrain to a certain extent the activities of any actual speaker or writer. This is a system that we get socialised into, and we use it quite unconsciously to produce our own thoughts and statements. It is apparent that languages change as new words and usages appear; yet no-one actually seems to be responsible individually for such change.

More technically, one of the great breakthroughs in modern social science came when analysts began to try to trace the rules of the system of language as a whole – how meaning is constructed and conveyed by a system of similarities and differences between sounds, for example, or how speakers seem to be able immediately to distinguish meaningful sentences (the detailed examples do not matter). These rules operate unconsciously in any competent speaker, of course.

Sociologists and anthropologists were quick to apply this insight and to search for other structured rules of social life operating collectively and unconsciously. There is an excellent and readable account of the development of the notion of 'structure' in social theory in Boyne's contribution to Turner (1996). Boyne traces the principles through Durkheim, but also via other exponents of the biological analogy such as Spencer and Radcliffe- Brown, through to modern structuralism and post-structuralism, encompassing the work of several theorists whom we shall examine in later chapters.

In the time and space available we have to make choices, and I have chosen to outline in more detail the work of Lévi-Strauss. This famous anthropologist explicitly based his 'structuralist' approach on the progress made in structural linguistics (see Part 1 in Lévi-Strauss 1977 – and there is an online reading guide), and thought he had discovered similar underlying structures and rules in the ways in which kinship systems were developed. As Figure 2.3 shows, certain basic units of relationship (adult–child, male–female, blood ties–marriage ties) can be linked in several ways (warm–cool, for example). Once you know the terms and the rules, you can explain large numbers of actual kinship systems: ones where biological parents raise their children warmly while getting cooler towards their own parents, for example, or ones where uncles raise the children of their sisters (since in that system, warmer blood ties between members of the same generation are balanced by cooler ones across the generations).

Naturally, as an analysis of kinship specifically, Lévi-Strauss's work is controversial (see the commentary in Leach 1970). As an obvious point, he seems to be showing how 'natural' divisions between sexes and generations underpin social arrangements. Indeed, he was to argue specifically that the domination of women was integral to this system – family structures are cemented, and, crucially, incest avoided by men giving away their daughters to other men. Of course, whether he approved personally of this practice is another matter, but for some critics there was insufficient critical analysis.

Let us stick to the principles of the analysis – that structures and rules underpin all the apparent diversity of activities seen in a number of specific societies and locations. These structures serve as a kind of collective, unconscious set of ordering devices, of which the participants need not be aware, but which proper social science can uncover and clarify. We have to uncover these structures by examining how classifications and the practices in which they are embedded are related to one another in whole systems. Empirical data are important in this process, but empirical study alone will not reveal these underlying structures, partly because they are never fully expressed in individual activity. We seem to have found a 'social' level or order behind the specific activities of actual individuals and groups.

Not surprisingly structuralism spawned a number of insightful studies into other human cultural practices. Lévi-Strauss himself analysed certain culinary practices as examples of symbolic structures – briefly, the few basic relationships between raw and cooked types of food symbolised deeper issues of the relationships between nature and culture, for example. The development of social practices connected with cooking (such as various rituals in the gathering, preparation or use of food) involved a kind of physical enactment of thinking about important philosophical issues such as where human beings had come

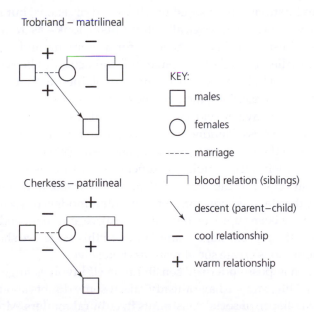

**Figure 2.3 Lévi-Strauss's structural analyses of kinship (Lévi-Strauss 1977: 45).**
**English translation © 1963 by Basic Books, Inc. Reprinted by permission of Basic**
**Books, a member of Perseus Books, LLC.**

from, and what was their proper place in the natural order. (This work is summarised and criticised in Mennell 1985 – and see the online reading guide.)

Lévi-Strauss's work on myths in non-industrial societies (involving the same approach of identifying basic units and their relationships and explaining specific myths as variants of this structure – see Boyne in Turner 1996) inspired work on the cultural practices of industrial societies too, including some famous work on the deep structures of the fashion industry (Culler 1976), or even on the underlying mechanisms and codings of the Bond movies (Eco 1982).

This story can be spelled out in more detail when we consider the 'linguistic turn' in social theory in later chapters. As we shall see, there is an ironic outcome with the linguistic turn. Briefly, instead of structural linguistics remaining as a helpful analogy to keep functionalist sociology in business, it became apparent that it had ambitions to replace sociology altogether. It might be clear already that the examples used above indicate a very wide range of application for structuralist linguistics, to include cultural matters as well as the traditional sociological concerns like kinship. As with marxism, studying cultural matters – art, literature, music or film – leads to the issue of determinism again. Cultural matters can be studied in their own right as autonomous areas of inquiry: is there really a need continually to refer back to social origins? Indeed, culture might even have escaped sociological origins altogether (if not entirely escaped structural linguistic rules and patterns).

We saw this in the previous chapter when we asked whether it was always necessary to refer everything back to the one magic original moment of creation in an economic system. This argument can be generalised to cover functionalist sociology too. Durkheim might have been right to insist that the origin of 'representations' lay in social practices and divisions, but is that helpful or necessary today? Sociological determinism looks as reductionist as economic determinism. To change theorists for a moment, and to return to a problem raised earlier: can all our popular cultural activities be seen as fitting into the AGIL model? Have we satisfactorily explained activities (a film by Tarantino, perhaps) by ascribing them to one of the four underlying functions?

Cultural meanings have developed 'on their own', as the particular cultural specialisms make progress. Paintings or films come to refer to other paintings or films, or to develop their own specialist languages and practices that no longer just refer back to their social origins or functions. Culture is no longer just a symbol for social order: in the work of Baudrillard (1983; and see the online reading guide), the stage where culture represented models of social life (as in Durkheim) has long been supplanted by more creative and independent periods until we arrive at the present stage – simulation. In this stage, we shall discover, cultural representations create social realities themselves.

Of course, such a 'postmodernist' sensibility itself involves huge generalisations about social life, and we have already raised some doubts about the extent of the apparent collapse of social constraints in cultural matters. More cautious writers (such as Crook et al. 1992) acknowledge the continued persistence of local constraints at least. To end on a Durkheimian note, is it conceivable that all social constraint will vanish, leaving people entirely free to invent their own lives? Or will new solidarities arise, maybe not as compelling or as long term in their effects, but still constraining?

## Concluding thoughts

Functionalist analysis has its problems and its critics, as do all the other approaches we will have discussed, but it is not completely worthless. Even though fashion has moved away from functionalist writers in introductory texts (in the UK at least), many other theorists still find it useful, and the works of Durkheim or Parsons are still frequently cited. More surprisingly, perhaps, I find that functionalist analysis has simply dominated numbers of political commentaries (including the debates about 'inclusion'), and it has swamped some of the 'applied' disciplines such as education. A functionalist perspective has become almost the 'common sense' of the modern manager, quite often in a peculiarly naïve form. Of course, we have to reject the claim that functionalist analysis is complete and sufficient on its own. None of the three main theorists we have discussed ever believed that it was, and it is possible to find all of them being much more tentative and self-critical than some of the summaries would have you believe. In a nutshell, all three thought of a fully functional society, tightly integrated around a set of common values, as a limit case, a matter of 'the last instance' only (to borrow a marxist term).

More recent commentators have used this sort of approach too. The contributors in Alexander's collection, for example (Alexander 1988), want to explore some current local solidarities in European and American societies using functionalist (Durkheimian) terms. For these analysts, tensions and splits between the sacred and the profane, analysis of mechanical and organic bonds, and the continued importance of social ritual continue to inform analysis of current society. Stripping off the evolutionary assumptions and the tendencies to conservatism in Parsons, Rocher (1974) believes, could also relaunch a programme to continue concrete investigations into patterns of tension and stability in areas of modern life. Sztompka (1986) says the same for Merton.

It is easy to be misled by some commentaries, especially those trying to establish that 'postmodernism' has made all classic sociology redundant. I was surprised to find, on rereading some of the classics, for example, the extent to which they do acknowledge the tensions, strains and contradictions of modern society (including a full awareness of the tendency of human beings to reflect upon their past actions and to act accordingly). The terms and concepts used still have a certain currency, for politicians, as we have seen, as well as for academics.

Of course, these modern appreciations involve selective readings of the authors concerned, and an awareness of the strengths and weaknesses of the approach, and that gets us into technical matters again. Which of these readings is the best one, for example? More generally, can we just leave out some bits of the account and reinterpret the others?

The one technical issue with which we might end this chapter is chosen with postmodernist commentaries especially in mind. Functionalist writers were able to analyse the threats to the smooth integration of industrial societies and to predict new forms of solidarity ('organic'), or new complexities for the social system (new structured strains, more differentiated sectors – greater autonomy for each of the boxes in Parsons' AGIL model). There might well come a moment when the tensions, autonomies and complexities take up more time to explain, occupy a larger part of the picture, than the functional, integrating and solidaristic or systemic aspects of social life. As with marxism, how much complexity can the model take while still remaining the same model? Is it best to think of our societies as basic adaptive systems with increased levels of complexity and autonomy, or as a series of complex and autonomous interactions with occasional moments of solidity and functionality?

# PART II

# 3   The Emergent Qualities of Social Life: Weber and Elias

I hope it is clear from what you have read in the last two chapters that there are two equally plausible (and equally problematic) general ways of looking at social life as a system with some sort of external quality, with a 'life of its own' to some extent. If the one approach (marxism) stresses the economic system as 'determinant in the last instance', the other (functionalism) similarly stresses the value system, or cultural level. Both approaches consider that their special elements, 'the economic' or 'the cultural', operate at two levels: specific forms of economic or cultural life, but also a more general economic or cultural level which more or less defines human activity itself. Humans are fundamentally economic or social/cultural. Both approaches have been forced to develop more specific levels of analysis to get to grips with the complexities of modern societies, but, for the enthusiasts, it is still always possible to trace back all the complexities to a deeper, less specific and less complex level of reality.

In Britain at least, this kind of argument can be seen as 'deep' in a 'bad' sense too – too 'philosophical', too abstract, too far removed from everyday perceptions. It is not uncommon for a kind of 'middle way' to be sought (the requirements of writing 'balanced' essays also lead in this direction).

Is it not possible for the 'good' sides of both marxism and functionalism to be combined in some way? Advocates for either approach have argued this already, but usually in a specialist manner – that all the points made by marxists can be incorporated into one of Parsons' boxes, for example. Functionalists might argue that marxism should be read as flawed systems theory. Marxists could reply that functionalism is obviously one of the 'ideological' social sciences, a bit like economics or philosophy, not entirely 'wrong', but flawed because it operates too readily 'at the surface', and generalises from these surface features – and because it unwittingly reproduces the conceptions of the dominant groups. In these specialist debates, clearly, there is also rather a lot at stake for academics and research programmes committed to one or other of the approaches.

Leaving these theoretical wrangles aside, though, and stepping outside of any organisational politics, any fair-minded, tolerant and interested persons might well want to say that it is possible to give each perspective its due, but remain uncommitted to the whole approach. Instead of abstract theorising and system-building, let us use the approaches more pragmatically, as heuristics, as tools to grapple with concrete social situations. We have already reviewed one famous attempt to compare the two approaches with a view to approaching some kind of creative way forward – Lockwood (1992; and its accompanying online reading guide).

On a more pragmatic front, there might be some areas of life which seem to be organised 'functionally', where values are important, and the effects of the economic system more remote. Religious behaviour might be an example here, or, to change topics for a moment, the behaviour of communities of academics such as scientists. The activities of these groups might well be rooted ultimately in the generation of economic surpluses, and their work used by dominant groups in some sort of struggle to subdue underdogs – but understanding their actual activities requires much more detailed analysis of their values and norms. What scientists do, why they choose one scientific theory rather than another, why they believe in scientific progress, how they go about recognising and citing the works of others (a very important issue for those in the trade) – all these aspects require more than a knowledge of the role of science in the economic or class system. We have already pursued this sort of argument in Chapter 1, of course, where we saw that modern marxists need non-marxist analysis to flesh out marxism to meet modern conditions (although they still think that everything can be packed back into the general framework in the end).

Exactly the same sort of dilemma affects functionalism too, we argued. When it comes to looking at actual conflicts, for example actual social divisions, functionalism lacks an obvious mechanism to explain the sort of systematic or social structuring of conflicts. We can see people like Merton in particular becoming interested in marxist notions of contradiction and structured or built-in social strain. Perhaps actual societies and actual social developments will reveal complicated and intertwined entanglements of economic and social or cultural factors: first economic factors might prevail and play the major part, and then cultural values, giving quite complicated sequences.

The classic illustration of this sort of approach heading towards complexity is found in the work of Max Weber and his analysis of the impact of religious belief on social change. The story is told in general in his massive study of major world religions (see Ritzer 1996). Let us try to illustrate the approach by considering two aspects of religious systems of particular importance to sociologists – their social consequences and their social origins. (Turner 1981 has a helpful summary, and I have included an online reading guide on this work on the website.)

To be very brief, all the major religions focus on developing a theodicy (that is, roughly, a theory to explain suffering in the world). It is clear that there are a number of broad possibilities here, however. To summarise drastically, religions can offer a view of the world where a good force is balanced by an evil one which produces suffering, or one where suffering in this world is rewarded by bliss in the next, for example. Even other-worldly religions differ: some offer no hope at all for this material world and urge withdrawal into the spiritual realm, while others urge strict rules of conduct for everyday life. Religious systems can suggest different routes towards achieving a state of grace (as Christians might call it), such as a commitment to a long-term process involving reincarnation and the accumulation of rights to a better world next time. For some religious systems, there is a divine presence at the heart of the world, but not for all. There may be one god or many – and so on.

Far from ignoring specific differences in favour of underlying common functions or structures, we should recognise immediately that the consequences for social behaviour are going to vary quite considerably as a result of these different commitments. Some people might find themselves urged by their religious conscience to ignore their material commitments and go on a pilgrimage (to use Christian terms) in search of enlightenment. Some would see constant hard work as a religious duty, where others would see only a futile distraction. In colonial times, of course, religious differences of this kind would be used to justify cultural domination in the name of 'progress', and there is still a tendency to perceive people with different religious practices as culturally inferior or irrationally exotic (see Sivanandan 1990 on this).

As anyone who has done any preliminary sociology will know, Weber's work on the connections between Protestantism and the growth of capitalism (see Ritzer 1996) tries to explore the rather ironic social consequences of a particularly stern Protestant tendency (a version of Puritanism). Protestantism always stressed 'rational' theological development – the systematic, scholarly and specialist explication of principles and their application to problems of the 'real world'. We have already proceeded a long way from the orgiastic and ecstatic elements of Durkheim's 'elementary forms', of course. As we have argued once or twice before, pursuing the logical and rational principles and issues in a specialist scholarly discipline (Protestant theology in this case) can lead far away from people's initial intentions. We have already tried this out on the emergence of scholastic social theory.

I am no theologian, but it is easy to imagine Protestant scholars beginning their labours imagining that they are merely going to clarify a few issues, only to find that quite new and surprising implications are appearing. Rational theology might even lead to serious questions about the very basis of the faith: serious scholarly inquiry trying to establish a firm historical basis for the Gospel stories, for example, might even lead to (and indeed has led to) a rejection of the literal truth of those stories. I am reminded of the issues raised by marxism and post-structuralism earlier, where writers like Hindess (1977) managed to test marxism to destruction (in their view). There are several other episodes described in this book too, of course – once we shift on to the specialist and technical grounds of the debates, things start to look more doubtful and more complicated, as the assumptions of 'common sense' are explored and tested, and, inevitably, stretched and rejected.

In Weber's work, the unexpected outcome of the labours of Protestant theologians appeared as the doctrine of predestination, which apparently held (in brief) that there were some people who were 'elected' to be saved on the day of divine judgement, but that no-one could know the mind of God in these matters. Thus whether you were among the saved or not was predestined and unalterable by any good works that you might be able to perform during your lifetime. Further, strictly speaking, success and well-being in this life was no safe indication that you had been favoured by God with election to the ranks of the saved – indeed, there were no reliable indications. This clearly lies at odds with the common and much more palatable and practical view that good works or attentive religious observances somehow buy you a place in Heaven, or that if you are successful, someone must have been 'watching over you'.

Protestant theology of this type urged believers not to waste their time on earth, of course, and to act responsibly and morally at all times; but it was folly to think that such behaviour would lead to guaranteed salvation. Even if we are not Protestants, we might be able to realise how strange and contradictory this surely must have felt to the believers themselves. They were urged to lead orderly and hard-working lives as a duty, and yet offered no comfort in terms of the crucial issue about whether or not they were to be rewarded for a good life by bliss in eternity. In those circumstances, it is not difficult to imagine a strong impulse emerging from the believers themselves to engage in a little home-made practical theology of their own to cover the circumstances of their lives, whatever the hard logic of the theological scholars might have concluded.

As Turner (1981) points out, this could even be seen as a kind of theory of ideology in Weber, not unlike some versions of Marx's. Briefly, people make assumptions about ideas weaving in some aspects of their own lives: in this case, it is clear that those who are doing well from existing arrangements in society are quite likely to see those arrangements as God-given, and, by contrast, those who are not prospering under the current arrangements tend to be drawn towards cults promising revolutionary changes. Further, if the perceived needs of the mass congregation turn towards something a little more passionate and exciting than stern and abstract theology, it makes sense for wise religious elites to turn a blind eye to any excesses or simplifications.

Indeed, this is the interesting thing about Christian religious belief for Weberians: one form of the faith belongs to the congregation as much as to the theologians, and there are times when the believers themselves take a hand, so to speak, and revitalise specialist theology with a demand for a more relevant and immediate theodicy. Evangelicalism and charismatic movements, 'house churches', the proliferation of sects or the emergence of the Christian gay rights movement might be current examples of moments when the congregations try to lead the official scholars in theological matters. Incidentally, this approach has also been used to grasp some of the specifics of Islam or of Soviet Communist Party doctrine.

The clash between the theological insistence on predestination and the more commonsensical views of salvation as a reward for good work was to have a classically ironic consequence for Weber: stark, puritan Protestant theology eventually was to become a practical 'work-ethic' as believers heard the doctrines but also 'applied' them to their everyday concerns, not abstractly or rigorously, but 'practically'. Even though there was no scholarly warrant for it, the belief grew that hard work would and must bring spiritual rewards. Religious belief came after all to sanction certain everyday behaviours in a clear and direct way, and encouraged hard work and an abstention from idleness and pleasure-seeking, honesty and ethical conduct in business, and high personal standards (work as a duty). This fitted some of the early requirements of capitalism very well indeed: you can easily see how such virtues would help develop people's faith in the probity of companies, for example, and it is possible to see major roles being played in these areas (in the UK) by well-known Protestant families such as Lloyds (banking) or Cadbury (confectionery).

It so happened that the social groups most attracted to Protestantism of this rather puritanical variety at that particular time also were the ones positioned to play a leading role in urban and civic life, and thus were well suited to develop their own capitalist enterprises. The kind of intellectual curiosity and the right sort of 'practical' ethics that attracted these groups to Protestantism also led them into reforming social and industrial practices. This spread the 'work-ethic' more generally. Of course, the material conditions had to be present too, such as a certain level of technological development, for example, but these were insufficient on their own without a cultural impulse to legitimate and encourage the application of technology and finance to actual enterprises. Thus the ironic and unintended outcome emerges in its final form – a stern, rather other-worldly doctrine preaching indifference to material success vitally assists in the development of capitalist enterprise.

This 'Protestant ethic' thesis has been much discussed since, both as a concrete account of the emergence of European capitalism and as an example of Weber's general sociology. There are considerable debates about the historical data Weber used, as well as about his methodology. For our purposes, though, it is the general approach that counts. To be brief, Weber's analysis can be seen as showing that actual social events are emergent, complex and quite often ironic or unintended, rather than being driven by some underlying laws or logics of social development. It follows that sociological analysis must operate with this complexity and concreteness, with the events themselves, rather than with developing general laws and trying to 'apply' them to concrete cases. Another implication might also be clear. For Turner at least, Weber cannot be seen as an uncritical or naïve advocate of 'action' approaches which privilege the subjective intentions of individuals, since subjective actions are always likely to turn into unintended consequences.

Weber clearly offered a number of broader generalisations about the fate of industrial societies. These included predictions about the growth of bureaucracy and calculative rationality in public life. These predictions also have connections with other commitments in Weber's sociology, including those to an individualistic theory of social action, but we explore these a bit further below.

Protestantism spreads and legitimises these forces, which eventually dominate public life and reduce any kind of religious belief to a merely private concern. Here we have the clue to Weber's entire sociology, says Turner (1981) – actions come to have the opposite effect from what was intended. This is one of the ways in which Weber can be rescued from the usual charges of determinism and reductionism which we have seen levelled against other approaches, and Turner (1992) has suggested that he can be very useful too in grasping the issues raised by recent debates about modernity (see the online reading guide on these debates summarised in the journal *Theory, Culture and Society*).We shall offer further illustrations of Weber's work in Chapter 5, where we change the focus of application to look at politics and class analysis

## Elias, figurations and civilisation

In recent years, the work of Norbert Elias has come to represent a particularly promising variant of the general 'emergent' approach we have outlined in Weber's work, and many people also find it far more optimistic. Mennell (1992; and see the online reading guide) offers a useful introduction, with some examples and extensions of the approach, but many students will have encountered the approach first, perhaps, in studies of leisure or sport, as in Dunning's work on football hooliganism (see Dunning 1990; Dunning et al. 1986; or the online reading guides. Another possibility arises with the newly codified specialism of the 'sociology of food', as in Mennell (1985), which also has an online reading guide). As these examples illustrate, Elias's work has helped to broaden interest away from the classic (and often privileged) concerns of more politically committed sociologies of stratification or of identity.

The examples also help us to understand Elias's work too, because they can be seen to represent a distinctive approach, which involves beginning with areas of social life and trying to theorise about them, rather than the other way round (which is characteristic of those trying to 'apply' marxism or functionalism). Of course, whether the approach is quite as innocent of theory as this is debatable. Elias and his followers use concrete and historical analyses of matters such as table manners, etiquette or sport to launch and illustrate a distinctive general approach – 'developmental sociology' or 'figurational sociology', a sociology of emergence, of social process.

A 'figuration', incidentally, can be thought of as the sum of the underlying social and psychological connections between people. These connections permit alliances and factions to emerge, on almost any basis (not just class or gender memberships). Mennell (1992) uses Elias's study of the royal court of medieval France to illustrate the concept. Court politics were the result of a constantly shifting series of alliances between the various factions – the nobility, the new aristocracy and the King. The King played a particularly skilled role in managing to preserve his own power by balancing the rival factions, allying first with one and then with the other. The actual social patterns or 'figures' that emerged depended on this underlying process of figuration.

Briefly, Elias is able to use the history of the figurations underlying the particular 'figures' shown in the areas of manners or sport to chart the progress of what he calls the 'civilising process'. It is important to realise that he is trying to develop a rather technical definition of 'civilisation' here, and not just reproducing the tendency of elites to call their behaviour 'civilised' (and the behaviour of others correspondingly 'uncivilised'), but the term does carry an unfortunate baggage of elitism and cultural domination none the less, which can be a problem. 'Civilisation' in its more technical sense means a gradual controlling of personal appetites, passions and impulses in human affairs, away, say, from the hot-blooded spontaneous behaviour of knights in the middle ages, always ready to seek adventure and violence, to the (allegedly) calm, impersonal and technical behaviour of the modern politician. Interpersonal behaviour becomes much calmer and less volatile as passions of all kinds decline and become replaced with a consideration for the effects of one's behaviour on others. These are, of course, generalisations, and Elias (1978) himself traces out much more complex patterns in the development of variants of this management of the emotions when comparing, say, France, England and Germany.

It is possible to detect this general change in the fascinating world of table manners, which gradually become more and more 'refined'. To cite Mennell's selection of Elias's examples, in medieval Europe it was considered perfectly normal at mealtimes to perform in public bodily functions like spitting, blowing your nose in the tablecloth, urinating or breaking wind, but then politeness suggested that these functions and their products were covered or at least not openly displayed or discussed. Later, of course, such functions were confined completely to private occasions, and it became very impolite even to name or discuss them (except in sociology seminars). Similarly, animal carcasses would once be brought to table, dismantled and devoured there, whereas modern tastes tend to lead us to cover such uncomfortable reminders of death and cruelty, even when we shop (for the ready-cut and pre-packed portions of 'meat', or, even more euphemistically, 'steak').

Sport also shows the same general trends, as when traditional football is compared with the modern games of soccer or rugby. Traditional football, which still survives in rural Britain, is a loosely structured game involving moving an object of some kind (a ball, perhaps, but also a barrel or a 'hood') towards certain prominent sites (like pubs or churches). Youths from adjacent villages compete, with no limits on the size of the teams, and only minimal rules. I have never played this game myself (although British schoolboy games like 'Murderball', 'Bulldog' or 'deck hockey' are probably close), but I can imagine how easy it is in such a game to experience a satisfyingly full range of emotions, from fear to gloating revenge. The modern game of football (whichever code is pursued) is much more restrained and regulated, of course, to suit modern tastes, but the player or spectator can still feel the emotional pull of the sporting contest;

indeed, that is why it is so popular, since it allows us a licensed zone of emotional discharge, even if it is second-hand or 'mimetic'.

Other detailed applications of this approach include Mennell's own study of the 'civilisation of appetite' (Mennell 1985; and see the online reading guide), which covers some of the material on the development of table manners, but goes on to offer a detailed historical account of the emergence of the modern menu, tracing a complex path through the various technical developments in cooking and eating (including the crucial stage of writing down recipes). At different stages, various elites in different European countries took up and sponsored new culinary or dietary fashions, techniques or possibilities, but there were growing pressures 'from below' as well, as affluence grew and tastes changed. These are general changes that can be explained in terms of the 'civilisation process' as preparing and eating food ceases to be a matter of the immediate gratification of hunger or indulgence of the coarser appetites (exemplified best, perhaps, in the medieval feast). Instead, eating becomes more and more 'cultural', so to speak, more and more affected by the need to communicate with others, which means anticipating their needs, empathising and, of course, entering into relationships of dependency with them.

For me, there are strong links with Bourdieu's work here too, which Mennell (1985) explicates in more detail (he also claims that Elias was the first to use the term 'habitus'). We have mentioned Bourdieu already in connection with this material on the 'popular' and the 'high' aesthetics and its importance in life in universities and colleges (Bourdieu 1986, 1988). It is easy to see echoes of the stages in the 'civilising process' in the demands for immediate participation and emotional involvement in cultural activity in the former, and the cool detached technical stance in the latter. Bourdieu's analysis of the processes of social distinction (maintaining differences between the social classes) in cultural matters would also fit as a special case in the relations of dependency involved. People do use these cultural stances to patrol social boundaries with other groups, but the two stances are also linked to each other at a deeper level – the high aesthetic makes sense only as an inversion of the popular forms, and without them it would lose its social power. In more popular terms, opera-goers need people to watch television soap operas to confirm their own superiority and to give them a kind of benchmark for their own values. More pointedly, the academic discipline of cultural studies relies on a non-academic interest in popular culture in order to demonstrate its superior aesthetic and technical grasp.

Although no-one to my knowledge has pursued an openly Eliasan approach, some of the classic work on human sexuality looks rather similar. Plummer, for instance (in Brake 1982), has suggested that human sexuality is far from being a simple matter of discharging biological drives, even though it is sometimes convenient to represent it in this way to ourselves or to others. Modern sexuality is clearly interwoven with our general cultural habits and interests, which provide the erotic impulses that are so important. As a result any human activity can be sexualised, Plummer argues (including watching a football match if this involves fantasising about having sex with the players), and any activity can be de-sexualised too (such as when doctors intimately examine patients, or when nudists encounter each other on beaches). There is no historical dimension in Plummer's analysis, although there is a view that cultural variations, cultural influences generally, are increasing as more and more people experiment with choosing different sexual identities.

The historical dimension is important, though, since it leads to a major theoretical claim for Elias and developmental sociology: it helps to focus on the underlying importance of social *process*. Process is easily overlooked in classic sociology and in recent concrete studies as well, and, as a result, matters get fixed and settled too early. It would be easy to generalise from Plummer's study above, for example, to arrive at some general support for 'action theory' of the kind discussed below, since sexuality shows the endless cultural creativity of human beings. For an Eliasan, I imagine, this would not be entirely true – *modern* sexuality might well show these attributes, but there is no guarantee that humans always behaved in this free-floating culturalised manner. Experimental sexuality has developed as a mode of forming relationships, as a result of an important underlying and unpredictable process of what might be called the civilisation of sexual appetites. Once developed, this 'civilised' form of social relationship is well described by approaches like symbolic interactionism; but it is wrong to conclude that human beings have always acted like this, or, indeed, that they always do so, or that all of them do so now: the civilising process is unpredictable and uncontrollable, and thus can go into reverse, as it were, or spread very unevenly, leaving pockets of more immediate and impulsive behaviour.

More general implications of the approach might now be pursued. The examples cited tell us something about the conduct of social life and the complexity of the processes that produce the forms we know and often take for granted. We did not always behave in the ways that seem so 'natural' now, and the processes that produced our current behaviours are not easily summarised. Certainly the kind of schematic functionalism of Parsons, with its 'pattern variables' and AGIL models (discussed in the previous chapter), can be seen as far too ahistorical and static, based on current American bourgeois culture at most. Of course, there is some dynamism and movement in Parsons (and the other grand theorists), but it is easily grasped as a change from one sort of pattern variable to another, or, at best, an evolution towards a more differentiated society.

Mennell (1985) makes the case against a number of other grand theories too in his useful Introduction, using critiques with which we should be familiar from earlier chapters. French structuralist approaches (especially those of Lévi-Strauss towards understanding the social significance of food) head unerringly for static universal variables as signs ('raw', 'cooked' and the rest – see the previous chapter), and avoid emergent concrete variations and significations. Marxist approaches over-emphasise the role of the food industry in forming tastes and thus risk the familiar charge of 'economic reductionism' we discussed earlier. Again, process is not entirely absent in these approaches, but it is too simple a process, within limits set by combinations of the universal categories, or tendencies within an overall logic of capital accumulation.

As hinted above, 'action theories' do not escape the charge of (process) reductionism either, with their tendencies endlessly to discover and rediscover static generalised qualities of human beings, such as our abilities to interpret and communicate in symbols, or the ways we use certain universal mental apparatuses to construct meaning.

Just about any general theory can be rebuked in this way, though, including Freud's, which abstracts from the historical processes of the taming of impulses and their traces, and turns these into the eternal structures of the modern consciousness – the id, ego and superego. In my view, much postmodern commentary runs similar risks as scattered examples of current behaviour are generalised into solemn static theories about the emergence of new forms of identity or whatever (see Harris 1996).

Elias suggests that the pull of social processes can be detected in any human being, and that they offer only temporary fixed points. We were all once 'uncivilised' in his special sense, as infants, simply pursuing our own impulses, seeking immediate gratification and unable to empathise or respond on a more interdependent level. We learn patterns of restraint, possibly of several different kinds as we enter different sorts of interdependencies. I have suggested already that, for some people reading this book, or attending a university or college for the first time might mean an encounter with different sorts of social restraint. Students taking sociology courses, for example, can find themselves personally involved in some ways in the sorts of social patterns under discussion in seminars; but instead of an engaged, personalised, perhaps even heated discussion, they are expected to show academic restraint, to operate in calm, moderated tones, to focus on the technical aspects of the problem (such as the evidence available, and so on). You could argue the following:

1   These new forms of discussion have developed out of a specific configuration of bourgeois male professional intellectuals developing a specialised form of restraint. This might help us solve a problem with the Eliasan notion of 'detachment', discussed critically by Rojek (1986), and featured in the online reading guide. Detachment is commended to us as an essential stance for sociologists, standing back from their immediate political or social commitments in order better to grasp the objects of their inquiry (see below) – but what is 'detachment', and where does it come from? One paradoxical answer is hinted at here – detachment arises from commitment, oddly enough, commitment to the specific academic values of the figuration we mention. Several implications arise, of course – 'detachment' is a value position, an aesthetic and not a general principle open to all. Of course, it is a useful and valuable aesthetic, a 'good' aspect of the 'high aesthetic', generating more than endless 'scholasticism' (and this can get lost in Bourdieu's analysis). Further implications arise for the notion of 'object adequacy', as we shall see.

2   The specific academic institutional context fosters these restraints, especially where objective assessment is essential, and 'professionalism' is
encouraged more generally. It has always seemed no accident to me that the
foremost exponents of figurationalism are also classically 'homeless'
Europeans, multilingual and international in their outlook.

3   These forms of social conduct are used to do social differentiation – some
individuals 'belong' straight away and others do not; some succeed immediately in relating to 'objective' assessment and detached academic
judgement, while others struggle.

If you are not one of those who have quickly adjusted, you might still be in a
position to be critical of these customs. Are there any clear processes of social differentiation involved underneath the cool exterior of 'objectivity'? You might be
able to see that academics are 'over-civilised' in these matters – too restrained
and 'objective' to the point of seeming uncaring. No normal person can remain
detached and objective all the time, you might think, and we all need 'moral hol-
idays' where we can go off and be nice and 'spontaneous', as we let our hair
down 'backstage' (where we can gossip scandalously about each other), or at
concerts, the opera, discos, parties, football matches or political demonstrations.

## Critical discussion

Like all the other approaches, Elias's has its critics, of course. Rojek (1986) offers
a good account here, we have suggested, but we might pursue an obvious objection first: figurationalism is such a powerful approach that it becomes possible
to fit almost anything into it, and, as with the other approaches, this should
make us suspicious. If we are equipped with a view that a very flexible social
process is at work which produces sometimes tightly constrained behaviour
and sometimes more loosely constrained behaviour, it is clear that we can
always find good reasons to make the theory fit any case whatsoever. As with
marxism, it seems possible to add on little bits of sociology or history to explain
actual complexities, while keeping the main structure intact. Just as with functionalism, there are also exceptions to the overall trends: far from offering a
problem for the theory, episodes of 'uncivilised' behaviour can actually confirm it, as 'throwbacks' or 'deviance', as 'exceptions that prove the rule' (which
is one way to analyse 'uncivilised behaviour' such as football hooliganism – see
Dunning et al. 1986).

   Van Krieken (1999) has offered a particularly acute criticism of the Eliasan
notion of 'civilisation' (see also the online reading guide to his article). Focusing
upon what might be seen as genocidal policies towards Australian Aboriginal
people by the European colonists, he points out that several problems with the
concept of 'civilisation' are discernible. Basically, the example shows the uneven-
ness of the civilisation process, not only in terms of suggesting that it can cover

for cultural genocide, as in this case, but also more technically. Elias has abstracted from a complex picture, and has thus omitted the simultaneous operations of barbarism towards outsiders when discussing the move towards self-restraint among Europeans in their relations with each other. He has failed to grasp European colonising impulses as important determinants of the directions of civilisation, the uses to which state-formation has been put in this case, even though his general position should have produced a more sensitive analysis of the actual figurations which can combine civilisation and barbarism. Ultimately, this is due to an inability to separate out different elements in the civilising process which can produce novel combinations – particularly the development of social constraint without any necessary mutual identification with members of other groups.

Nevertheless, it is easy to see why Elias's work has attracted some powerful adherents. It seems to have solved certain theoretical impasses, and to have opened the way to some interesting and detailed studies of social behaviours that have been neglected by the classic concerns for social order. This ability to suggest new work and to set new agendas is obviously important to professional sociologists, who have to develop their subject and to generate new research programmes. Elias apparently advocated a new flexibility by inviting his students to explore sociologically something that interested them in the first place – sport and food are two examples which have successfully emerged – rather than teaching theory first and letting the theory set the agenda, so to speak. This approach puts the object of inquiry first, and directs us to complexities to be explained, rather than privileging certain theories first, and then seeking confirmations or applications: it urges us to think of 'object adequacy', in Elias's phrase (see Mennell 1992).

## Object adequacy

We have discussed this issue already in the previous two chapters. In Chapter 1, we examined claims made by marxism especially that we need proper theory to make sense of the everyday objects of our experience (markets, or commodities). Readers of that chapter might recall some of the arguments here – that these objects present a misleading 'surface appearance', a deceptive simplicity. Commodities appear to be simple objects, exchanged in a simple way (but, crucially, labour is a special case), and the economic system seems to be a 'natural' method of producing and exchanging goods (but there is a systematic form of exploitation built into it which is not immediately apparent). Functionalism also has its variant of this 'deep/surface' metaphor, we argued: things which appear inexplicable or strange on the surface might be understood better once we think of possible social functions. Apparent complexity can be reduced once we can see the underlying 'structures', as in Lévi-Strauss's work on kinship (see the previous chapter).

Action sociology also has its objections to such 'naïve empiricism', or 'positivism' as it is often termed – 'facts' are already interpretations, as Blumer argues (in Manis and Meltzer 1972 – see the online reading guide). Garfinkel also has a famous piece in the Manis and Meltzer collection on the ways in which 'facts' are interpreted in the form of a document (and there is an online reading guide for this piece too). I find that these are the arguments most readily accepted by new students, sometimes for aesthetic reasons as well as technical ones.

These sorts of argument are often used against the simple view that we can just go out and gather or observe 'the facts'. Such a view would be seen as naïve positivism, and I do not think that this is what Elias is advocating – certainly it would be incompatible with his views on the importance of process and emergence. 'Object adequacy' seems to mean something more like a suitable respect for objects, part of the process of detachment we discussed above, an alertness to possibilities somehow contained in objects of analysis themselves. I may be taking this view having been influenced by Adorno's essay on subjects and objects (in Arato and Gebhardt 1978), where a similar respect for the objectivity of objects, so to speak, is used to remind us that our concepts cannot be simply fused with objects without further reflection.

A lack of respect for objects can lead to a loss of meaning, or to the complete domination of theoretical concepts which are just imposed on actual patterns of behaviour, or to the abandonment of any attempt to explain any actual events at all (and here theory gets elaborated and extended for its own sake, as a kind of purely intellectual exercise). We have already seen both trends in the material we have examined. They are detectable especially in recent work in cultural studies, in my view, but let us examine some examples in a little more detail.

## The politics of identity

The management and negotiation of personal identities was a theme in some of the classic work by the 'interactionists', to whom we shall soon turn. However, it is likely that for many younger students, this topic will have been introduced using some of the classic marxist and feminist work associated with cultural studies, and this kind of work has migrated into other academic areas and into journalism too. The basic themes are relatively easy to identify, once it is accepted that identities are not just matters of personal choice, but are important areas of social control. We shall be exploring this issue in greater depth later, in the chapters on social life as politics in Part III.

Clearly, feminist writers have done much to alert us to this area by suggesting that the identity of 'proper woman' (as heterosexual, submissive, wanting to have babies and live in nuclear families, and so on) is clearly one that favours men and permits a level of social control to be exercised over women. The racialised identities of ethnic minorities can be explained in a similar manner – dominant white groups have liked to think of minority black groups as inferior in some way (less intelligent, more emotional and 'natural', less civilised, and so on). Clearly, identities associated with social classes can be understood in this way too – the images of loyal but deferential and conservative agricultural workers, or of sexually promiscuous and violent industrial workers demanding 'instant gratification', have helped install social regimes aimed at preserving the civilised and modernised values of elite groups (once more, the British education system is a good example of such a regime). We have explored some marxist work which suggests that the notion of 'the individual' does the same sort of work, helping us reconcile ourselves to the system by assisting us to read our submission as the result of 'choice'.

This theme of personal identity as a major location for social struggles can come to dominate the work. It has appeared in a number of 'applied' studies in education but also in leisure, families and popular culture. To take a study which I happen to have at hand, Mac an Ghaill, in Woods and Hammersley (1993), reviews some work based on the experiences of black and Asian girls and how they react to the regime of their (British) school: briefly, they perceive its values, expressed in the school curriculum and in the informal social settings of the school, as racist, and react in different ways to try to preserve their own identities via a series of actions which Mac an Ghaill describes as 'resistance and accommodation'. Here, gender and 'race' are combined (and probably social class is involved too, although this is not highlighted). Work like this has led to a tendency to see social interactions of this kind as fundamentally concerned with the three main or 'condensed' identities – class, race and gender.

A whole tranche of work exists on the ways in which popular leisure locations like the Disney theme parks expose visitors to these dominant values, for example (see Bryman 1995), and some work attempts to suggest how visitors can resist them. The whole approach is based on intertwined themes of domination and resistance with some local variations.

This approach has also influenced the study of mass media, as many students will know – practically the only thing my media students could recall from their courses (when I asked some once at Graduation Day) was how the news introduces 'bias' (that is, a set of ideological values), and this is, of course, a major theme. Scores of influential studies have also examined how mainstream Hollywood films, including Disney films (see Byrne and McQuillan 1999 for a recent example), develop adverse images of women or black people, or quietly privilege the values of dominant genders, or national or ethnic groups. For me, some of the best work here is still that on the James Bond movies (see Bennett and Woollacott 1987). Just about every sort of television programme, from soap operas to advertisements, can be subjected to the same sort of analysis.

I hope it is clear, though, that I am implying that there are some problems with these analyses. There are two main ways in which such analyses can come to over-simplify or reduce the complexity of the objects they are studying.

Firstly the 'texts' themselves are simplified, whether we are talking about school curricula, news broadcasts or Disney attractions. To keep faith with marxist or feminist traditions, contradictions in those texts can be overlooked.

As an example, school curricula might well express dominant values, but they also feature more universal values, or even critical ones. American schools also stress civil liberties, for example, and teach students how to be assertive individuals and how to be critical, to quote one study (Gintis and Bowles 1980; and see the online reading guide to this and allied pieces by the same authors). Black people or females exposed to schooling will therefore encounter contradictory values not monolithic dominant ones favouring the status quo. After all, the education system has also spawned the very radical critics who analyse it – how have they managed to escape?

Films and television programmes also offer mixes of values and other complexities to viewers. The media are often less racist than other sectors of public opinion, for example, and news broadcasts offer insights into how television works and how stories are put together, rather than straightforward indoctrination. Even classic Hollywood films offer far more than just dominant values.

The famous debates about realism can be cited here, briefly (we return to them in the discussion of 'Otherness' in Chapter 9). One classic approach (MacCabe in Bennett et al. 1981; and see the online material) argued that mainstream films commonly offer a hierarchy of viewpoints to explain the world to the viewer (to deliver an underlying sense of the reality of the social world – this is the sense in which the debate features 'realism'). Most of the viewpoints are attributed to the characters in the film, but there is a less obvious narrative that comments on those individual viewpoints and tells the viewer which is the more believable (if, indeed, any are). In this way, a set of values (invariably conservative ones) is worked into the very narrative structure of films, and, because it is not consciously perceived, the viewer gets seduced into accepting it. There is no time to explore this view in greater detail, but Williams (1994), for example, has suggested that this sort of approach first reduces the effects of films to one of narrative (leaving out matters like plot or characterisation), and then further focuses upon particular effects of this narrative to the exclusion of matters like how the films manipulate emotions or refer to other films.

Let us illustrate and parody this debate by considering a film like *Jurassic Park*. It would be possible, clearly, to 'read' this movie as offering standard ideological representations and narratives – of women, or capitalism or of modern technology. A critic of a feminist persuasion might draw attention to the ways in which the female personnel are depicted as intelligent but still caring, vulnerable and sexy at heart, or to the ways in which the conventional heterosexual family emerges as the 'natural' unit, despite the initial scepticism of the male hero. Marxists might want to suggest that the message of the film is that capitalists are rather cuddly if misguided individual men, and that only perverted technology that tampers with 'nature' is to be rejected.

You might wish to try out these readings a little further for yourselves, and, as you do, think of what else the film contains – the way it builds suspense or terror, deploys special effects (including the use of sound), depicts other groups (ethnic groups or the villains), and makes references to other films (most obviously to *King Kong*). How do these other elements work – to reinforce, or contradict, the values we began with? Or perhaps they do not really 'fit' with these readings at all, and if this is so, what should we do with them – ignore them as less relevant than the issues of ideology, perhaps? But then what makes the ideological issues more important exactly, and more important for whom?

My own unpublished work on Disney suggests that the same sort of complexity can be found in Walt Disney World (in Florida). It was possible in 1996 to find there an attraction that offered a rather negative view of modern corporations, for example (and an even better one, based on the *Terminator* movies in the Universal Studios theme park), and the same kind of knowing references to the obvious construction of the effects. For me, the clever work in Marin (1977) or in Eco (1987) on the effects of controlling the gaze of the visitor by careful landscaping was immediately exposed on my first visit – right at the end of Main Street USA looms the Disney castle, which rather spoils all the careful attempts to reconstruct Main Street 'realistically'. If you visit in August, there can be no doubt that you are visiting a specially designed tourist attraction and not some 'real' place: tourists swarm all over the sets!

Secondly, the audience's reaction is simplified too. For the mechanisms constructing identities to work, there must be a real effect on actual people. Yet people's reactions are hardly ever pursued adequately in this work.

Indeed, it used to be common not to investigate them at all: it could just be assumed that ideology was all-powerful, and the problem simply became one of isolating and specifying its effects in schooling or the media. This was accomplished by the critic standing in for the audience, offering a skilled theoretical reading, ready-armed, so to speak, with the relevant concepts, already primed to find the sexist or racist codes in the Disney movie. The viewer or visitor was just assumed to be the victim of this sort of ideological mechanism, innocently consuming ideology as he or she studied 'Distory', sat back and watched a film promoting Exxon or followed the officially marked routes around the park.

In some recent work, especially in media studies, there has been a turn towards a more active viewer who is able to decode and oppose the dominant values of the texts involved: female viewers who can watch programmes like *Dallas* ironically, for example (Ang 1985), or adolescents who can impose their own narratives on electronic games (Fiske 1989). Even here, despite some useful work which deserves wider application, there can be a limit to complexity, as reactions still tend to be classified by the analyst as 'resistance', 'incorporation', 'accommodation' or whatever. Reactions that do not easily fit the theoretical framework of domination and resistance are left out altogether.

Critics sometimes report that their students will dismiss much of this analysis as far-fetched, overdone, a lot of fuss about something that is only meant to be fun. This sort of reaction gets explained as showing only too well the deep ways in which Disney has managed to domesticate and indoctrinate its victims, who have drunk so deeply of Disney values that they literally cannot criticise the company. Nevertheless, there might be good reasons to listen to those sorts of reactions differently, to take them more seriously: they might be interpreted as a sign of a different sort of pleasure altogether, an emergent one, outside of the framework of resistance and domination. Incidentally, I have also tried to reread the reactions of the critics as demonstrating a refined kind of academic pleasure with Disney too – referring to Bourdieu, academic condemnation can be seen as a pleasurable demonstration of one's own sophistcation.

## Concluding thoughts

There are many general issues raised by this discussion, of course, and we cannot pursue them further here. As with the other chapters, I am going to try to argue in favour of the perspectives we have reviewed in this chapter, or at least with their emphasis on 'emergence'. Briefly, I think it is important to argue that theoretical endeavour need not involve only the manipulation of theories (their clarification or classification, or attempts to improve their logical coherence or to synthesise different approaches, and so on). For social theory, it becomes important to remain open to the complexities of the 'real world' too, difficult as this is. The positive function of the location of social theory in universities is precisely to permit and socially support this kind of openness, in my view.

We have seen how the 'classic' approaches in marxism or functionalism can turn to reductionism of complexity in order to make events fit theories, but this is a tendency affecting all theoretical systems. 'Postmodernist' theorising can operate in a similar way, for example, as some of the social commentaries of writers like Eco or Baudrillard show: armed with concepts like 'hyperreality', such writers set out to explain the postmodern condition by way of a kind of 'poetics', spinning out the possible meaning and significance of everyday events. For Eco (1987), the events can range from visiting tourist sites in America to witnessing voodoo ceremonies in Brazil or sporting ceremonies in Italy, while Baudrillard's (1983) commentaries cover crashes at the Paris air show as well as architectural styles and how they have changed.

All alike are treated primarily as symptoms with some deeper significance. These events, examples or processes are never analysed or grasped in any depth, but that is not the point, apparently – we just catch the sense of the argument in them, much as a telling phrase in a poem suddenly gives us an insight. Much of Giddens' recent writing (see Giddens 1991; and the online reading guide) offers the same kind of poetics. The analyst unpacks the meaning of 'texts', such as the contents of lifestyle manuals, the memoirs of a body-builder, newspaper articles on anorexia, imaginary case studies, historical materials on mourning rituals, or whatever. In some way, this sort of material supports the general diagnoses of the times on offer.

Of course, this sort of approach can be insightful, but the actual objects and events only have a walk-on part to play. The strategy seems to depend upon we readers simply recognising and agreeing with the analyst's interpretation, agreeing to 'see' anorexia as a matter of addiction, or accepting that the pursuit of lifestyle is a dominant concern in reflexive modernism, or whatever. Personally, I am still doubtful, and I require more of an analysis before I agree to be swept along. I think that lazy and rather circular theorising is likely to be the result otherwise.

I accept that there are problems with a stance of putting 'the objects' first. These include serious philosophical objections to empiricism, of course, of the kind raised by Althusser (see Hindess (1977) and the online reading guide for a succinct account). There are no objects in the social world independently of the theoretical (and political or personal) interests that generate or make sense of them. However, it can help to proceed as if there were such independent objects, even if only as a kind of exploratory sensitising device (an heuristic, to use the technical term). If we do not investigate these seemingly empirical, objective or emergent qualities, we seem to be left with two unpleasant and unprofitable alternatives – we remain with an entirely abstract and scholastic theory of concepts and their connections, or we smuggle back in conceptions of the empirical social world, often in an uncritical way. We shall see these dilemmas revealed in quite a lot of the theory that follows, especially in the chapters on the more politically engaged approaches.

# 4 Theorising Subjective Action

If you have followed a course in sociology before, you will be able to anticipate the opening arguments in this chapter. If not, it is possible that you will have thought of a particular objection as you followed the accounts of classical sociology earlier. In the general task of 'applying' sociological insights to their own lives, my students have often decided that these accounts do not leave enough room for 'the individual' in general, and for individual choice in particular. This might have arisen while you were reading the previous chapter on 'emergence' and 'object adequacy' as well – both seem to imply that we need a much richer model of human action (or 'agency', to use the technical term).

Let us start at the homely level, though. There are many occasions on which anyone can encounter the force of these objections, of course. It is true that I feel I belong to particular social groups or trends, or collectivities (even short-lived ones), and I am constantly surprised by how widely shared are my views, opinions and feelings about issues. However, I can also feel very much that I am an individual person. Much of this turns on matters like personal feelings or memories, for example. Our lives have provided us with a unique stock of memories and experiences. On many occasions, I am aware of the peculiar ways in which experience affects my actions. Memories, and their uninvited intrusion into the present, indicate what a number of writers have called 'subjective time'. This is far less regular and predictable than objective time, the 'clock time' we all use. Instead, moments in the present are united with moments from the past, and the meanings that emerge develop from this process of unity.

There have also been many examples of sustained and mutual misunderstandings of those with whom I work or live. In one case, a misunderstanding with a colleague about what we both thought the other had believed over an incident in the past had apparently persisted for eight years, and, rather as in one of those existentialist novels by Camus or Sartre, it was a shock to realise how persistent and consistent the alternative perceptions had become, although neither of us realised this at the time.

In these circumstances, I became aware that it is very easy for others to misunderstand my personal reactions, since they do not share my biography. In principle, we might have been able to explore each other's reactions, try to reflect upon them and talk about them, or compare reactions to events in the present, but this sort of activity is likely to be reserved for people we feel especially strongly about, rather than for those we meet in the course of doing our jobs. An orientation towards mutual understanding can take too much time and effort for most of our contacts.

The same sort of experience of oneself as an individual can come about when making those important choices that arise at turning points in our lives. There are moments when we become aware that our personal actions can make a difference – we can choose one partner rather than another, one university rather than another, one career rather than another. The social system might structure these choices in a broad and general sense – people tend to choose as partners those from similar social backgrounds, for example – but this still leaves important elements of choice between persons in that same category. Think of the discretion available to us at work, when we decide whether really to help a student or really to try to teach a topic, or just to go through the motions until the problems go away: social structures, economic compulsions or professional value-systems might keep us at work in general, but only personal commitment keeps us trying to do our best.

It is clear that a detailed and concrete understanding of social action cannot ignore personal meanings. Of course, it is not always necessary to understand people that fully, as we shall see when we look at the work of Schütz (1972). For most interactions, such as those between myself and the postal worker, which is one of Schütz's examples, a fairly anonymous 'ideal type' postal worker will do (and an ideal type customer for him or her, of course): typical motives and typical meanings held by both sides will be enough to permit effective limited social interactions.

Again, though, it is different for sociologists ,who need to probe a little more deeply into subjective meanings in order to understand at a deeper, or at least a different, level from participants. There are a number of special reasons for this: human interaction is rapid, fleeting and often achieved in particular circumstances that leave little time for research or reflection. To understand means to retrace and to spell out what is often taken for granted. As with our example of capitalism in Chapter 1, many participants are simply glad that things do happen fairly predictably, without being especially interested in why they do. Sociologists need to know why. As usual, however, the reasons for needing to know why can shift us on to a theoretical terrain and bring additional questions which arise in that specialist area alone – such as which theory best explains human interaction, or which model of social interaction helps us grasp what we are interested in.

Pursuing what looks like a simple interest in deeper understanding can lead into some strange areas. In particular, all the examples I have given so far are well within the boundaries of common-sense experience. Action is not seen as a concept that particularly challenges our understandings of the social world, and usually we do not have to rethink our knowledge of that world. On a more abstract note, the same might be said about quite a lot of 'action sociology', incidentally: that it leaves too much of the social world unexamined. This leads to marxist criticisms that action sociology is too uncritical (see Gouldner 1971 or the online reading guide to this work), for example. It can also lead to a more technical criticism, that action approaches can be fully compatible with functionalist conceptions of 'the social', despite the common view (in A-level Sociology at least) that 'action' and 'structure' are somehow always opposed conceptions. We have seen the work of Parsons as an example of how the two might be seen as compatible 'levels', though, both equally explicable by the same concepts (the AGIL model).

## Towards a theory of action

There are some serious problems in organising a discussion about the many and varied theories of action. If you have taken an elementary course in sociology, you may not be aware of the considerable variation that exists, since the differences are often collapsed into an overall 'action perspective'. This is often just associated as an alternative to the other 'perspectives', such as marxist and functionalist ones that occupy an equally condensed 'structural perspective'. Students might be aware that there are different names or approaches within this overall perspective, but it is not common to explain how they are all connected together, or why they actually vary from each other. It is common to see 'action perspectives' as standing for individualism, free choice and free will against the various constraints and determinisms offered by the other approaches. To add to the appeal, action perspectives are commonly illustrated with reference to a number of fascinating studies of deviance, of cases where 'underdogs' stand against official institutions, or of what we used to call in the sixties 'happenings' (temporary dislocations of social order).

We have at least learned something from this condensed account, perhaps – that subjective meanings and actions are important; that they cover a wide range; that there are many empirical studies; that there is a special method commonly used, usually called 'ethnography', which is an alternative to 'positivism'. In my view, it is also very difficult to improve on matters with a 'proper' account of how the various approaches developed, and how they might be connected together. We have something like a network, with different clusters in it to examine. Teaching the topic is akin to plunging your hand into a box containing a net and lifting out some of the clusters for inspection. It would be possible, in principle, to explore more clusters, and to see how all the clusters were joined together into an overall network, but this would take a great deal of time. Instead, we can only explore some clusters and some connections, and the ones we haul out might not be the choice of everyone. My task as a writer is to start the exploration, but point to other ways to trace the network. As usual, the references and the online reading guides are there to encourage further exploration, but you will have to teach yourself if you want to follow these initial connections.

Turning to specifics, I have decided to focus my attention on two well-known sources of specific theories of action – American pragmatism, which led to the Chicago School and to symbolic interactionism; and 'social phenomenology', which connects with the work of more European theorists, especially Weber, but which has also inspired more recent American work such as ethnomethodology. Incidentally, I postpone a lengthier discussion on ethnomethodology to Chapter 12, where it seems to fit better. I end this chapter with a discussion of Giddens and 'structuration theory' as an example of an influential, current British approach. I am sure a fascinating account could be written showing how these specific theories relate to each other, but there is not the time or space to do it here, and it is an area of some controversy.

## American interactionism

This is a large topic too, but I am relying largely on the discussion in Joas (in Giddens and Turner 1987), and to a lesser extent in Manis and Meltzer (1972), and Fisher and Strauss (1991). There are online reading guides to each of these pieces for those interested in further details. These authors vary in the accounts that they give of the main developments associated with the Chicago School, but one agreed source is the pragmatist philosophy of Peirce and his associates.

This philosophical approach looks very appealing to sociologists because it seems to perform an important task in moving away from endless speculative philosophical discussion into something more sociological and concrete. Joas gives a number of examples of how philosophical problems were dealt with by this approach – abstract problems such as reconciling the dualism between mind and body were to be replaced by studying how concrete individuals solved immediate, concrete, personal and social problems; the mysterious notion of 'collective representations' in Durkheim's work, which we have discussed, was to be replaced by an examination of actual signs and symbols found in public discussions of religion or politics.

We end up with some important notions for a sociology of action – a creative, problem-solving individual, on the one hand, and a tolerant, democratic pragmatic community, on the other. To be very brief, the result of a good deal of thought about these different poles led to some of the specific work found in most of the common accounts. I am thinking here in particular of the work of Mead, for example: it is common to think of this work as involving a 'split self' (with a reflexive problem-solving 'I', and a more concrete and active 'me'), and emphasising the importance of symbols in interaction. Human beings have this capacity to express their meanings as concrete symbols – gestures, words – and once expressed, such meanings can be reflected upon by both parties to an interaction. We can therefore learn to understand others and ourselves. This capacity leads on in turn to acts of imagination such as 'taking the role of the other', or even constructing a Generalised Other to guide and orient our actions in anticipation of real interaction with real others. This is the part of Mead's work that sociologists know, but Joas argues that it had a much more general scope than just face-to-face immediate interaction – this is how human beings solve all their problems, including those when encountering the natural world.

It also seems to be the case that the intention was not just to build a model of a reflexive individual, but, as hinted, to draw implications for social collectivities too. This is often missed in those elementary glosses that attempt to confine action theory to modern notions of individualism alone, or to those moments of face-to-face interaction between isolated individuals. Individual problem-solving needed the support of a collectivity, it could be argued. The democratic and collaborative community that is implied could lead to real politics, or it could be seen as an important additional and far more optimistic possibility for advanced industrial societies, quite unlike the generally gloomy predictions of European sociology.

Joas goes on to argue that these conceptions could be 'applied' in a number of more concrete ways. Empirical research could be launched to discover exactly which forms of community were taking shape in city areas, and how exactly actors such as immigrants were developing problem-solving forms of interaction with hosts, an obvious project for the 'melting pot' that some people identified in Chicago in the middle of the twentieth century. Research need not confine itself to city communities either, but could focus on interaction inside organisations, and, indeed, this is where some of my favourite ethnographic work has taken place. Of course, ethnographic studies often fail to sketch in the wider theoretical context for their approaches, but this pragmatist thread, sometimes combined with European philosophy, and sometimes manifesting itself in combination with other forms of psychology or sociology, might be common to them.

If there were to be one study that seemed to summarise many of the themes we have been discussing, as well as being of immediate relevance to all of us involved in education it is Becker et al. (1995). This is a marvellous collective ethnographic study, involving all the great names of symbolic interactionism of that period, and it focuses upon university life. One story about the study is that it began with the intention of examining the impact of academic life upon students and their thinking, but, as with all the best ethnographic studies, a 'surprise' was waiting. When listening to students discussing how they were solving the pragmatic problems of coping with university life, the ethnographic team soon discovered the existence of a semi-deviant collective solution to the main problem that was perceived. In a nutshell, students were primarily concerned to maintain a good 'grade point average' in their studies. A good 'GPA' was important for both academic and social success, but it was terribly difficult to achieve one by reading all the suggested books and attending all the classes in the official manner. Instead, students were adopting solutions that were quite deviant in terms of the official university conventions for assessment – they were, for example, collective solutions and not the results of individual efforts, showing the effects of the collective accumulated wisdom of the student subculture. They involved strategies aimed at delivering the best possible grade in the time there was available, and the strategies often involved techniques which would meet with official disapproval, ranging from the 'selective neglect' of elements that were not assessed to attempts to 'psych out' individual tutors in order to affect their grading. Implications for universities were also drawn: basically, universities were simply demanding too much, placing too many obstacles in the way of student success, and thus, in effect, challenging their students to develop collective coping strategies, as intelligent people in structurally loose organisations will always tend to do. It is worth adding that this study is a model for ethnographic work too, with its careful attempts to sift 'spontaneous' comments from those that might have been prompted by the presence of the observers, and its careful pursuit of ambiguous or negative cases.

I have pursued a controversial strategy here, perhaps, in not discussing other American interactionists in much detail. I think readers can be referred to the excellent summarizes and discussions in the usual collections – Ritzer (1996), Turner (1996) or Waters (1994). I have included some histories and some typical pieces in the form of online reading guides on the website, taking examples of the work of Becker, Blumer, Cooley and Garfinkel. I have selected these to emphasise the methodological arguments in symbolic and other kinds of interactionism.

This approach struck me at the time as quite compatible with several main qualities of American interactionism itself – that they are not primarily concerned to put a theory of subjectivity at the centre of their work, but, rather, interested in demonstrating the flexibility and subtleties of human interaction. If you read some actual examples you can catch this concern at work. As Cohen puts it (in Turner 1996: 112) 'theorists such as Harold Garfinkel and Erving Goffman begin with little regard for philosophical problems at all'; and: 'Given the multiformity of action . . . it should be expected that each theorist of action will argue that certain characteristics of action about which he or she has something interesting to say matter more than others'.

Another key piece that reveals one such set of themes very clearly is Blumer (1976; see also the online reading guide). Blumer is credited with inventing the term 'symbolic interactionism' in the 1930s, and in narrowing its focus. This piece illustrates this well, reading at times like a pretty straightforward empirical (possibly an 'object-adequate') attempt to describe central features of human action, despite his formal acknowledgement of the central theoretical tenets of Mead; and much of the argument relies on contrasting the approach to others and claiming some greater sensitivity.

To borrow an elegant work by Habermas (1984), who was much influenced by American pragmatism too, it might be possible to classify action approaches in terms of how far they want to see action as compatible with, or opposed to, functionalist notions of social structure, rather than just to operate with a simple 'opposition' between the two.

We can even try to trace a connection from action theory back to the more general analyses of politics that are to come. It is clear that for some theorists, for example Parsons, interaction takes place within a framework of overall social norms and values, and can be seen to reinforce those norms and values. The notion of interaction ending in structured and persistent conflict is missing, although Parsons does discuss conflict arising from various kinds of social mis-understandings or social inadequacies in terms of grasping the central norms and values.

For analysts like Goffman, there seems to be a different goal for interaction, perhaps summarised best by remembering the title of one of his most famous books: *The Presentation of Self in Everyday Life* (1969). Goffman is describing a world of pretty intense interpersonal rivalry and constant conflict, where rather anxious and insecure individuals are constantly defending and preserving their status. They do this by a calculating attention to presentation, controlling the little details of action and behaviour that create an impression of themselves which will give them some advantage in their conduct with others. Swimmers on the beach constantly wish to present themselves as 'proper men' to both male and female onlookers, to cite one of Goffman's actual examples. On another tack, medical professionals constantly engage in impression manage-ment, at least when 'on stage', so as to persuade the public of their competence and occupational status.

In Habermas's hands, this notion of impression management could be extended to meet more traditional and critical notions of politics too, however. We can see how this works by referring to another very well-known area of impression management these days, the activities of professional politicians and their associates, the spin doctors. Most people are familiar with this kind of activity, perhaps the most famous example in Britain being that of a spin doctor attempting to 'bury' bad UK political news in the middle of the extensive cov-erage of the 11 September attacks on America. In other examples, various glosses are placed on press releases, for example to announce large increases in government spending while underneath the glosses, the totals are massaged by including previous expenditure. The record of governments is played up and their failures played down by a selective presentation of facts and by placing strong favourable interpretations on those facts. Again, this can take place in some detail, so that an environmental campaign can be countered with a 'cam-paign for jobs'. The US military invented a number of famous euphemisms to create a favourable impression of their activities, say in Vietnam – 'interdiction' meant a large-scale bombing strike, for example, while 'collateral damage' was a term referring to the unavoidable death and destruction of civilians involved.

In fact, Habermas (1976; and see the online reading guide) identified two main types of this sort of politically inspired communication, which he thought were common in political discourses in modern states: 'strategic communication' was intended to mobilise support for a particular political strategy, while 'dis-torted communication' was a particular kind of communication that attempted to represent particular interests as universal ones. As an example of the latter kind, any politician's speech that uses the word 'we' needs to be examined very carefully to see exactly what is meant by this term. Does 'we the people' really mean 'we politicians', or 'we members of the ruling elite', or even 'we wealthy white people'?

Just to round off this aside from Habermas, he points out that very few of those interested in action sociology have grasped the real political potential of interaction, which is to use speech to challenge the existing political system. In his famous 'ideal speech situation' (see Chapter 12), which is akin to the democratic collectivities in pragmatism, the participants are able to raise questions about the validity of any of the claims being made by the others. The point is that any competent speaker can raise such issues of validity: they can question the sincerity of the speaker, the social appropriateness of what is being said, and, of course, the validity of the utterance in the usual sense (whether it corresponds to the truth of the situation being described).

This notion has run into criticisms of its own, mostly centred upon the unusual nature of such situations, their rarity and the difficulties of actually organising them (think of the problems in trying to organise a critical discussion of something in sociology seminars!). Nevertheless, the ideal speech situation remains as a kind of useful extreme, and we can use it to contrast with other, much more limited forms of interaction which we are permitted, but which have serious constraints. My own favourite examples are so-called 'consultation' exercises at work, where we file in to be confronted by a management that has already made up its mind and which wants to limit discussion to 'constructive' matters only (that is, those related to tweaking some of the minor problems with the policy, but not those that radically challenge the policy, or suggest a major alternative).

Before we get to discuss Habermas more fully, let us consider some of the more radical implications of an emphasis on subjectivity, sticking to the traditionally defined accounts. What is subjectivity, and how does it work to produce action? How much of the social world is produced by subjectivity, and how much is objective, beyond its reach?

## European action theory

I hope it will be sufficient briefly to sketch out the usual concepts associated with Weber by way of an introduction, leaving you to follow up the discussions in the major textbooks we have mentioned, like Ritzer (1996) or Waters (1994). We have also mentioned aspects of Weber's work in Chapter 3, and we shall do so again in Chapter 5. I shall not attempt to enter into the discussion about how these aspects of his work might be connected, or how Weber might be connected with his peers – this is another bit of the network that you can pursue for yourselves, starting, perhaps, with Turner (1981).

Weber developed an interest in subjective meaning, it is argued, in an attempt to preserve some kind of subjective (or 'value-rational') action in an increasingly rationalised society, and to stand with his colleagues in the methodological struggles against positivism. His work offers a classification of types of action – traditional, affectual, 'purposive-rational' and 'value-rational' – and some comments about how we might understand how subjective meanings get 'attached' to action. Weber also has a definition of social action covering the case when individuals attempt to orient their action to each other. Having identified this as the major focus for sociology, Weber goes on to discuss some ways in which we might begin to understand such subjective meanings.

This discussion begins with a rejection of some obvious approaches. We should not assume that action is always functionally connected to meaning, for example, partly because intentions are not always realised in actions as we would wish. Nor can we use the appealing option of 'empathy', where we try to place ourselves imaginatively in the position of the person we are observing. Incidentally, this rejection surprises students sometimes, since empathy is not only a common technique to use in ordinary life, but is even occasionally suggested as a method in modern history syllabuses. Weber thought it was much too speculative to serve as an adequate method, and recommended a more rational and testable technique instead – *verstehen*. This involves building a kind of model of the actor, attributing 'typical' motives to actions and then testing the adequacy of this construction in two directions – the model must be 'causally adequate', that is, conforming to what is known already about behaviour and its 'laws', and 'meaningfully adequate', which involves consistency with what is known about meanings. The model in question is a special one, of course, an 'ideal type', with a mixture of empirically typical behaviour and some statement about what is 'ideally' or 'essentially' at the heart of the action. It follows that constructing such ideal types is easier in some cases than in others: the activities of rational actors in bureaucracies or markets can be modelled in a predictable way because typical action is strongly supported by what might be called the 'logic of the situation'. One curiosity that often strikes students encountering this work for the first time is that Weber does not seem to advocate any actual communication with the people being studied, no interviews or questionnaires – instead, detached observation and theoretically guided speculation and type construction will deliver.

Naturally, the approach has attracted a great many criticisms, including some pertinent ones which have a much more general application. Where is the role of social conflict for example, and how might we discuss the differential power of the actors? As an attempt to be scientific about subjective meaning it reveals a great deal of uncertainty and paradox: subjective meaning has to be dragged quite a way on to the terrain of sociologists before it can be studied, so to speak.

## Social phenomenology

We are trying to avoid excessive scholasticism, but I do want to take a more 'philosophical' route here, in examining one writer whose work has relevance for several of the approaches associated with action sociology. We might begin this topic with a discussion of the work of Husserl (such as Husserl 1973; see also the online reading guide to this piece on the website). There is a rather abstract beginning to this account, but we will get to the issue of subjectivity soon.

Husserl wanted to ground science and social science on really firm, unshakeable, indubitable foundations in order to sort out what he saw as recurrent crises, demonstrated best, perhaps, by the occurrence of so many alternative approaches and debates about how to proceed. The *Cartesian Meditations* (Husserl 1973) begins by discussing how (social) sciences try to ground theories on evidence, but argues that this is usually a process riddled with assumptions. What we should do instead is to try to establish some unshakeable ('apodictic') first principle and then proceed.

These unshakeable principles could not be found in sense data, because the senses obviously frequently mislead us. Nor should we start by making some simple assumptions about the world – that it contains real events, or reflects some human nature, or that it is mathematical in its regularity, offers an expression of Christian or humanist principles, or whatever. Already, we have raised serious doubts about positivist approaches, and we can begin to question some of the classic works in sociology, such as Durkheim's, with its odd assumptions about what counts as 'the social', or Marx with his unprovable notions of economic determinism, or even Weber with his unclarified notion of a 'social relation'. Obviously, this critique applies equally to all 'common-sense' views that see the world affected by superstitious forces, or populated simply by unique individuals.

There is one undoubted starting point for the study of human beings, however, and that is that they are conscious, or, more pointedly, that their consciousness constitutes their world. This is not an immediate denial of realism, since there may well be real objects out there. The point is that we can never finally separate out what really is real (so to speak), and what is merely real for us. We cannot rely on the usual test which consists of trying to manipulate things and then, when we fail, awarding them some objective status (which is more or less Durkheim's cheerfully operationalised approach). Everything that looks real must be re-classified as 'phenomena', that is 'things as they appear to us'. This view departs from the usual one of consciousness as a matter simply of awareness of the world – consciousness does much more than just register and mimic a real world.

Consciousness in general constitutes the real world, the social world and our ordinary notions of ourselves. That is, it somehow constructs these areas, in the sense of making them possible, of providing a reservoir of possibilities that are then selectively used to create what we see. We can grasp this notion if we reflect on it, and notice that we attend to the world differently at different times, and that we even perceive and define it differently. Thus this object on which I sit is a chair when I decide to sit on it, but it can also be a stepladder when I climb on it to change a lightbulb, a weapon if I use it to defend myself against a burglar, a commodity if I decide to auction it, and so on. My consciousness is responsible for these different aspects – that is easy to see. But Husserl wants to argue that consciousness actually also imposes a unity on all these different intentions, that it constructs the object in question as a discrete object, a chair. Normally, this is not a very consistent unity, because it is not significant for me to explore this aspect of 'chairness', but I can make it more systematic by theorising explicitly about what it is that unites together all my intentions towards an object. That is precisely what social and other sciences do to get their theories. As we shall see, this involves taking a particular perspective on the world, a 'theoretical attitude'.

Ordinary consciousness lives in the world as it is immediately accessible to us, the world of our intentions and working knowledge, but, for Husserl, it has another dimension, revealed by further reflection. This is the transcendental dimension. Its existence is necessary and presupposed by our discussions of ordinary consciousness. The transcendental realm constitutes ordinary consciousness, that is, makes it possible as a more concrete realisation. It also constitutes ordinary egos ('personalities'). It follows that if we want to study consciousness in its pure sense, without building in all our everyday assumptions which we take for granted but which actually are assumptions nevertheless, we have to focus our attention on the transcendental realm of consciousness – that is, to see how consciousness works, to see how it constructs a sense of reality for us. This is a necessary task if we want to understand how individuals, including scientists and social scientists, construct their reality.

To cut a long story short, the end result of all this investigation of the transcendental is to produce 'structures of the lifeworld'. These include processes like systems of motives, and 'relevance systems' (which enable us to direct our intentions towards aspects of phenomena): these guide our actions, including the construction of theories. There are also mechanisms such as intentionality and certain inner connections of subjective time (which help us to unite in our minds past experiences and current perceptions), and these provide our main ways of understanding the world. These mechanisms produce particular patterns, particular constructions and understandings – but these become habitualised, the processes are forgotten, and our understandings come to be seen as the real world itself.

Schütz uses this basic apparatus initially to clarify approaches to consciousness found in the 'action sociology' of his day. This clarification seemed urgent to him, because most of the existing sociology simply assumed, or gave common-sense definitions of, important terms such as intersubjectivity, communication, accounts of action and how these might be linked to motives, and so on. (There is an online reading guide to Schütz's major work on Weber – Schütz 1972.)

Here, Schütz argues that Weber proceeded on the right lines by focusing on social interactions, subjective meanings and the importance of human consciousness. He was quite right to prefer this to positivist accounts that try to sidestep the issue of meaning altogether. But at the very heart of his account there are certain terms and processes that have not been adequately analysed. To take some examples:

1   Weber is interested in 'subjectively intended meanings'. To understand these, he proposes to place actions in a context of intentions and motives (although he also seems to believe that we can somehow 'directly under-stand' meanings as well). He is not very clear, however, about how motives and intentions are actually connected to action, how the one leads to the other. Here, says Schütz, we might consider how individual actors them-selves describe what they do – they fantasise, they project their actions into the future, or they manage somehow to connect a past event with action, so that the past 'causes' action to take place in the present. Of course these con-nections are possible only if consciousness has a mechanism to do this, an ability to 'synthesise' experiences. This is where Weber needs Husserl's work on consciousness.

What makes things worse is that it is not at all clear how these connec-tions are actually made, even to the actors themselves (unless actors can be persuaded to philosophise). The observer has far less a chance of under-standing. What observers often really do when they offer explanations of subjective action is to try to integrate bits of action, and a set of assumed motives, into a meaning-context of their own (an 'objective meaning con-text', for Schütz). To see this as an explanation of the intended meaning of others involves making a massive assumption that actions relate to the con-sciousness of the actor in the same way as the observers relate them. This is a very powerful critique that can be applied to ethnographic observational methods and their claims as well.

2   Weber refers to 'social action', that is, action which is meaningfully related to others. This is along the right lines, but there are in fact several ways of relating to others. There are also several categories of others to whom one relates, depending on how intimate a relation one desires. Thus contempo-raries can be related to in a much richer way than predecessors or descendants. Not only that, we can perceive others in our everyday social world quite differently according to our motives and intentions towards them – we can see them as objects in an environment, clever machines or as fully human active persons like ourselves ('Thous'). Schütz's example turns on the different ways in which we might relate to a person of minor impor-tance in our lives, such as the postal worker whom we encounter for a few seconds every morning, compared to the person we live with in everyday intimacy. This is an important point for sociologists to remember, because they so often assume that particular forms of social action are dominant (including a strong tendency to privilege face-to-face forms). In practice, it may not be at all easy to establish which of the many possible forms of social action are being played out for us to observe.

3   Weber's method turns on the notion of the 'ideal-type'. He is right to see

these as the only methods available for social sciences. Social scientists have to simplify and make assumptions about others, about their typical motives or their typical intentions. The only danger arises when sociologists forget how riddled with assumptions ideal types actually are, and come to see their ideal types as real individuals, whereas they are in fact sociological constructs. Weber himself strays into this mistake. He thinks he can build ideal types and then test them in some objective way, to assess their 'causal adequacy' and 'meaning adequacy', in his terms. Schütz carefully analyses these conceptions (as the material in the online reading guide indicates) and suggests that what this really means is that ideal types have to be predictable, that is, to conform to the 'laws' of sociology. In other words they have to be properly constructed in sociological terms, using recognisably sociological constructs, to fit in with existing sociological abstractions. It is not surprising, therefore, that ideal types usually are causally adequate, because they are constructed that way in the first place! As for meaning adequacy, Weber thinks he can test ideal types against the meanings of real individuals, but this is absurd because we have already argued that we can never know real individuals, but only ideal types of them. So checking ideal types against real individuals really means checking one more general ideal type against a more detailed one. Again, it is hardly surprising, given the tendency of consciousness to impose a unity on the social world, that ideal types will mostly turn out to be meaning-adequate. Overall, Weber is mystifying the issues and deluding himself if he thinks that ideal types can lead to some objective test for sociology, somehow outside the motives and intentions of sociologists: this is radically impossible.

Let me summarise some implications for sociologists trying to study the meaningful actions of individuals:

(a) Real individuals cannot be studied in their full complexity, but only as ideal types. Even intimates only appear to be more fully understood by us because we have a far more detailed ideal type of them than we do of postal workers. The problem is that some ways of acting may well be typical, so we can understand them fairly easily (a lot of economic activity falls into this category). But there are always highly complex and individual sets of meanings and individual accounts of them, and we have far less chance of understanding these: even the actors themselves cannot always understand them.

(b) Sociologists are not above or outside of the social world, although they do have a different perspective on it (see below). They do sociology in much the same way that any individuals impose meaning on their world – that is, by attempting to typify it, albeit more rigorously, by using special constructs called data, and by pursuing special projects and procedures, validated as 'science'. Sociological understanding is still the product of typical motives, intentions and relevance systems, however; it is just that these are collectively owned by sociologists, and not naïvely held as 'common sense'.

(c) The key method of sociology, the ideal type, is therefore not unique to sociology. Sociologists use the method more systematically, and try to make it more of a systematic unity than ordinary people do, and they probably deploy a greater range of ideal types, including very general abstract ones (such as Economic Man, who engages in 'rational' action, as Weber understands it). Sociologists are deluding themselves if they imagine sociological ideal types are objective in some positivist sense, however. Bringing sociologists back into the normal social world is not necessarily a bad thing, especially if it helps to dispel self-delusion and encourages a reflective account of doing sociology.

(d) Sociological studies occupy a different place from common-sense understanding, however. For most of us in the everyday world (taking the 'natural attitude', as Schütz calls it), the world is arranged around us in a series of concentric circles, based on our ability to interact fully with others, and it also occupies a definite space – the 'Here and Now'. Sociology occupies a different stance, organised around an impersonal detached observer and a generalised abstract viewpoint – the 'theoretical attitude'. In this way, sociology does not simply replicate common-sense understandings, but can provide us with knowledge about the social world that ordinary actors do not have. But again, this must not be misunderstood – sociology simply occupies another 'province of meaning'. To be useful for ordinary human beings, it must go on to explain how its special perspectives relate to their common-sense ones. This is usually not accomplished very well: sociologists simply assume their ideal types are the same as real people, or they try to persuade people to make them see the social world in the same way that they do.

There is a more promising alternative for sociology, Schütz thinks, based on a more reflective approach, drawing on classic phenomenological techniques. We might begin by investigating how we ourselves switch from a sociological perspective to a common-sense one, for example. We often experience this simply as a 'leap' from one province of meaning to another, as we leave the lecture room or office and re-enter ordinary life, or stop reading philosophy and feed the cat. But if we reflect on this leap, perhaps we will discover that sociology is closely tied to mundane life after all, just as affected by ordinary motives and naïve assumptions. If we pursue this reflection on ourselves, thinking about the details of our own biographies, for example, we might discover what it is we have in common with 'ordinary' individuals. Of course, to understand how this is done in a more technical sense, we will also have to understand how consciousness works, how motives are connected to attractions, how apparently logical theorising depends on a pre-logical understanding.

I must say I have experienced the shift between theoretical attitude and natural attitude as a 'leap', but only after a long process of becoming a professional teacher, and being socialised into the theoretical attitude in the first place. For newcomers, getting into the theoretical attitude can be a major problem, and it can take a great deal of time and struggle. This process is not well examined by Schütz, and I think we need something more like interactionist work on professional socialisation. The classics here include work by Becker et al. (1961) on how medical students come to take on the typical professional perspectives of their occupation; work on the professional socialisation of teachers as in Ball and Goodson (1985; and see the online reading guide to this collection); work by Goffman (1969) on how the experienced professional learns to manage the drama of everyday professional life, with its 'on-stage' and 'off-stage' regions. I cannot resist making here the point that recurs again and again in this book: this socialisation takes place in special institutions called universities, which are designed partly to facilitate it, with a number of social rituals to support socialisation of this kind (seminars, practicals and assessment, for example). For me, university life would be the neglected 'material base' for such shifts in perspective. For practical purposes, it is the Timetable that tells me when to 'leap' into and out of a theoretical attitude.

Reflecting on our own subjective activity seems a very promising and interesting project still, if rather an abstract one, partly pursued in the more reflective styles of sociological thinking, including feminism, as we shall see. Of course, there are also some problems with Schütz's work, including the accusation of abstractness cited by American pragmatism. The project seems very uncritical about the mundane world, for example, unprepared to comment on the different sorts of action found in it. The listing of universal characteristics of action tends to ignore important differences between them, such as differences of power, for example. More abstractly, there is always a problem with two-stage arguments like this. To comment on Schütz directly, the transcendental realm clearly is a very important one that operates somehow 'behind' ordinary consciousness, and this raises problems of theorising the connections between the two levels (as critics like Hindess [1977] have pointed out – try the online reading guide). This 'surface/depth' metaphor is virtually universal in sociology. For critics like Foucault, it is important to move away from such a two-level explanation, as we shall see in Chapter 10.

Some initial problems can be detected immediately, however: this important transcendental realm simply cannot be accessed directly. We have to get to know about it through rather dubious processes such as sympathetic reconstruction. As one implication, we can only ever operate with plausible explanations, and never with fully argued and justified logical ones. The split between levels therefore introduces an inevitable 'incoherence' into sociological explanation.

Hindess (1977) has become famous for pointing out that such incoherence is usually managed by some dogmatic assertion about how one level affects the other. I suppose such dogmatism might just be detectable even after a quick summary of Schütz. It is not so much that he dogmatically insists he is right, more that the arguments make a great deal of sense when he pursues them, but are rather difficult to develop for oneself. This, for me, is often an indication that there is something more than logical arguments being deployed; something that involves unclarified personal judgements or argumentational manoeuvres. Recourse to authority is often implied in such skilled expositions – we know that Schütz speaks with a particular authority as a student of Husserl, and we know of his great reputation from the references and endorsements on the covers of his books. Schütz is by no means the only theorist against whom one could level this mild complaint, of course!

There is also another very powerful critique that can be brought to bear, in the work of Derrida (see Kamuf 1991). We shall be examining this work (in so far as we are able) in Chapter 13, but we might just float it here. Derrida's main point is that phenomenology (he has in mind Husserl in particular) misunderstands the role of language and consciousness. If we assume, just for now, that Derrida wants to replace the notion of consciousness as some sort of transcendental realm which 'constitutes' the world with a proper account of language as the source and fount of meaning, this begins to make some sense, but it still looks like a pretty abstract argument (and it is developed in a pretty impenetrable way, alas).

However, what is at stake is quite important. Language is a social practice from the very beginning, so we have immediately escaped from the isolation of consciousness and from the odd realm of transcendental subjectivity into the social world (and, as a result, we can do without a lot of philosophical baggage concerning speculation about this unknowable level, and concentrate instead on nice tangible practices like writing). Husserl is closely examined on this matter, and Derrida finds him wanting. Husserl tries to confine language to a development of some originating internal dialogues with oneself within consciousness, so to speak, but Derrida (Kamuf 1991) insists that this is impossible to sustain, and that many features of language contain irremovable references to others and to social relations. This has important consequences, one of which is the turn away from consciousness to language, which is a feature of several major and later social theorists' work, as we shall see.

But let us not run before we walk. We can linger a bit, and focus on the implications for action sociology of social phenomenology, which are important and interesting. Let us postpone the scholarly (scholastic?) agenda, which wants to operate all the time at the most abstract levels of European philosophy. For now, we can politely resist and reimpose our own agenda. What can we learn about action sociology from social phenomenology? How has it been developed?

There is one other important attempt to apply the insights of Husserl (and Schütz) to sociology – the work of Berger and Luckmann (1967) on the 'social construction of reality'. There is an online reading guide to this famous account, and those readers interested in pursuing this project in more depth might want to consult it. A brief account might be given here, using a 'thought experiment' deployed by Berger and Luckmann themselves. It goes like this:

Let us imagine that we are all on a journey together, and that we are interrupted by an accident that causes us to land on a desert island. Rescue is impossible, and so we have to construct a social life for ourselves. What we decide to do would clearly reflect our own subjective preferences, motives and intentions, and we would draw on the amazing capacity of subjective experience to unite past, present and future actions, just as Schütz suggests. As a result, we might develop some rituals that obviously imitate the past lives we have led – still celebrating the traditional feast days, for example. On the other hand, we might also develop very eccentric forms of social ritual, involving, say, the ceremonial consumption of mind-altering vegetables, on the occasion of the birth of the second male child in a particular family. We would also have to produce more 'normal' institutions to develop the equivalent of kinship systems, religious systems, education systems and occupational systems of our own as a response to the 'functional prerequisites' of social life on the island. It would be interesting to see just what is 'functional' here, and what is the result of the values of dominant groups amongst us, as we suggested in Chapter 2. What we produced would be clearly traceable to our own subjective activities and preferences, if not entirely determined by them. We could imitate the institutions we know, or, again, branch out and do something really novel – choosing marriage partners of alternating sexes every five years, or whatever. Of course, we might not all agree, and we would have to develop some kind of political system to solve these differences too. We might decide that since motherhood is the most important function in our society, for example, we would rely upon the judgements of a panel of wise women to settle disputes. In any event, our society will clearly have been 'socially constructed'.

Of course, for any descendants of ours, society will look very different. It will take on an objective reality 'of its own'. It will become thing-like, or 'reified', apparently existing independently of human consciousness. Its origins in human action will not be perceived or experienced directly, although it would be possible to detect the way in which newcomers had their consciousness adjusted, so to speak, to conform to social institutions.

Using this simple thought experiment might permit us to trace out the rest of the argument in Berger and Luckmann. Future generations might well turn to sociological models to try to understand their social life, for example, and they could well reproduce the existing divisions between marxism, functionalism and action sociology. Each of these approaches would be partially correct, depending on which stage of the social construction of reality is being analysed, but none of them would be universally applicable, capable of explaining the whole process. In this way, Berger and Luckmann claim to be able to offer a new kind of unity between the different sociological approaches, giving each one its due, without fully endorsing the claims of any of them.

## Giddens and 'structuration'

This model bears a certain resemblance to a much more modern and influential formulation of the same project – Giddens' 'structuration theory'. Again, much has been written about this particular approach, including much criticism of it. Only a brief summary can be offered here, but there are some excellent commentaries (including Cohen in Turner 1996).

In its simplest form, Giddens offers a two-stage model of social action (see Figure 4.1 and the discussion in Waters 1994). At the individual level, actors engage in social relations with each other, and form various kinds of social bonds between themselves in the process. Action sociology explains this process very well. Individuals express meanings in their actions, and because they have the capacity to detect meaning in the actions of others, in various ways, including assuming a 'reciprocity of perspectives', or 'internalising the role of the other', they can generate mutual understandings. These can take the forms of customs, habits, norms or laws, depending on how binding they are expected to be, and what institutional support they can attract.

However, there is another level to the model as well, the systems level. Individual actions can be reified, more or less as Berger and Luckmann have described the process, taking on some external life of their own. What is more, actions sometimes have unintended consequences, some emergent property, as we have described it, which 'surprises' the participants themselves and again takes on some objective existence. The usual examples here include occasions like the ones Weber describes in his account of the Protestant ethic and its unintended effects on the growth of capitalism, as we discussed it in the previous

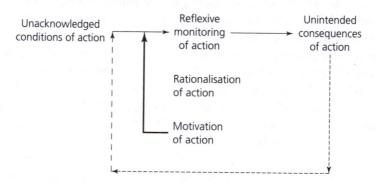

The duality of structure (Waters 1994: 105)

'**Structure** consists of rules and resources which provide the formulae and the means for action;
**Systems** are the accomplished relationships between actors/collectivities which are organised, regular, and relatively enduring;
**Structuration** consists of the conditions and the media by which structures are transformed into systems.'

**Figure 4.1 Models of structuration in Giddens (1984: 5). Reprinted by permission.**

chapter. On a more personal level, it is common experience that casual friend-
ships sometimes have consequences that neither of the participants originally
intended – marriage and parenthood, fits of jealousy and violence, an interest in
mortgages and life assurance, for example. However, these localised and limited
unintended consequences are also patterned by social structures – by social
class, ethnicity and gender, for example. The theoretical implication is that this
is a new way to avoid the old splits between 'agency' and 'structure' and overcome the problems of each, as May (1996: 107) argues: '. . . functionalism and
structuralism fail to see society and social life as the product of active subjects,
whilst action theories consider only the production, but not reproduction, of
social systems in social relations.'

In Giddens' work, 'social structure' in the usual sense – social patterns and
institutions – is accomplished through action (although it can influence the actor
in turn), but this leads to another implication. There is yet another dimension
'behind' social structure, however, a rather more mysterious 'philosophical' level
existing in a 'virtual' dimension. We can understand this dimension fairly simply,
as what May (1996: 108) calls an open set of 'opportunities for innovative social
conduct . . . the possibility of always being able to "act otherwise"'. This level can
also be thought of as a set of 'rules and resources', or capabilities and knowledges, to guide action at the individual level. What action does is to take these
rules and resources and give them concrete shape, actualise them, or 'structurate'
them (that is, turn potentials and possibilities into tangible structures). The combination of the concrete level and the level of potentials is what provides a
necessary 'duality of structure'. Just as we saw in Chapter 1 with the case of the
dualistic nature of the commodity, this necessary duality is just not picked up by
'positivist' approaches, or by 'static' ones that fail to employ an historical dimension (compare this with the idea of 'process reduction' in Chapter 3, pp. 77–8).

Giddens uses the marxist term 'praxis' to introduce some optimistic politics
here, denying structural determinism, although he is not saying that it is a
simple matter to change social structures, because of the 'unacknowledged conditions of action [including unconscious motivations] . . . and the unintended
consequences of action' (May 1996: 109), which tend to reproduce existing social
patterns. Considerable reflection for active individuals is needed to effect
social change, and sociologists can obviously help by analysing the 'duality of
structure', which is not immediately apparent.

This might seem rather mystical at first, and it is difficult to understand this
argument on its own without considering the substantial theoretical labours
that Giddens has undertaken in order to try to develop this view against the conventional major sociological approaches. This groundwork was done in a series
of highly influential books written in the 1970s, which took in turn functionalism
and structuralism, marxism and action approaches, and subjected them to some
very searching critique. I have some online reading guides to aspects of some of
these pieces. The example explored best here is the account of the 'structuration'
of class relations, which is to come in Chapter 5. The argument is that some

process is needed to explain how the underlying structural forces (found, in marxism, in modes of production) actually produce concrete social groups 'on the surface'. 'Structuration factors' bridge this gap, as we shall see. The same general argument can be detected in Giddens' critique of functionalism, which we have mentioned (and on which topic there is an online reading guide) – again, functionalism can be criticised specifically for not operating with a properly dualistic notion of 'structure', and thus confusing the actually existing social institutions in the social system with the evolutionary and social forces which are claimed to act at a deeper level.

Some critics have likened this to Derrida's project, sketched above, or to the project inaugurated by the German philosopher Heidegger. This project can be summarised as an attempt to establish the 'ground' for the specific cultural and philosophical activities that were around at the time. Simply, establishing the ground in this case means trying to conceive of some underlying background that would explain each of the specifics (in Heidegger's case, this leads to the curiously abstract project of trying to uncover the ways in which Being tries to express itself in various concrete forms and traditions). It finds an echo in Husserl's work – which we have discussed above too – to describe the transcendental realm of consciousness that 'constitutes' the activities of normal consciousness, providing raw materials, as it were, for specific activities. Perhaps Giddens is embarked upon the same quest, suggesting that there must be some level of social and cultural 'raw materials', at the level of potentials, to provide for specific actions and institutions.

To refer to a homely example, the rules and resources of a game could be seen to operate at some general, 'virtual' level: the rules might be written down somewhere, I suppose, but not the specific moves and manoeuvres. Any actual game would clearly draw upon such rules and resources and put them into a concrete practical form – but that concrete practical form would be better understood by realising that there is a virtual level 'behind' it.

As an aside, a similar argument is sometimes advanced to defend a version of realism against the excesses of postmodernism, usually traced to the work of Bhaskar (see Benton 1981 for an effective critical discussion). This often also crops up in the discussions about Foucault and the notion of 'discursive' and 'extra-discursive' elements, as we shall see. Briefly, while actual discourses about social reality can be clearly seen to be relativist, that which they discourse about can be seen as a kind of 'real', non-subjective but 'virtual' level.

A more common application, perhaps, is often found in elementary sociology textbooks as well, where structuration theory is used as some 'last word' to round off the familiar story of eternal conflicts between action and structuralist 'perspectives'. (My own view, for what it is worth, is that this eternal conflict has its origins in a teaching strategy anyway, rather than in some accurate history of sociology – it is used to generate a nice simple debate so that students can display suitable levels of open-mindedness by discussing 'both sides'.) If only to open up this narrative closure, it might be worth considering a few brief criticisms of Giddens' structuration approach (for more detailed criticisms, see Bryant and Jary 1991; Craib 1992; Dallmayr in Giddens 1982).

To begin with, as you might expect, advocates of the different approaches have objected that the structuration model does not do sufficient justice to their preferred approach: it is not marxist enough for marxists, not sufficiently well developed at the individual level for action theorists, and so on. Unkind commentators have seen the whole project as a matter of 'raiding' other positions, and 'bolting on' new dimensions as the work progresses. The model certainly is ambiguous here, and different critics have suggested that the approach is 'really' grounded in both action and structural approaches, somewhat to the delight of Giddens himself. He does remain elusive in his own (hugely extensive) writings, I find.

One important criticism echoes the argument about incoherence that we have seen above, however. Dallmayr (in Giddens 1982) suggests that the problems start by lumping together both rules and resources as characteristics of the virtual level. May (1996) explains that Giddens does this in an attempt to marry the structuralist notion of 'rules' to an account that brings power back in (since 'resources' can be, and nearly always are, unevenly distributed). We might take this as a typical attempt to synthesise, incorporate and transform earlier perspectives; these are really quite separate, though, it might be argued.

Specifically and partly as a result of trying to do too much, Giddens hesitates between seeing the 'structural' level as a genuinely 'virtual' level, and seeing it merely as a 'contingent and essentially irremediable constellation of "present" and "absent" factors . . . "structure" tends to merge imperceptibly with "system"' (Dallmayr in Giddens 1982: 21). This is the same problem as that faced by functionalism, and runs the same risks of a 'conservative' justification of what exists already.

As for the conception of action or 'agency', Giddens has another dilemma. He does not want to use it in the ordinary (Weberian) sense, as subjectively intended action, because that would commit him to the conventional and uncomfortable view of a dualism between 'life sciences' (analysing humans with special techniques to grasp subjective meaning) and 'natural sciences' (analysing everything else with the more powerful and general techniques of causal and empirical analyses). But he is content to use the concept to describe 'everyday conduct understood as "activity" or "doing"' (Dallmayr in Giddens 1982: 22). This risks an uncritical description of every activity alike as somehow all dignified by expressing some universal humanist 'agency'. I think Giddens does get close to this in his later work on life in modernity (Giddens 1991, for example – try the online reading guide), where the human ability to exercise 'choice' describes almost every human action, from poor people 'choosing' to spend their meagre budget on food, to pampered celebrities 'choosing' plastic surgery to change the shape of their bodies. We have here some general problems that we have encountered before – the problem of incoherence, and also the problem, which arises again and again, of managing both theoretical and concrete levels.

## Concluding thoughts

As we shall see, Giddens is by no means the only one who finds it difficult to maintain high levels of academic inquiry when returning to the details of every-day life. The material he has produced in response to more practical and political agendas can seem both uncritical and theoretically unsophisticated (see his work on The Third Way, such as Giddens 1998). There seems to be a tendency for action approaches, as well as functionalist ones, to reproduce this uneasy accommodation with the status quo. Perhaps it is that general theories of humanity, consciousness and agency cannot lead logically to an analysis of con-crete actions either, without bringing in some naïve and uncritical acceptance of common-sense categories first.

# PART III

# 5  Weber, Class and the Politics of Closure

In this chapter we pursue the notions of both 'emergence' and 'action' that we have seen in earlier chapters, and begin to consider the issues of political activity. Political activity is no mere distraction, but, arguably, the very social glue that binds us together into social groups. We take sides. If we have any public life at all, it is by joining associations of various kinds – professional, interest-groups, even committees to run our favourite sports facilities. It is with these activities that we are likely to encounter first social and economic constraints, or to experience the force of figurational emergence, or to be able to formulate and co-ordinate social actions of various kinds. We are discussing politics in a very general sense here, of course. We do not want to limit the term to refer just to conventional national politics, the struggle between Conservative, Labour and Liberal Parties in Britain, or between Democrats and Republicans in the USA, or Liberal and Labour in Australia, although not long ago these were far more like mass organisations than they are today.

We can still head towards the sort of everyday politics we have in mind by thinking of the technical sense of the term 'party'. Although we think of the official political parties, the term has always had a much more general usage to mean any group that is organised so as to achieve particular advantages for itself.

This usage of the term was popularised first, arguably, by Weber. Consider his famous discussion of social stratification. The usual story is that Weber wanted to add additional dimensions to the notion of social class, perhaps to counter the obsessive focus on class on the part of marxists. There is the additional dimension of status, for example, which refers to one's position in some less 'economic' system of social ranking. Thus certain occupations have always held quite high prestige – such as priests, doctors and, perhaps once, teachers (Weber refers to some local aspects of this by telling us that, for example, bookbinders were often held in high esteem in certain parts of Germany). This dimension can cut across matters such as income and wealth, since despite low levels of income or wealth, these occupations enjoy high local status.

The other dimension, though, is 'party'. Here, Weber is reminding us that political power need not be always associated with social class. Paid bureaucrats and officials have power, for example, by dint of their occupation of official posts. Trade union officials or the leaders of pressure groups can also wield power. In modern nation-states, political parties in the familiar sense wield power independently of the class position of their members – they have to be elected and legitimated through a separate political process.

## Classes

To go back to the category of class first, we can add some detail (from the selections of Weber's work gathered in Giddens and Held 1982 in this case). Weber suggests that classes can be subdivided according to class situation (how they go about procuring goods, position, or satisfaction), which produces three main types – property classes, commercial classes and social classes.

Property classes, incidentally, include those people able to monopolise educational privileges as well, but Weber clearly has in mind economic property mostly, owning the usual forms of wealth such as land. There are both 'negatively' and 'positively privileged' groups here, such as debtors and lenders, tenants and landlords (the characteristic types for Weber). There are also middle classes, literally acting as middlemen between these two groups. These classes can form the basis of social associations as well as being merely formal or analytic categories – landlords can band together into associations to pursue their common interests, for example, and can even come to develop some sort of common outlook. However, revolutionary conflict between the classes, as predicted by marxists, is likely to be rare. Some kind of radical social polarisation is required, enabling immediate contrasts to be drawn, and lines of battle clarified. Conflict between these classes is more likely to be aimed at redistributing property and rights between them rather than at a social revolution.

We might add that most political struggle takes this non-revolutionary form, and includes the activities of status groups and parties as well. Weberian analysis gets much closer to actual forms than does marxism in this case, and has provided much more of a foundation for modern sociological analyses of actual struggles.

The commercial classes are formed on the basis of being able to monopolise entrepreneurial opportunities. Negatively privileged groups here include labourers in commercial operations, while the positively privileged ones, obviously, are entrepreneurs (although there are different types here again). There are also middle classes, such as the self-employed, or craftsmen (who are in a much better position to use their rare skills).

The third category, the social classes, are much larger and more holistic. They include the classic proletariat as in Marx, and Weber has a very interesting section about how technical progress is deskilling proletarians and consolidating them into a more homogeneous group as a result. Other social classes include the petty bourgeoisie, the intelligentsia or specialists, who gain their privileges partly because of the connection between social class and education. Class conflict between social classes is possible if the groups are immediately opposed and likely to come into constant contact and conflict, if there is a degree of concentration, and if they can be organised on the basis of their workplaces, and led by the intelligentsia. This does not sound very different from marxism, of course, although Weber seems to have been much more sceptical about the possibility of these conditions arising.

## Status

Status seems to be quite a different grouping, based on style of life, education and hereditary or occupational prestige. Status can be expressed through various forms of social association, including marriage, 'outlook' and the ability to monopolise modes of acquisition, or to forbid others (so that only craftsmen printers can work in the print industry, and then only after a long apprenticeship, while others are kept out). This ability to monopolise depends in its turn on whether a group can marshal support from cultural and social conventions or traditions. Status distinctions may rest on social classes, but class does not determine status, or vice versa. Status groups engage in some interesting struggles to gain an advantage by closing off opportunities for themselves, and there may be conflict between those performing such 'closure' through a claim based on heredity and those claiming privileges through a style of life or occupation. Status groups, rather than class, can be the dominant form of political struggle. However, annoyingly, status groups can be identical to social classes, and can be created also by property classes (although commercial classes are unlikely to generate status groups – they are too unstable and too competitive internally).

Generally speaking, status groups of the more traditional kind are threatened by industrialisation, because the whole area of prestige based on heredity or tradition, the sort of thing that is claimed by the royal family in the UK, for example, is clearly at odds with the process of rationalisation and modernisation that Weber saw as so important. In fact, many critics have argued that the whole dimension of status is likely to be much more regularised and organised in modern conditions. For one thing, it can come to depend increasingly on the ability to consume and acquire status goods, and thus gets connected much more with markets and the ability to secure a favourable position in them. For some commentators, like Parkin (1979), the modern state becomes important too, in conveying types of legalistic status on certain groups. What has come to be known as 'credentialist closure' is a good example of this, where the state permits only credential holders to enter a profession. Examples include graduates in school teaching, registered members of an association in medicine, and so on. Parkin also suggests that Weber diminishes the active role that groups play in trying to effect social closure, as a deliberate political struggle, we might say: perhaps this is a sign of a limit provided by a specific social context to Weber's writing, of course.

## Parties

Parties are yet a third possible basis of stratification. They establish themselves in the sphere of power, regardless of their specific goals, attempting to acquire influence in general. They must be rationally organised, however (in the Weberian sense of pursuing the 'scientific' rationality of means and ends, as in the general thesis on rationalisation), and thus take the form of definite and explicit associations. Parties can represent classes or status groups and their interests, or they might be mixed. They vary according to the tactics they use and the structure of domination in which they find themselves – and there are connections here with Weber's analyses of different types of authority (such as traditional, legal-rational and charismatic). Because of their very general nature, some commentators have seen 'parties' not just as an additional 'dimension' to stratification, but as the most fundamental units of stratification and of politics, as we shall shortly see.

My favourite discussion, still, is found in Giddens (1974). Drawing on the main sections of Weber's work as above, which he read in the original German, Giddens suggests that there are both abstract and concrete models of stratification, for example (explored below). When it comes to the concrete level, we can operate with the three main types of social classes (upper, middle, working), defined around the three major 'class situations', based in turn on property ownership, commercial opportunities and social groupings. We can add in the status groups, similarly subdivided according to the claims their members make about their inclusiveness and the attached rights. It becomes an important task for concrete sociological investigation to describe the various specific combinations of groupings, life chances and lifestyles in any actual society at any given time. For example, it might be important to see whether all the specific struggles between the different groupings are being reduced or polarised into main struggles over the control of the means of production (as Marx predicted), or whether they are being simplified and reduced as a result of the emergence of rationalised ' structures of domination' (another possibility predicted by Weber – and sounding very like one reading of Foucault, whose work we shall examine in Chapter 10).

## Classes and class closure

The legacy provided by this concrete account of class formation has been very rich, but rather diverse, depending on which elements are to be seen as the major ones. For empirical British sociology, Weber's emphasis on occupation and status has led to the usual working definition of social classes as 'socio-economic groups', and this definition informs the huge amount of official statistics that are gathered on social and economic inequality (and other distributions and patterns) in Britain. Such data have often been crucial in the political debates about inequality (or similar terms such as poverty, or social exclusion), and in debating what level and type of inequality are to be encouraged. These debates in turn underpin many of the more 'applied' discussions on the value of 'social class' as an analytic device, its usefulness in describing social mobility patterns or conventional voting behaviour, and so on, which we discussed in Chapter 1, and to which we return here.

More abstract developments have also proved very fertile. Weber's remarks on the processes of class formation (deciding on who can be included, or how the barriers around classes may be 'closed') have led to the development of various 'social closure' approaches to stratification.

Parkin (1979), for example, develops Weber's emphasis on how social classes are defined by the way they actively relate to other groups, how they engage in strategies of closure in drawing boundaries around themselves. This allows us to see politics, and much social life in general, as a matter of how groups organise and compete for power, especially how they manage to admit some people as members and exclude others. Social closure becomes an active process of class formation: classes are not just the product of social forces, but active organisations, pursuing various types of closure strategy. Such organisations need not take the form of conventional and formal associations, of course: support for policies designed to restrict entry to chosen professions is also part of a closure strategy. Teachers and lecturers engaged in the efficient provision of educational credentials might also be pursuing a closure strategy designed to retain privileges for graduates.

There happen to be two major types of closure strategy. Parkin calls the first type 'exclusion', where people are denied access to desirable life chances unless they possess some particular characteristic. What they actually need to possess could be anything that is socially important, but it usually refers to the ownership of capital or educational qualifications. This strategy is clearly detectable behind the important distinctions lovingly preserved between the working class and the bourgeoisie, but we can use it to discuss 'new' forms of social division as well. Thus people can be excluded from full membership of the working class because they do not 'own' certain characteristics, such as the 'right' skin colour, gender or ethnic background (so there may be two subtypes of exclusion here, in fact, according to whether 'ascribed' or 'achieved' factors are used to exclude). A good deal of political struggle takes place around attempts to get the state to forbid or legitimise these exclusionary strategies, to ban discrimination on the grounds of 'race' or gender, for example, while encouraging and institutionalising the ownership of private property, or meritocracy.

The excluded can sometimes try to mobilise power to fight back, using their own closure strategy – 'usurpation'. This refers to the classic working-class practice of trying to close off particular occupations on the basis of trade union membership and the 'closed shop'. Here, collective strength is used to dominate markets. This sort of usurpationary power is the real abiding type of working-class power, for Parkin, far more important than the development of conscious revolutionary political parties as in marxism. Rather riskily, however, he argued that usurpationary power would remain as a real force in capitalism, which seemed very vulnerable to strategies of this kind in the late 1970s because of the complexity of the production system. Although we are continuing to see strike action as the most explicit demonstration of usurpationary power, Parkin's analysis was written before the onslaught on trade union rights by the state in the UK in the 1980s and 1990s, and probably over-estimated the persistence of the wave of industrial militancy of the 1970s. Nevertheless, it is true that a great deal of political struggle ensued over the protection, reduction or extension of working-class usurpationary power, and we may be seeing a revival of this form of politics in the UK at the moment.

Since closure is a device that affects the formation of a number of groups in capitalism, marxist models of class formation can be included as options, but should not claim any privilege. Any group can exclude or usurp, and so new for-mations and new forms of political struggle are always likely. The same concepts, for example, can be used to account for gender politics, or conflict between ethnic groups, and these have been almost entirely neglected by the old theories, Parkin (1979) argues. The argument is turned against functionalist accounts too because they under-estimate the importance of struggle and con-flicts over power, and assume that societies are held together by common values instead. Above all, we can move to a more specific level of analysis, without wondering about the effects of dark and mysterious social forces operating below the surface (Parkin is particularly rude about Poulantzas here). Finally, the analysis looks appealingly neat and simple, since a few basic principles can explain a wide variety of concrete social class formations.

Of course, there are criticisms, and we can consider one that raises some very general implications as well as focusing on Parkin specifically. Barbalet (1982) suggests that Parkin really lacks an explanatory mechanism – in effect, one that explains the origin and the need for class closure in the first place. This is also an attempt to rescue marxist analysis, by insisting that there are important differ-ences between struggles based on exploitation and struggles based on competition. Parkin is accused of an excessive interest just in description – in other words, of making the same ideological mistakes that an earlier generation of political economists made when they took the categories and distinctions that appear 'on the surface' as self-sufficient. (Murphy (1986) makes this and several other important points, and I have summarised them in an online read-ing guide.)

Thus if closure really is a matter of power, we need to explain the social ori-gins and patterning of this power first. It is clearly not enough to stay with Parkin's examples where the state empowers particular groups, since class struggles can occur despite the explicit discouragement of the state. It is not dif-ficult to see that marxists would want to suggest that it is a capitalist mode of production that lays down the conditions for state acquisition and distribution of power here. If the bourgeois ability to exclude people from the ownership of capital depends on exploitation, this needs to be explained as well, using the classic marxist categories of appropriation, the conditions under which surplus value is extracted, and so on.

The usurpationary power of the organised working class can also be of two types: either a purely localised, reactive and disruptionary power, or something more ambitious and threatening to the entire system. Finally, it is a mistake to see the barriers between segments of the working class (between skilled and unskilled, or black and white) as the same as the barriers between social classes in the classic sense. Barbalet's preferred explanation for these intra-class struggles is to see them as the effects of the labour market, whereby white, male or skilled workers are able to get a better deal. Be this as it may, there is a need for an account of the labour market and its workings, at least. This sort of debate has continued to the present, as indicated by a glimpse at the recent work of Bottero and Prandy (2001), which is summarised in an online reading guide.

## Conflict theory

Another approach, more of central interest to this chapter, perhaps, retains Weber's emphasis on the issue of 'party', and tries to move decisively off the ground of economic relations. The clue here is Weber's insistence (in the collection in Giddens and Held 1982) that the notion of political domination is the 'central phenomenon of all social organisation'. We might remind ourselves that, in this sense, parties are the fundamental unit of social analysis, not classes as implied above. Parties can be seen as social groups organised so as to gain an advantage, acting so as to increase influence. Since some sort of social organisation is usually necessary for these groups to form, they are connected to class and status groups, but they assume greater importance.

One legacy of this argument became known in Britain as 'conflict sociology', associated with writers such as Dahrendorf (1959) or Rex (1961). In the USA, it might be possible to include writers such as C. Wright Mills in this camp as well (see Horowitz 1967). For these writers, conflict became central to social life, but not necessarily the large-scale schematic class conflict predicted by marxists. Instead, all of us were engaged, in various ways and in various groupings, in the struggle for advantage.

The problem was that classical marxism represented a particular snapshot of a particular form of general relations of authority. In the 1840s, European societies might have been becoming polarised into two major camps organised around the ownership of capital, but modern societies are far more diverse. In Dahrendorf's terms, the major classes have become 'decomposed' (capitalists are split into groups of owners and managers, for example, while the classic working class has been subdivided into smaller rival groups such as skilled and unskilled workers). A new middle class has grown enormously, to blur further the sharp boundaries between capital and labour. The end of polarisation means the 'end of ideology' (and in a popular modern variant, the 'end of history' as well). This slogan is central to the emergence of 'New Labour' in the UK, it could be claimed.

Conflicts over authority are likely to be far more widespread, but take a different form: they are no longer closely associated with social class (because there are now separate strata of people who have authority and influence, but do not own the means of production). Any class conflict that remains is likely to be both localised and institutionalised, and thus revolutionary class politics is very unusual. An implication of this view is that conflicts over authority are indeed to be found in any organisation that involves the exercise of it (as all organisations do, of course). This helps us focus on a routine aspect of everyday life – conflict – which is ignored in both mainstream functionalist and marxist positions.

Conflict need not be 'deviant', for example, confined to those on the fringes of social life, as functionalists might argue. Nor should conflict always be on the verge of escalating into major revolutionary disputes about the very nature of society, as predicted in some of the earlier works of Marx. Conflict is both normal, everyday and often institutionalised, operating within strict limits, before it gets out of hand. The study of conflict becomes a normal part of the study of politics of everyday life.

Conflict theory originally made progress in explaining some of the more significant aspects of social conflict in modern Britain, including 'racial' conflict (see Rex 1970, where localised 'racial' conflicts were analysed in terms of all the social factors and disputes at work, including the crucial conflict over access to desirable types of housing). However, although there was always a tendency in conflict theory to emphasise these rather large and disruptive forms of conflict, it was not at all clear why these should be privileged by the theory itself. Why not focus on everyday petty disputes and conflicts, like those between neighbours over the planting of hedges, or between members and committee members in a local cricket club (to cite some of the critics' examples)? Lockwood (1992; and see the online reading guide) takes the view that conflict theory is limited by its initial interest just to 'invert' functionalism, and thus never really develops any sound or extensive sociological theory of actual conflicts. As Giddens (1974) points out, conflict theory also needs some explanation of 'large' conflicts in particular. Giddens accuses Dahrendorf specifically of missing this dimension in his interest in abandoning 'philosophy', and heading for 'scientific' accounts instead. This is another example of a general dilemma we have noted before (and shall do again) – the need to grasp everyday routine examples of social interaction without just describing them.

## Back to social class?

As you might expect, Giddens' view is more or less the line taken by marxist critics as well. We have already hinted at the work of Poulantzas (1975) in

Chapter 1, and seen in outline his attempt to explain the apparent diversity of class formation in terms of the model of the social formation which offers economic, political/ideological and cultural 'levels', each of which has a determining effect on surface forms. (I have online reading guides on this work, and also on Turner's [1981] argument that says Poulantzas has simply borrowed bits of Weber to modernise Marx.)

It might be appropriate here to summarise Giddens' own approach very basically. There are two levels on which we might analyse his work on social classes (Giddens 1974): as a specific intervention in the debates between marxists and Weberians on the nature of modern social classes, but also as an initial step in the clarification of the much broader 'structuration' project, as we hinted. Let us stay at the specific level for the moment.

According to one summary of the larger work (Giddens in Giddens and Held 1982), the real issue is how economic differences become social classes, how technical market relations turn into social structures which pattern people's lives. Weber's analysis suggests that the emergence of social classes arises from social overlaps between economic and prestige groups, but this is still not a full account. Instead some analysis of 'structuration' is needed to explain how abstract social forces and possibilities are developed into concrete social groups, how they combine to produce social groups as an emergent effect.

The details of this specific structuration process on class can be outlined systematically. There are both 'mediate' and 'proximate' structuration factors, and these intervene to join a merely formal market position to a more significant social class as such. The mediate factors concern the chances to undergo social mobility. Social immobility certainly produces a way of life that is strongly reproduced from one generation to another, producing definite class-based cultures. Social mobility can disrupt those cultural and social groups, and possibly form others. Whether social mobility takes place depends on different types of market capacity: the effects of property, educational qualifications and labour power. As we saw, the effect is to produce a basic three-class model.

However, there is never complete closure of social classes from these factors alone, and we also need to look at the 'proximate' factors. These consist of the division of labour in productive enterprises, patterns of authority and distributive groupings. For example, the actual division of labour can lead to a social separation of manual and non-manual groups, as a kind of prelude to and continual support for class formation. As many management consultants have pointed out, local social divisions like this are very likely to produce a situation where groups call themselves 'us' and 'them'.

Such a division can also be reinforced by particular authority patterns (for example, where bosses or superintendents dominate workers on a daily basis). Authority relations can also split the ruling class into upper and middle levels, as in the division between 'senior' and 'middle' management. Incidentally, this kind of division according to whether or not one exercises authority has been incorporated into one of the newer forms of class classification used in UK government research (the 'Hope–Goldthorpe' scale) to provide a way to separate classes I and II.

Distributive groupings are reflected best in consumption patterns, and this covers one notion of status, as we have seen. Distributive groupings reinforce market separations, as when the opportunities to acquire different types of housing close off communities and neighbourhoods into, say, 'public' (in the UK 'council-provided') and 'private' estates.

These different structuration factors can overlap, and point in the same direction, reinforcing each other to produce a closed class system. More usually, however, they pull in different directions, producing many concrete variations according to the level of economic and political development. The boundaries between them are liable to shift and to change, leading to a clear role for empirical research to pin down the actual forms they take. Ethnicity is treated best as a separate factor, Giddens (1974) thought, but it can overlap with class structuration, producing, for example, an 'underclass', where those who lose out on all dimensions end up clustered together in areas of major deprivation. We need to investigate some of the trends, such as the divisions emerging in the class that owns property, those between the grand and petit bourgeoisie, and the possibilities of mobility between them, and the dynamism introduced by the emergence of new skills. Giddens was writing at the time that a major study of social mobility of this kind was being undertaken in Britain, the 'Nuffield studies' (see Goldthorpe et al. 1980; Halsey et al. 1980; and the online reading guide associated with them).

Giddens' work has been seen as over-formalist, and failing to explain the active politics of class struggle (Barbalet 1982). The publication of this work also led to rather more technical differences in interpretation, to try to uncover the relative influences of Weber and Marx in Giddens' analysis, for example. There is no time or space to pursue this very far, but a contemporary review offers a useful analysis for the really enthusiastic (Breines and Cerullo 1976).

## Class and class politics in modern commentaries

It is intriguing to note that these neo-Weberian or 'conflict' accounts of modern industrial societies and their 'decomposed' or flexible class structures have remained popular in the current era, thirty or so years after they first appeared, and despite the move away from class analysis in so many sociology courses. Indeed, class and class politics seem constantly to crop up in some renewed form – in debates about post-industrialism, or the musings of the 'New Times' theorists, or advocates of the 'Third Way'.

You would expect politicians to adopt something like Dahrendorf's conflict theory as a convenient working ideology, of course, and it must resonate in some way with the ideologies of many journalists and commentators too. Yet it also appears in rather surprising company like sociologists discussing class (see

Pakulski and Waters 1996; or the online reading guide that summarises it), or even with leading postmodernists like Lyotard (1984; and see the online reading guide on his work). What might be seen as the usual retorts, common when Dahrendorf's work was fresh, the kind of thing we have seen in Giddens, Lockwood or Poulantzas, are surprisingly absent. The rediscovery of empirical complexity seems to suffice, and no attempt is made to consider, let alone research, any current equivalents of 'structuration factors' that might explain such complexity.

Finally, as we suggested at the start, this neo-Weberian work lurks in the background of a good deal of modernised Marxism. It is to this tradition that we now turn.

# 6  The Turn to Gramsci

Oddly enough, the sort of revival of interest in marxism that influenced cultural studies in the 1970s and 1980s barely referred to the specific debates about class discussed in the previous chapter. A vague interest in political 'activism' was pursued, but marxist conceptions of social class as the privileged root of cultural politics were simply abandoned. I do not remember much discussion at all, but any arguments that were advanced seemed to borrow pretty uncritically from the 'decomposition' views we have seen in the previous chapter.

The supposed origin for the new kind of activism is the wave of student unrest that affected Britain, Europe, Japan and the USA in the late 1960s. It is very difficult to describe what it was like to experience and to participate in such unrest. For me, as a student at one of the centres of British activism – the London School of Economics (LSE) – in the late 1960s, it seemed as if a number of struggles at different levels had somehow coalesced in some new forms of social grouping. There were large-scale external political struggles, such as the opposition to US involvement in Vietnam and to US imperialism more generally. Support for colleagues was offered in their various struggles against governments in Germany, France or Japan. There were national issues such as the policies of successive British governments towards immigration and civil rights.

There were also institutional concerns, centred on the struggles at the School to resist what we saw as excessive managerial bullying, principally the suspension of our Student Union President for organising protest meetings; the subsequent suspension of students who supported him; the decision of the School governors to go ahead with appointing as a new Director a man with what we saw as a flawed political record in the then apartheid state of Rhodesia (now Zimbabwe); and the general drift towards uncritical and pro-business university degrees and courses. Some of us were also engaged in personal struggles to assert ourselves and to experiment with our social or sexual identities, often against the wishes of family and friends. We saw these different struggles as somehow linked, and a great deal of 1970s social science also pursued the links between struggles like these.

Of course, a loose and absurdly romantic vision that was around at the time just somehow imagined it was all one big struggle to assert humanist values against various opponents. Student activists would be urged to think of themselves as 'brothers' of those at war in Vietnam, and 'fraternal greetings' were solemnly exchanged between protesters at the LSE and Black Panthers in the

USA. The cosmopolitan nature of the student body made it very easy to think of oneself as part of a great struggle at large, somehow, and the nightly TV news showed widespread cultural unrest and agitation in Berlin, Berkeley, Tokyo and Paris.

A popular but actually little-read book at the time was Marcuse's *One-Dimensional Man* (1968), which seemed to launch an impressive but very general critique against the economic and cultural aspects of the entire capitalist system, and to offer support for anyone organised to agitate about it. This was probably a misleading impression of the politics of the piece, in fact, but a major theme certainly was that the organised working class had been incorporated into dem-ocratic capitalism, and that the torch of dissent (if still burning at all) might have passed to more marginal groups. A new kind of agitational cultural politics was available, most visibly in the politics of the symbolic street demonstration, or the political 'happening'. I was present on one occasion when students filed into the room in the LSE where all the portraits of past directors were hung, and simply turned them to face the wall. Outcry followed, with porters and police called to evict the deviants, and with much anguish and invective directed against them by lecturing and administrative staff. The point was to show – not merely to argue but to demonstrate – that the real values of the School upheld private property as some sort of sacred institution, despite all the radical aca-demic critiques it peddled – and this was certainly achieved, to my satisfaction at least. Similar tactics may be around today in the street politics of protests against multinationals. Plant (1992) has an excellent analysis, with some hilari-ous examples, of situationism, the artistic and political movement that inspired many of these tactics. The situationist tradition is also closely connected to the arguments about the unregulatable 'excesses' and natural indiscipline of the 'everyday', as we shall see in Chapter 11.

Of course, academic consideration took a much more serious form. Fay (1975) suggested almost that it was human nature to struggle against whatever blocks and frustrations hemmed you in wherever you were – at home, at work, in your own history. At one stage, it looked as if a new species of human being was evolving, 'Struggling Man', to take his place beside those other fictitious cre-ations such as 'Man the Tool User' or '*Homo Ludens*'. Of course, for professional social scientists, the project was to become far more ambitious. The apparent unity of these struggles and movements had to be founded on something much more concrete than fantasy or arguments about 'human nature'. The scholastic impulse led to general social theory.

An early phase involved attempts to collect together a variety of radical themes from very different social theories, in order somehow to inform or legit-imate new activist practice. We already knew of marxism, but in those days it was associated with a distinctive focus upon working-class struggle, a tendency towards social closure and authoritarianism, and an unfortunate association with the disastrous regimes of Eastern Europe. (For many demonstrators, it was also far too 'serious'.) If marxism were to become useful to explain and to guide the kinds of general cultural struggles that seemed to be emerging, it would need to be modified first.

## Modernised marxism

Luckily, an attempt to rethink marxism in a much more suitable 'philosophical', and thus general, direction was under way at the time. Again, there were a number of special influences at work. In France, especially, attempts were being made to develop new dimensions in marxism, to make it somehow conform much more to the kind of humanist liberal traditions with which we were familiar. A great deal of emphasis was placed on the relatively unknown early writings of Marx, mostly a series of notebooks completed in his early career, during his stay in Paris – and thus sometimes known as the 'Paris Manuscripts'. These manuscripts contained a number of useful early pieces, displaying Marx's comments on the kind of philosophy he had studied in Germany (see, for example Colletti 1975).

The jewel in the crown was the famous account of alienation. This concept already sounds familiar to us. It has become an everyday word, commonly used to indicate the status of general frustration and the feeling that we do not belong, or that we are not able to express ourselves as well as we might. I hope you can already see how this concept might serve admirably to link together the various struggles that I mentioned earlier.

There seemed to be different types of alienation in marxism: classically alienation from production, from product, from 'species being', and from self. The first two help us to implicate in this process the capitalist production system. That system absorbs the human creative power of individuals and uses it to create products, which are then assumed to be the property of someone else, and which are subsequently sold on the markets (one of the early technical connotations of the term 'alienation' implies selling off property). The other two connotations suggest a much more general 'philosophical' dimension in alluding to some proper state of human nature, in which human beings can live without treating each other as objects. Not to put too fine a point on it, that state, where alienation had ended, would be communism, where people might herd cattle in the afternoon and philosophise in the evening, just as they please, to paraphrase Marx and Engels (1977) in the *Communist Manifesto*.

We seem to be a long way away from Russian communism with its institutionalised oppression, scarce consumer goods and dour five-year economic plans. The discussion of alienation would appear to bring Marx back into the tradition of the great humanist philosophers, who also advocated that states be based on Reason; that all individuals be treated as ends in themselves, and not means; that policy be guided by the pursuit of the greatest happiness for the greatest number of individuals; or even that all shall be equal in the Kingdom of

God. Of course the details might vary, but the early Marx seemed to be recognisable and acceptable to people in modern Western societies at last.

Modern reinterpretations of marxism, based on the discovery and publication of some of the more obscure works, became a major theme of academic social science. Another strand in this development was the growth of the group of academics and radicals in Britain calling themselves the 'New Left', and clustering around an influential journal – the *New Left Review*. The story of this group has been told before in several ways, but one of their most famous projects involved making connections between British radicals and Continental theorists. Roughly, the argument went that the native British radical tradition unfortunately had flourished before Marx was able to develop his work. This partly explains the peculiar nature of British society, which had never had a proper bourgeois revolution and thus had remained curiously conservative, but it also explains the isolation of British social sciences, which had not incorporated marxism to the same extent as those in France, Germany or Italy. It was to academics in those countries that British academics turned in particular in order to try to acquaint themselves with the latest developments in marxist theory.

Initially, a number of Continental theorists were read with interest, and with a great deal of scholarly effort. It is also true to say that a number of other radical social sciences were rediscovered and popularised. In the early days, virtually any approach that appeared to give some insight into the general conditions of 'alienation' was considered of value. This included American radical work, like some of the pieces by Becker or Goffman, which we have reviewed earlier. Becker (1963; and see the online reading guide), in particular, announced that he stood with the underdog and thus could be seen to be exposing the ways in which deviants, including political deviants, were socially controlled and managed in important cultural ways.

All sorts of liberal philosophy could be added in and explored as well. Action sociology had popularised the work of modern social phenomenology, as we have seen, and that too seemed to offer support to the radical project. After all, phenomenology offers a series of powerful techniques to doubt the world, to dissolve the facticity and thing-ness of social arrangements, to encourage new and radical thoughts of possibilities. Scholarly projects promptly sprouted to investigate possible connections between phenomenology and marxism.

## The gramscians

I have outlined the project of one particularly influential set of British activists before (Harris 1992; and see some of the online reading guides and files on my website, which are grouped under the names of major activists like Hall and Willis, or under the heading of CCCS). I call this group the 'gramscians' because they accord a key role in their project to the writings of the Italian theorist Antonio Gramsci. As much of the early work was carried out in a particular university department, they are also known as the 'Birmingham School', the 'Birmingham Centre' or the 'Centre for Contemporary Cultural Studies' (CCCS). However, much of the key work was performed after a significant move to the UK Open University (OU), where the core CCCS members formed the OU Popular Culture Group.

In Birmingham, the major members produced a number of publications, sometimes in the form of annual collections of papers, published in the usual way (such as Hall et al. 1980), but also as 'occasional papers', or 'stencilled papers' produced on in-house presses, and circulated as pamphlets. When they moved to the Open University, however, they were able to produce a substantial and highly influential university course for undergraduates – the legendary *Popular Culture*, or *U203* (Open University 1982), as it is known to aficionados. Several other Open University courses, in education studies, and in media studies, also featured input from the leading member of the group, Professor Stuart Hall, and his colleague Professor Tony Bennett.

There is a lot of work that has been produced by this group, so I am going to select a few pieces to illustrate key moments. In 1976, members of the Birmingham Centre produced a famous book on youth culture (Hall and Jefferson 1976). Various (early) groups and youth cultures were analysed in this collection, including Teddy Boys, hippies, punks, mods and bikers. The overall theme of the analysis, however, is particularly relevant to this chapter. The authors were going to argue that the emergence of these groups and their characteristic conduct could be understood in terms of a political struggle, rather like the student movement.

The press in Britain had accorded such groups very little respect, and had tended to focus upon aspects of their behaviour that seemed unacceptable (drug-taking, bad behaviour and fighting). The authorities tended to regard members of such groups as mindless hooligans. Well-meaning sociologists had begun to point to factors such as growing affluence and periods of excessive freedom between school and work as responsible for the growth of such youth cultures. Other popular explanations involved mysterious biological and hormonal changes in adolescents, which somehow caused young people to wear unusual clothes and adopt increasingly bizarre hairstyles.

The CCCS line was quite different and rather novel, however. Joining a youth culture and taking part in its rituals and activities could be seen as a political response to the changes that were taking place in modern Britain. We had to see joining a youth culture as a symbolic or cultural act, with values and a rationality of its own, once you looked hard enough. The characteristic clothes, mannerisms and activities of youth in those youth cultures had to be decoded first, and the intention was to use some high-powered and influential European social theory for this purpose. It had been used already to understand the similarities between a variety of myths operative in the various Indian societies in South America, or to clarify and understand the apparently baffling types of kinship structure in those societies (as we saw in Chapter 2). Now it would be used to understand the costume and the characteristic weekend rituals and activities of male youths in southern England.

Those costumes and activities made sense if they were seen as expressing a kind of alternative society. In the case of mods, the smart clothes and the close attention to appearance and grooming could be seen as expressing some kind of protest against being assigned a working-class status, and a yearning to join a classless society instead. The allegedly characteristic mod weekend activity – going clubbing in London and having an entirely hedonistic weekend, fuelled if necessary by amphetamines – was another expression of a wish to escape into a more futuristic pleasure-seeking society away from the dull routines of (clerical) work.

In fact, the article written on mods in the 1976 collection argued that much of this picture of the typical mod was a mass media construction. Hebdige used an 'alienation' metaphor, borrowed from Norman Mailer, as the key to explain the mod instead – as the 'White Negro', pursuing 'cool' ways of life in an urban environment. There was also an earlier more conventional piece by Cohen (summarised in Hall and Jefferson 1976), which had attempted to see youth cultures as more of a functional adjustment to the stresses and dislocations produced by social change. These changes included the demolition of the docks in the East End of London and substantial rehousing and restructuring that destroyed the old working-class communities. This in turn had presented certain problems of identity to young people (and real material problems too). Two sorts of symbolic solutions were on offer. The 'upward' solution was shown best by the flight into some fantasy future, as I have described it above. There was also a 'downward' solution, which involved an attempt to re-create some imaginary working-class community, borrowed from the past. This explains the activities of groups such as skinheads, and, to some extent bikers, who lived a kind of exaggerated and idealised working-class life, celebrating working-class values of rough industrial dress, territoriality, aggression and the defence of working-class technical and mechanical skills.

Just about any youth subculture could be 'read' in this way, from hippies, with their symbolic rejection of the work ethic and of objective time (according to Willis 1978), to Teddy Boys, with their provocative transgression of class-based dress codes (according to Jefferson in Hall and Jefferson 1976). Although this leads to a more sympathetic attempt to understand youth cultures than was common at the time – perhaps too sympathetic an attempt, some critics have argued – marxist analysts would still be critical. After all, these youths were only engaging in 'symbolic', or 'imaginary', politics, whereas what was needed was real (marxist) politics.

The paradox was explored best, perhaps, in a famous book on male working-class school students, Willis's *Learning to Labour* (1977); and see the online reading guides on this work). In fact, Willis's work was not a classic gramscian one, and he expressed reservations about the key term 'hegemony' in a footnote. Nevertheless, we can summarise him as a useful introduction to the themes.

The disobedience and disruption enjoyed by 'the lads' was not mere mali-ciousness or negative mindless behaviour, Willis argued. His interview transcripts showed that 'the lads' were quite intelligent and insightful about their predicament. They knew that only a few lads from their background ever succeeded through the education system, and thus withheld their support for it, as a perfectly rational thing to do. Instead, they sought their future in skilled manual work outside school (there was much more of it around in Britain in those days) and kept up their spirits in school by trying to build a kind of clas-sic working-class masculine identity for themselves. They were tough, manly, aggressively heterosexual, 'hard', and so on. In maintaining this identity for themselves they developed rather negative views of teachers (soft, feminised 'poofs') and of the women they knew, their mothers and sisters and their girl-friends. The real problem and tragedy, says Willis, is that this rejection of all things 'soft' included a rejection of any kind of strong politics or social theory. Thus, in the end, the lads were forced to accept a very conventional destiny for themselves as hard working-class men doing hard working-class jobs. What began as a joyful symbolic resistance ends as a kind of consolation and con-formity.

Whatever the concrete conclusions and theoretical reservations, the overall general project seems to have triumphed in showing that apparently ordinary everyday activities, like leisure activities undertaken by youths, really can be seen as a form of politics. Of course, this impression was strengthened when youth cultures bumped into conventional politics in a highly visible way – when the police turned out in large numbers to confront, arrest or intimidate members of rival youth cultures gathering at seaside resorts, or when conventional politi-cians started to call for legislation to ban drugs or regulate clubs. Taking these examples, it is not too difficult see how other activities might be shown to be political in the broadest sense as well.

Broadcasting and journalism are obvious examples. In Britain, we like to hold a myth that our news media are 'objective', rigorously sticking to a political balance, and trying to tell 'both sides' of any important story. It might be possi-ble to justify this when looking at conventional party politics, where, indeed, the media do attempt to balance the contributions of various spokespersons for the two major parties rigorously and to the last second. But in the broader political struggles, the media were seen to play an important but far more conservative part. For example, press and television played a major role in stereotyping and demonising anyone who was likely to offer a threat to the authorities. The case of youth cultures demonstrated that role quite easily, as youth cultures were crudely defined, stereotyped, and then had their members denounced as mind-less thugs requiring strong police action.

The role of the media in cultural politics could be easily seen elsewhere too, as a number of analyses of news and current affairs programmes attempted to show. To cut a long story short, these programmes appeared, on the surface to be neutral, to give contending parties a chance to speak, and to criticise equally.

However, a deeper look revealed that the media were important constructors and purveyors of ideology.

This term is an important one in modern marxist analysis, of course, but it is not easy to pin down an exact definition. As we have seen in Chapter 1, for some marxist traditions ideology arises from a false perception of social reality, while, for others, it is not so much a matter of perception as a problem of the mislead-ing appearance of social reality. In some cases, ideology means virtually the propaganda of the ruling classes – as in the views of Britain as the united, calm, confident and conservative country of British propaganda films made during World War II, for example (try the dreadful film *This Happy Breed*). In other usages, any view of the world that does not look deeply or critically enough (in other words, that is not marxism) can become ideological. This sort of charge is often made against rival social sciences, which try to develop critical categories, yet which also include very uncritical ones, as we saw in Chapter 1. It is largely in this sense that the media are accused of being ideological in this particular tra-dition.

Thus it is clear that British current affairs programmes do (or once did) permit ruthless and aggressive interrogators to question leading politicians about their policies, and do their best to root out any inconsistencies, failures, evasions, and so on. In the USA, even presidents can be impeached and find their per-sonal, financial and sexual details broadcast and discussed on the nightly news. However, the issue turns on the categories and concepts, the theories that are used to maintain this criticism. Criticising individual personalities does not offer much of the criticism of the ways in which politicians are elected, which interests are represented, who is left out, and the powers that politicians can use after their election. Indeed, criticising the personal morality of one politician can even be seen to strengthen the system as a whole. Thus, to paraphrase one analysis of current affairs programmes (see Bennett et al. 1981), while the British media criticise politicians, they leave uncriticised the parliamentary system as a whole.

In the same way, analysts were to argue, the deeply ideological notion of Britain as some naturally united nation somehow escaped scrutiny. Everyone knows, even journalists, that there are substantial inequalities and important dif-ferences among the people of Britain. It is not that these are ignored in favour of some propagandist message about how we are all one people. Rather, the dif-ferences are shown but explained away using rather dubious uncritical categories. (Here I am summarising and simplifying a famous article by Stuart Hall [1977] on the 'ideology-effect'. You might try the online reading guide for a longer summary and some critical discussion.) Scenes of poverty, for example, are shown as occurring in the North of England, as if geography were responsi-ble for poverty. Alternatively, the poor are described and represented as old or inadequate in some sense, as if poverty were their fault. Black people in Britain are often described as 'immigrants' or as members of 'ethnic' communities (implying strange, religious, exotic or otherwise un-British cultures).

Given that these divisions are explained away in these curious terms, well away from the only categories that make sense to marxists – class divisions – the solutions to them also become mysteriously simple. National television can overcome geographical differences; charitable acts can assist the poor to make the most of their chosen lot, demonstrate a more successful lifestyle, or compensate for some of the inevitable effects of ageing; multicultural events and understandings can reduce barriers between ethnic communities; at Christmas we can forget all our differences in the name of some mystical unity; and so on. There are many other examples showing how the concept of 'the nation' is defined in this way by the codes used in the media. Even televising a national sporting occasion like the FA Cup Final can be read as offering symbolic politics of this kind – the rival teams can stand for important geographical divisions, while the game itself offers a resolution of those differences and permits spectators to become unified in watching the spectacle as a national occasion.

We can see just about any struggle in terms of cultural politics, in other words. Going back to the original examples of mods and bikers in conflict with the police, it becomes straightforward to see at least some criminal activity as a form of symbolic politics as well. We are all familiar with cases involving black persons, for example, who get arrested and charged in disproportionate numbers, or are particularly badly treated by the police, where there are clearly political dimensions. Any criminal activity involved can be combined with racist ideologies (such as beliefs that tend to see black people as more likely to be criminals, as closer to nature, as more like animals than white people, as not fitting into British society, or whatever).

This has led some British activist theorists, such as Taylor, Walton, Young and others, in their various works (see, for example, Taylor et al. 1975; and the online reading guides on the website) to argue that criminologists should not be researching criminals so much as researching the activities of the agents of law enforcement, and ultimately of the state. These are, after all, the people and institutions who decide which acts should count as criminal ones (the theft of items from a shop, for example), and which should not (asset stripping after a financial takeover of a rival company). For some critics, of course, this would be an absurdity, offering an excess of political analysis, so to speak. Crimes would receive universal condemnation, and victims are often members of the same social class as the offenders, for example, and to insist on a purely political analysis is to sidestep these important moral and social issues (see Cohen in Downes and Rock 1979; and I have an online reading guide to this critique too).

Members of the CCCS entered this particular controversy with a famous discussion of their own on the phenomenon of 'mugging' (Hall et al. 1978; and see the online reading guide). The first part of the story is easy enough to understand. Following a public scare, fostered by the press, fears of unrestrained street crime were heightened and elaborated (the borrowed term for this effect is a 'moral panic'). At the height of the scare, three black youths in Birmingham were convicted of fairly minor street crimes, but were given excessive sentences by a judge keen to play his part in preventing a perceived crime wave. Some of the people who were then students at Birmingham got involved, and organised some research combined with a campaign to get the sentences reduced. This was the 'Mugging Project', summarised in Hall and Jefferson (1976). At the risk of seeming heartless or unfeeling, I must say that this is the kind of thing that activist academics dream of – at last, a chance to connect with the real issues in the community, and to help by bringing to bear one's particular skills of analysis and critique.

The first account of this Project set out to provide a rival explanation for the involvement of young black people in street crime, to counter the 'mindless thugs' version of events. Criminal action could be explained as a combination of social impulses, stemming from the structure of society and the culture of the participants, mediated through their individual biographies. In less abstract terms, these episodes could be explained partly as a reaction to the unpleasantness and discrimination offered by British society to black kids, and also as an unfortunately misunderstood consequence of their cultural legacy.

In the much more substantial piece *Policing the Crisis*, Hall et al. (1978) set out to offer a systematic analysis of the mugging phenomenon, showing how the term had arisen in the USA, been imported into London by a police officer returning from a course, and had been taken up by both police and press as a conveniently vague yet threatening term to describe street crime. The press had created a classic moral panic by adding particular themes to give the story maximum interest, or 'legs' in their terms (what critics might describe as the development and 'articulation' of an ideology). Early on, for example, mugging became seen as a 'black' crime, which enabled all sorts of anxieties about black people to be added in. Such anxieties included fears induced by social change by black people living in inner cities, anxieties about jobs and educational standards, and other aspects of what might be termed low-level racism, like fear and suspicion of outsiders. In this way street crime had been politicised, and the police and state were able to build on public concern to demand greater powers to police inner cities This enabled them to feel reassured about their own peculiar fears – that various crises in British capitalism would lead to social disorder, and perhaps even revolutionary upsurge, the CCCS writers thought (with little empirical evidence to support them, it might be added).

As I have argued elsewhere, however (Harris 1992), *Policing the Crisis* also addressed a number of important theoretical concerns, as well as the substantive matters of mugging, white racism, policing and economic crisis. As we examine these, it is important to remind you that, from the point of view of practical understanding or analysis of politics in everyday life, much of it must have seemed completely irrelevant. To the parents of the black youths convicted in Birmingham, the point of the Mugging Project must have been to deny that their children were mindless thugs, to offer a much more sophisticated explanation of what they did, and to explain to the judiciary that the atmosphere of moral panic which had been generated by the press had led to an over-reaction on the part of the judge when sentencing. To anyone reading *Policing the Crisis*, however, there are obviously far more extensive theoretical sections engaging in debates with various marxists about science, ideology, the status and nature of the individual, and so on. It is still tempting to see these as an academic indulgence, an irrelevant piece of scholasticism. However, it is important to try to explain these sections first, as representing genuine and important interests for theoreticians, possibly even (professional) 'political' ones.

A theorist's agenda was always present in gramscian work, at least after the early phase of enthusiastic collection of radical writings. In the excitement of launching their novel political analysis of youth culture, Hall and Jefferson were content, in their Introduction to the 1976 collection, to cite a large number of writers as supports for what they were doing. However, as is common with collectors, a secondary task soon appeared, involving the sorting and classification of these theories. This is something that theorists are particularly interested in doing, and it separates them from activists or politicians in general, who typically want to gain as much support as possible for what they are doing, even if this involves some pretty shaky alliances between different groups. For theorists, however, this kind of cheerful patchwork of theories will not do, that is, if they wish to be loyal to the scholastic conventions of university-based social theory (which include the view that one should try to define powerful theories accurately and hold them consistently).

Professional academics have two important tasks to do. First, they have to teach undergraduates, exposing them to a wide range of theories, following conventions of balance not unlike those of media professionals (who were criticised, of course, in the work), while maintaining some consistent story, narrative or approach. Secondly, they have to compete with other groups for research funding and publication opportunities. In the case of research findings, the necessity is for a successful programme that will yield consistent opportunities for research over a number of years. This in turn can involve having an ongoing series of problems that have to be managed within some sort of consistent framework. It is for reasons like this, as well as inherent interest, of course, that the theorists involved began to examine other theories, to try to criticise and evaluate them, to try to sort them according to certain preferences.

In addition, marxist theorists in particular are often inspired by the example of Marx himself, of course, who spent many years of his life doing precisely this: he read, criticised and incorporated elements from a wide range of alternative political, economic and philosophical positions, and spent rather less time on picket lines and barricades. He did this partly to develop a superior position of his own, one that could preserve the insights of rivals and yet proceed to solve problems that had stopped them from progressing (including the problem of the origins of surplus value, as we have seen in Chapter 1). Yet this also had a political function itself. It enabled rival, flawed and ideological positions to be decisively rejected by argument, thus helping in some way the wider struggle, at least at the level of ideas. Marxists could expose the flaws in arguments that saw capitalism as a natural stage in evolution, and thus inevitable, for example; they could see through the trick embedded in the slogan 'a fair day's work for a fair day's pay'; they could argue with philosophers that European states were based not on Reason but on the interests of dominant groups.

We saw above that the ability to engage in practical politics was certainly one factor in the original developments of the Mugging Project, but what practical political benefit might be generated by some of the more esoteric debates about the rival merits of Althusser and Gramsci? And, as we all know, political issues are not just decided by the better argument. As we student militants in the 1960s soon learned, when the authorities lost the argument, they simply turned to force, which they were much more successful in mobilising.

Pursuing some sort of theoretical systematisation seemed an equally important task to the gramscians, and it was one that was to preoccupy them. The CCCS group incorporated some conventional sociology, especially ethnographic research techniques, into their work, but also some bits of theory relating to social strain, and some conventional history, seen best, perhaps, in Clarke's and Critcher's accounts of 'rational recreation' in the British Victorian era (Clarke and Critcher 1985; and see the online reading guide). These conventional disciplines had to be reinterpreted, basically by attaching them to a marxist framework. Thus ethnographic work showed cultural struggle and resistance, as we have seen; 'social strain' was reinterpreted to refer to the contradictions in capitalism; conventional history was reshaped to indicate some underlying pattern of political 'settlement and crisis' as class war developed and abated.

In many ways, though, the most indigestible approaches were rival marxist ones. Some earlier work could be dismissed fairly easily, if not entirely fairly, like 'critical theory', which we shall be examining in the following chapter. However, the approach associated with the more modern work of the French theorist Louis Althusser proved surprisingly resilient, and led to a much more intense and prolonged struggle, both with Althusser's writings themselves, and with his British disciples. The battle raged at a very general level, in publications such as *On Ideology* (CCCS 1978), for example, and at more specific levels, such as when discussing ways to analyse films or education systems. At a more specific level, some useful criticisms of the 1976 book were listed by Coward (1977), and replied to by Hall (in Hall et al. 1980). (I have online reading guides to both pieces.)

We cannot possibly do justice to this much-discussed controversy here. But let me offer a very quick sketch of some of the issues. In a very influential piece, Althusser had argued, as we saw earlier, that the category 'the individual' was central to understanding ideology in general in Western societies. That is, the way in which we are made to think of ourselves as individuals with freedom to choose, free will, our own individual preferences, and so on, had a major political effect in reconciling us to capitalism. This feeling of individual freedom is seen as a major political benefit, of course. However, the paradox was that we could only be individuals by submitting ourselves to the power of various 'ideological state apparatuses'. Althusser's own example (see the online reading guide on this) refers to the ways in which Christians first submit to God's Will, and only then, and in exchange, as it were, receive a full sense of themselves as individuals in God's sight. I have also used a possibly more familiar example, that of the education system: here, we receive individual awards, plaudits, praise, and so on, but only after submitting to the judgements of the system in the first place. For the gramscians, this was unusual, and also rather unfamiliar territory. They preferred to see ideology in older and more conventional terms, applying not to individuals, but to social classes, and involving some mystification of the real political situation.

I do not expect this sort of dispute between rival perspectives to fill anyone other than a theorist with immediate enthusiasm or interest, but it did make a difference in terms of how one was to analyse aspects of culture, for example. All marxists might agree that commercial films are suspiciously ideological, for example, but how exactly was this to be demonstrated? Followers of Althusser, who for a while managed to dominate the influential journal *Screen*, decided to try to analyse the narrative structure of films in order to demonstrate how viewers came away thinking of themselves as free and knowledgeable individuals. We discuss this a bit further in Chapter 9. In one particular analysis for example, (MacCabe in Bennett et al. 1981), 'realist' films in particular delivered this kind of effect for viewers, offering to explain some mystery about reality at the end of the film, typically after examining a number of rival approaches first. The mystery would usually be some banality, such as that it was natural for human beings to be competitive, or that troublemakers came to no good in the end, or whatever. Viewers would walk away at the end of the film believing they had 'discovered' this eternal truth for themselves (see the online reading guide on MacCabe and realism).

Gramscians, on the other hand, were more inclined to take a 'culturalist' approach, seeing films as offering particular concepts and categories, which would enable particularly politically loaded views of social reality to be developed. From this perspective, Althusserian analysis looked both abstract and insufficiently activist (the two most commonly cited criticisms). The apparent lack of activism was compounded by the overall pessimism of Althusser's analysis, at least in the original essays, since the power of ideological apparatuses seemed total and complete, and their effects irresistible. Indeed such was the power of ideology that it would take a particular effort to break through its hold and develop a proper, 'scientific' understanding of the social formation. This would require a particular specialist body, with intellectuals of its own, and yet with a substantial mass membership as well – in other words, a body rather like the French Communist Party.

No such body existed on anything like this scale in Britain, leaving radical intellectuals without much chance at all to contact 'ordinary' people and engage in conceptual struggle to help them throw off the effects of ideological practices. Gramscians tended to believe that the everyday experience of such ordinary people would predispose them towards radical thinking, a view which looks nostalgic, romantic and rather artificial, as if this simply 'must' be the case in modern times, just as it might have been once in the past. In the absence of a Communist Party, only a few options for contacting such people remained: some might knock on the door, as did the parents of the Birmingham muggers, perhaps, or encounters might be arranged during the activities of splinter groups organised by socialist teachers, or among fringe members of the Eurocommunist wing of the declining British Communist Party, or at congenial seminars with academics and journalists helping to organise a new journal.

More systematic contacts seemed to rely on the education system again. Founder members of the New Left had enjoyed taking adult education classes teaching history to coalminers; Hall has suggested that 'organic intellectuals' (highly trained but devoted to the activist cause) were being produced on the postgraduate course at the Birmingham Centre (in Hall et al. 1980). Some optimists, including myself at one stage, saw a radical role for the UK Open University in disseminating critical material to a wide range of unconventional students, some who were working full-time in industry and who might be expected to try out their new knowledge in their local circumstances.

I have tried not to be too dismissive here, and I accept that forging links between intellectuals and 'ordinary' people is always difficult. Yet the proposals of the gramscians did look pretty optimistic at the time, and, gradually and inevitably, interest in contacting groups of people outside the academy diminished considerably. First, the organised working class seemed to let the intellectuals down: they were too conservative and unable to see that society had changed (rather in the direction suggested by neo-Weberians in fact). The focus turned instead to other dispossessed groups such as ethnic minorities or women. These groups also showed some reservation in accepting the gramscian line, however, shown best, perhaps, in the production of alternative accounts of social conditions by groups of black students and women at the Centre itself (see CCCS 1982 and Women's Study Group 1978, respectively: I have online reading guides to both pieces, and we are going to discuss gramscian feminism in Chapter 8).

The last group to be seriously addressed, it seems, was the disparate readership of the journal *Marxism Today*, although hope remained for the revolutionary potential of various 'new social movements' (ecological protesters, supporters of Nelson Mandela, Rock Against Racism, and so on). Only the educational audience seems to have remained constant, but whether the takers for the new Open University Masters degree in cultural studies see themselves as headed for a life of activism must surely still be in doubt.

Althusser's analyses also seemed tainted by other undesirable connotations and arguments, some of which are detectable in the influential essay with which we began. Althusser seemed much more 'orthodox', for example, and willing to reinstate some central marxist concepts, such as economic determinism (redefined as a matter of limitation, as we saw). He seemed much more interested in

asserting marxism to be a science, which initially alarmed some of the human-
ists, and was far less willing to countenance the claims of rival non-marxist
positions. In his attempts to winkle out the signs of a mature science in Marx's
own work, he urged us to downplay, or even abandon, some favourite pieces,
including the work on alienation or the famous introductory section on commodity fetishism in Volume 1 of *Capital*. In his attempt to claim a scientific status
for marxism, he offered some powerful criticisms of the theoretical basis of
rivals, but came to some initially unpalatable conclusions (ably summarised in
Hindess 1977; and see the online reading guide).

To round off this story, it is clear that certain aspects of the Althusserian work
were indeed finally incorporated into the gramscian project nevertheless. Clear
signs of Althusserian thinking are found in Hall's essay on the ideological effects
of the media (Hall 1977), and in *Policing the Crisis* (Hall et al. 1978). By the time
of the construction of the 1982 Open University course, it was possible to represent the two positions as manageable academic options – a 'culturalist' and a
'structuralist' option, both with their strengths and weaknesses, laid out for students to examine and debate, although it is not really difficult to see which
approach is preferred by the course team.

## Summary and comment

We have tried to trace a trajectory from an interest in activism to a search for
some suitable theoretical grounding for that activism. The story also involves
gaining an initial independence from the university system which ends in major
incorporation into the same system, or a modernised version of it, and an optimistic faith in its activist power. It is, finally, a journey from a project that seemed
to offer much in terms of a broad cultural politics, to a demonstration of polite
educational politics. For in the end, this was the ironic fate of gramscianism, in
my opinion. Weber could have warned them, as could Critical Theorists.

The work of Gramsci had proved valuable in the earlier stages since it seemed
to offer a very flexible set of concepts, such as 'hegemony', or 'articulation', and
offered a licence to pursue 'extended politics', away from conventional party
politics and spreading into culture and everyday life. To give some simple examples, 'hegemony' (usually taken to mean a drive towards establishing or
maintaining cultural leadership) seems to provide much insight into the way in
which political consent for the system was organised. There was no simple,
fixed, ruling ideology, reflecting the interests of the ruling classes, and imposed
upon the subordinate classes. Instead, a much more dynamic process of cultural
interpretation was at work, where emerging concerns and demands were somehow incorporated into an overall view that preserved the system. The more
applied analysis, such as that of 'Thatcherism' (Hall and Jacques 1983), showed
how a number of political themes, some of them contradictory, were woven
together, or 'articulated', in order to support the Thatcherite project of

modernising British capitalism, while managing the inevitable social disorder that this produced. One theme was a 'return to traditional values', while another urged full-scale (and broadly very popular) modernisation of British institutions; nationalism was combined with a resistance to European economic integration, and, on occasion, with old anxieties about 'race' and immigration.

The task for the Left was to develop an activist version of such articulations instead, not just a set of political statements but a project radically to reform, perhaps eventually to smash, capitalism. The person of Gramsci himself seemed to show how theory and activism could be combined (after his political activities were suitably interpreted for modern conditions, of course, which might help remove the embarrassment of the major role played by the Italian Communist Party). A new version of 'Popular Front' politics could be developed, uniting all those oppressed by advanced capitalism, and providing the theoretical labour to link up all those protest groups and new social movements with a potential for change. However, although it might sound churlish, it is important to realise that during Gramsci's lifetime it was Mussolini who won the battle for hearts and minds in the end.

On the theoretical front, gramscian concepts and developments seemed quite capable of incorporating and reinterpreting other concepts, as we have seen. 'Social strain' translates as the inevitable tensions within drives toward hegemony, history can be rewritten as a series of crises and settlements within hegemony, and Althusser's account of the social formation can be seen as an unfortunate, static and pessimistic 'moment' in the ongoing process of hegemony.

However adversely the success of these projects might be judged as politics, there is one area where, ironically, gramscianism has been an outstanding success — in the founding of a new academic discipline or 'teaching object' (British Cultural Studies). I think this strange fate, more than any other single point, shows a major flaw in attempts to focus on activist but highly scholastic politics of this kind: cultural activism is very easily absorbed and incorporated into 'hegemonic' culture. Gramscians could see this coming for the youth cultures and other phenomena they analysed, but failed to notice it happening to themselves.

# 7    Critical Theory, Positivism and Critique

This is quite a different radical tradition, one that might be seen as a rival, at one time, to the gramscian work we have just summarised. Unlike gramscianism, Critical Theory (CT) sought a deliberately marginal place, trying to avoid being located in any base in universities. According to legend, one of its leading advocates, Theodor Adorno, turned down several prestigious university appointments in the UK and in the USA, and preferred to make a living as an independent music critic. This helped avoid 'incorporation' of the kind gramscianism fell into, it could be argued, but at a price, as we shall see. Before we go any further, it is useful to point out that the leading advocates of CT founded the Institute for Social Research (from independent finance), based in Frankfurt, Germany. They left for the USA at the outbreak of World War II, and only some returned to Frankfurt – but they are still sometimes referred to as 'the Frankfurt School'. In order to sidestep any controversy about which phase of the work was more important, or whether Adorno, Horkheimer, Marcuse and the others were sufficiently in agreement to be called members of a 'School', I shall use the term Critical Theory throughout to refer to the project.

To take a major and well-debated concept to begin with, 'reification' refers to the tendency for human relations and products to become things, or thing-like. There are clear links with Marx's account of alienation, and with Weber's account of rationalisation. The concept leads to a very powerful way of understanding and criticising modern social and cultural events. Familiar 'applications' include trying to understand the growth of mass culture or mass politics, especially of a fascist kind. The latter interest is hardly surprising – as did Gramsci in Italy, the early exponents of CT had a real struggle on their hands in the Germany of the 1930s and 1940s. Fascism combined a ruthless, 'scientific', 'rational', 'positivised' administration (in intention anyway) with a set of dangerously irrational commitments: official culture featured notions like cults of leadership, intense hatred of outsiders, notions of 'folk community' (based on mystical notions like 'blood' and 'soil') and an extreme nationalism. These commitments led to political consequences such as war, extermination of minorities, the policing of internal dissent, a corporate economy and a propagandistic popular or mass culture.

'Reification' implies that cultural phenomena, whether the product of mass media or of modern politics, can be criticised as being thing-like, that is, fixed, natural, real and therefore beyond criticism, leaving no alternative. The point is to show how these apparently fixed characteristics have developed from deeper social processes. One early parallel is the work of Marx on commodity fetishism, but a good deal of Freud was also drawn upon, partly to explain psychological drives towards uncritical authoritarianism and mass obedience. These trends affected 'normal' societies as well as fascist ones.

The tendency of social activities and relations to become represented in things or products is indeed partly a natural and inevitable development, essential to social life itself. Complex events and processes have to be simplified, or objectified. However, there is something specific to advanced capitalism that is not innocent or natural. Here, reification is different: it entails the politically loaded substitution of objects for processes. It has an ideological effect, concealing social and historical processes, and closing off the possibilities for revolutionary change.

Reification takes effect in advanced capitalism not just in the marketplace, where exchange relations are frozen or fetishised, but in certain processes of thought too. This tendency is seen best of all in modern positivism, and its effects on science, social science and philosophy. These disciplines also reify the social world, turning experiences into data; letting objects stand for processes (scores on a test stand for some human capabilities or qualities, for example); labelling people, categorising and classifying them. This is not done innocently, or in some 'value-free' way, but in order to control people, directly, in the form of straightforward manipulation by political agencies or corporations, and indirectly, through the cultivation of political passivity, a kind of political consumerism, where people lose interest in critical and creative forms of politics.

It becomes important politically, therefore, to oppose positivism with relentless expert critique. This critique should embrace negativism, continually denying that social relations ever do completely fit simple concepts, and continually pointing to repressed alternatives and new possibilities. This might seem a purely 'philosophical' task, and a very abstract one, but it is connected to the political goal of emancipation from reified social relations.

Critical Theory recommends no actual political programme, partly for the same reasons that are hinted at in Weber – a specific programme would involve a further closure of possibilities. So it remains ultra-critical – and also clever, profound and obscure. We see in this sort of politics a paradox: in order to escape the contamination of reified thinking, which so deeply affects everyone else, Critical Theorists need to keep a substantial distance from ordinary life, and the ordinary categories used to grasp it. There are clear dangers here of elitism (to use the usual disparaging term – but then all theory is specialist, which may not be the same thing), or of critical theorists becoming a detached intellectual stratum unable to link closely with any actual revolutionary agent (a much better criticism, but one not confined to CT).

Perhaps we should begin with some general points outlining CT's basic stances:

1   CT is characterised by a suspicion of 'scientific rationality' as the hallmark of capitalist thought, which involves not only the growth of positivism in science and social science but also the reification of social life.

2   CT celebrates the negative, the critical and the oppositional, such as: the 'negative side of the dialectic'; the suppressed alternatives that have not been 'realised' (in the sense of being turned into reality); the human processes (including nasty things like domination of people and 'nature') which produce the supposedly neutral and objective world.

3   CT expresses this as a desire to operate not just as philosophy but as a material practice, a form of social analysis, and maybe even a politics.

4   It engages in a search to find and establish a basis for such critique. The authors vary a good deal here (Connerton 1976 provides a useful account of the different positions – try his Introduction). Authors like Marcuse will want to comb through Hegel and even phenomenology for materials to be used in critiquing 'positivism', as we shall see. Horkheimer will want to take Marx's critique of political economy as his guide. The work of Lukács is also influential here, especially in his admiration of 'bourgeois social science', as in Weber (the incorporation/critique of Weber appears in Marcuse and Habermas too).

5   Although we are not going to discuss him at all subsequently, Lukács' position was influential in the background of several Marxist analyses. It seemed to provide good grounds for a faith in a revolutionary working class to re-establish some actual totality in social life, as the only class able to see the whole. This attributed mission must be abandoned according to CT though (and gramscianism too), since the working class had lost its chance for revolutionary politics, certainly after World War I. It has been defeated, incorporated, 'saturated' with reified thought forms, 'massified' as in 'mass culture'. As a result, re-establishing totality, materialising purely 'philosophical' demands as politics, is a task now for the theorist who occupies a 'committed' but 'marginal' position at the same time – lots of problems arise from this, of course.

Thus Critical Theory can seem to be an unusual project in its relentless pursuit of the critical and the negative. The critique it offers ranges from internal or 'immanent' forms (where contradictory, often ironic, possibilities are demonstrated by taking the claims of capitalist thought and practice seriously: on a homely note, try musing about how you can be charged money for party tickets and then be offered 'free' drinks). More familiar forms of argument included external or 'material' critique, where bourgeois thought is shown to be inadequate by using non-bourgeois categories that have been suppressed but which are technically better.

The basis of the critique and the targets of it are many and varied – German fascism is critiqued by using even liberal concepts of freedom; then post-war popular culture is critiqued using classical philosophy, empirical research,

Freudian theory, Weber, Nietzsche and (well-disguised) marxism. For the latter, the usual sort of marxism is rebuked as 'scientised' and extra doses of Hegel are recommended – and so on. For some critics this makes CT hopelessly eclectic, groundless and incoherent. For admirers, this shifting is necessary since new threats to 'liberation' emerge and must be confronted. This, plus the deep pessimism of CT, leads even to accusations of 'conservatism' – as Marcuse says, though, even this can be better than rampant modern versions of capitalism. Nevertheless, CT is seen as the worst possible example of unconstructive, unhelpful and elitist theorising by a most odd amalgam of critics, who include positivist sociologists, administrators and planners, Althusserians and gramscians.

There are considerable variations between the different approaches held by the different theorists. We can examine two different opening statements defining Critical Theory, by Horkheimer and by Marcuse, to illustrate this.

It might be best to start with Horkheimer's account, 'Traditional & Critical Theory' (in Connerton 1976). 'Traditional theory' is the classic mode of theory elaborated by Descartes. 'Critical theory' is based on Marx's critique of political economy. It investigates problems that somehow just appear 'naturally'. CT takes as its problem human activity and men (apologies for gendered pronouns) as the producers of their own life. It studies 'matter' (facts, reality), and the human processes of creating, interpreting, understanding the 'material world'. CT is, thus, the heir of German Idealism, but it rejects the notion of some abstract Ego or Subject as the agent of history. Instead, it focuses on the real world of men and, especially, of their work. Since Marx shows that work in capitalism is a form of domination, CT must seek to expose hidden relations of domination in order to achieve emancipation. CT is thus not just another specialism out to add knowledge, but is inherently political, as good philosophy always used to be (in the Greek Golden Age). CT is a demand for freedom for individuals to undertake a rational (re)construction of their social life, based on understanding themselves and their potentialities. Capitalist work, with its fetishism, alienation and reification, represents almost the exact opposite of freedom in this sense. The (marxist) critique of political economy shows us the way to proceed, although it needs to be amended as well.

To spell this out further, the goal of traditional theory is the achievement of a set of self-contained, logically derived, non-contradictory propositions, ideally in a mathematical form. Science is supposedly like this. Much conventional social science tries to be like it too – even seemingly non-positivist social sciences (Horkheimer has some learned and critical things to say about Durkheim and Weber here). The search for logical rigour, conceptual control and order is very closely connected with the domination of the world by technology. This connection occurs in two ways: (a) traditional theory openly embraces a desire just to study this world at the surface as it were, not bothering to inquire how the world has been affected by (produced by) technology; (b) theory, just like the familiar physical commodities, is also produced as the result of work:

theory construction is but a 'moment' of the wider totality of social productions.

Traditional theory has to operate with most unsatisfactory categories – like 'subject' and 'object', 'individual' and 'society', 'fact' and 'value', 'objectivity' and 'subjectivity'. This produces tensions within it, manageable at the abstract level, but particularly obvious when approaching the actual world. (We know in social sciences the contortions and embarrassments when concepts are 'operationalised' as a prelude to 'scientific' research.) Philosophers like Kant and Hegel tried to find a solution to these tensions, but did so only in thought, as it were, by postulating some transcending world where all is calm, pure and united. What we really need is to understand the social processes that have produced this contradictory reality. We need to de-reify reality, and see it as produced by contradictory events and struggles, by processes of alienation and recovery.

Critical Theory, by contrast seeks the proper solutions to contradictions in reality. Of course, this is not going to be at all 'useful' to those who do not want reality to be understood, demystified or exposed as contradictory. We must learn to be critical of existing notions of reality (and of categories like 'useful'). The constitution of reality, facts, events, constraints, and so on, is our interest, not just gathering knowledge about it, and definitely not just finding out what 'will work' and be 'helpful'. Horkheimer pokes fun at bourgeois 'sociology of knowledge' here. It is not enough just to establish a connection between social conditions and conceptions or ideas: we have got to grasp these connections, control them, and then do something about them to assist emancipation. Investigations and politics are united. If this means the sociology of knowledge loses some abstract objective value-free 'ground' for its investigations, that is a price worth paying. There are no 'grounds', no taken-for-granted 'facts' like individuals or 'social structures'. What we have is a process, a dialectic that constitutes humans as individuals and as members or victims of social structures. We want to clarify and understand this process of alienation or reification totally, so that all is transparently the result of (past) human activity, never just 'things', 'events', 'forces'.

Marcuse (1972) begins his account with the argument that the history of the concept of reason in philosophy shows an original marked separation from immediate reality (back to these splits and dualisms in classic philosophy – essence v. appearance, freedom v. necessity, etc.). This separation is what helped classic philosophy to be critical of reality. Actual reality was to be compared critically with abstract, universal, philosophically purified categories to reveal the limits and deformities of actual existing current notions of 'freedom', 'truth', and so on.

However, traditional philosophy could not maintain this critical separation. We know, for example, the fate of Hegel's theory of the state and its unfortunate but inevitable compromise with the 'bad present' of the Prussian monarchy. For other strands (Kantianism or phenomenology), the flaw was to focus upon the individual and on individual consciousness as the source and seat of reason. Critique then became a personal, private matter. The separation of critical consciousness from social reality turned into a split between 'individual' and 'society', 'private' and 'public'. This leaves social, public reality as an unanalysed 'necessity' which individuals can only retreat from or speculate about in private. With these flaws, traditional philosophy loses its critical potential: it cannot be used as a substitute for new critical theory.

'Materialist analysis' ('science') seems much more promising. It does address social reality, criticises it as unliberating, and demands concrete social changes. However, it faces the danger of becoming too absorbed in the world, too infatuated with and saturated by the existing material conditions, losing that crucial separation and distance which is necessary for qualitative changes of social reality. This is exhibited best in the sadly conservative fate of positivist social science (which even helped the Nazis manage Germany), but there are also clear dangers here for marxism. Marxism can become too closely committed to mundane and immediate analyses and politics, too concerned with organising the immediate demands of the working class, allowed to drift away from general analysis and critique.

This 'practical' orientation for marxism means that, because material concrete struggles can fail and be defeated, if identified totally with these struggles, marxism can be defeated too. (Bourgeois critics have always wanted marxism to be totally identified with the communist regimes of Eastern Europe, it might be added.) What is more, struggles to emancipate the working class from the immediate processes of poverty, disenfranchisement, and so on, can succeed, and be achieved within capitalism, especially advanced capitalism. The abolition of private property, rises in the standard of living, increases in personal freedoms, a general tolerance of private activities, and so on, can all be achieved within a society which is still unjust, still founded on domination. Later, in *One-Dimensional Man*, Marcuse (1968) argues that these 'freedoms' have not only been achieved but have become integrated into domination. Thus excessively immediate and concrete demands can lead only to redundancy for marxism.

Pure and simple philosophy, 'concrete' marxism, or positivist social science cannot be used. Instead, CT hopes to use the reawakened critical bits of these traditions. This produces some seemingly odd, eclectic, conservative conclusions:

1   We find Marcuse stressing the strengths of Idealism, of all things, welcoming its emphasis on pure, universal, uncontaminated categories that cannot be simply assimilated into existing reality. The negative side of Hegel is to be celebrated, and Weber is to be criticised here for not being 'value-free' enough!
2   Marcuse admires the achievements of bourgeois culture (before fascism arrived). Again, the admiration is directed at bourgeois philosophy (but also 'high culture' generally). There are truths in such cultural achievements; they are not just 'foggy ideas' hiding class interests. What bourgeois philosophy does is attempt to critique ideas and concepts, not simply account for them as in some mere sociology of knowledge.

3   Critical theory is, and must be, utopian (whatever Engels says about the flaws in utopian socialism), reviving and stressing human potential, holding out hope for the achievement of justice and freedom. These utopian demands must be grounded in material analyses which locate and explain domination, but they cannot be turned directly into 'realistic', 'practical' policies and demands without risking distortion or incorporation.

4   Nevertheless, Critical Theory does not just preach a 'social theology'. The task is to do critique, show how utopian demands could be realised, and what blocks their attainment. Here, Marcuse still sees the revolutionary proletariat as the only possible bearer of a programme of realisation, although he knows you have to do far more to activate them than just redesign a programme for the Communist Party or expect rational persuasion and rhetoric to carry the day.

It might be useful to pursue this with more detail of Marcuse's critique of positivism (Marcuse 1972; and see the online reading guide). He begins by pointing out that, for Comte at least, positivism initially had an important critical dimension. It was used to dispel some of the more obvious lunacies of metaphysics and endless philosophising, and still has a considerable appeal today. Comte urged us to abandon mere speculation, vanity and endless discussion, and get on with grasping the world as it is: we should stop worrying about questions such as what facts actually 'mean' in some deep sense, and simply get on with accumulating positive and useful knowledge. This is still a common refrain sung by politicians, university managers and, indeed, many university students when they encounter social science courses or undertake teacher training – why not just acquire useful and positive knowledge, without getting in too deep?

However, Marcuse points to some unfortunate tendencies already built in to this project. Trying to avoid useless and wasteful philosophising is one thing we might all agree on, but there is a danger of throwing out all philosophy. Taking a very uncritical stance towards 'facts' appears to save time, but runs the risk of being highly uncritical (and thus of mystifying). In capitalism, the 'facts' of social life are going to be produced by definite social relations, including relations of domination. Thus to operate simply with, say, existing types of social inequality, measuring them without inquiring where they came from or how they arose, is to be part of the political process of domination by not asking awkward questions about it. The same point might be made about approaches that do not inquire where profit comes from, or why bureaucracies are organised so rationally (and Weber himself makes this mistake, according to Marcuse: see the online reading guide for a critique ).

Positivists do not like to inquire about these processes, not because they are all evil capitalists but because questions like these tend to make their sciences messy and uncontrollable. However, they have to pay a price, according to Marcuse. Neat sciences where facts are facts and everything is neutral and objective (and conveniently divided into discrete subjects, like sociology, economics and history) appear to gain cognitive order and neatness, but do so by turning a blind eye to the forces of social order and repression. Eventually, those forces will burst through on to the agenda anyway.

The alternative, Critical Theory, can look very 'philosophical' by contrast. Critique of this deep kind is rather specialised, and only intellectuals can really be expected to do it. Rather ironically, Marcuse's work was embraced as a kind of guiding philosophy by student radicals of the 1960s, as we saw (in Chapter 6). In a way, this makes sense, since he seemed to be supporting the turn away from science and technology towards more 'alternative' or counter-cultural beliefs. However, Marcuse himself probably thought that while such marginal groups could demonstrate an opposition to capitalism, revolting students would attempt to be far too libertarian (nothing could be achieved by liberating individuals from social constraints, since individuality itself had been so crushed and distorted in capitalism). They were also too ill disciplined and not learned enough really to see through capitalism, and thus likely to find themselves easily accommodated, as a mere 'way of life' for example, tolerated, even celebrated, and then incorporated. Seeing so many former radicals in the ranks of government, big business and the entertainment industry, I cannot but think Marcuse was right here.

We might risk a quick assessment of the work of Adorno and Horkheimer now, in order to show perhaps the most 'philosophical' version of the critique of positivism. In his contributions to the famous dispute about positivism (in Adorno et al. 1976), Adorno argued that science distorts the world by grasping it with simplified categories. Positivism then has to rely upon the activities of the scientific community to make these concepts fit the complexities of the real world. The scientific community actually plays a very active part, attempting to simplify reality in order to make it fit chosen theories. It does this by using processes such as operationalisation, measurement and laboratory experiment. Because there is a view that positivism is a neutral and objective method, these crucial processes are little understood, largely unclarified and barely discussed. They are 'banished' in a sustained campaign to remain 'value-free'. This might gain useful publicity and state support, but even positivists themselves fail to see how values really deeply affect their work.

This sort of criticism is part of a more general strategy to expose 'identity thinking' in a range of rival approaches. To be very brief, no matter how critical the approach sets out to be, there is always a danger of a premature end to critique as presently existing institutions are simply 'identified' with philosophical concepts. This usually arises when a particular approach attempts to 'apply' itself to the 'real world'. There is constant pressure to do this since few theorists would feel happy to claim a complete disinterest and detachment, not least for the reason that they are constantly being asked to justify their existence by their paymasters or clients. The myth of the committed intellectual, somehow 'speaking for the rest of us', also haunts theory.

Adorno offers no comfort to those who believe in such myths. No theory is ever going to 'apply' easily to the existing world, or, as he put it: 'The name of negative dialectics says no more, to begin with, than that objects do not go into their concepts without leaving a remainder' (Adorno 1973: 5); (and see the online reading guide). It is a delusion or betrayal of critical thought to ignore this point. As for political commitment, he was to point to an important yet still-neglected paradox: 'For the sake of political commitment, political reality is trivialised: which then reduces the political effect' (in Arato and Gebhardt 1978: 308).

Adorno is so keen to avoid simplification and operationalism in his own work that he adopts an obscure and very 'literary' style, designed quite deliberately to show how difficult it is to attempt to grasp the full processes of social life, instead of just accepting common-sense categories and reified appearances. Underneath this is an argument that posits a social totality capable of many potential appearances or realisations. This totality can only be grasped through its appearances, yet these appearances are only one set of possibilities that cannot be taken simply as 'facts'. (This argument, in fact, is common to a number of theoretical and philosophical positions.) Relying on this ungraspable totality makes it possible to insist that any more specific concrete approach must be limited. Thus, for example, both 'structuralist' and 'action' sociology could be seen as tending to abstract particular qualities from this underlying social totality and 'hypostatise' them (roughly the same as reifying them).

In order to make this point, Adorno sometimes uses deliberately open-ended literary devices such as irony or chiasmus (roughly, a sentence or phrase containing a deliberate contradiction which suggests that a simple thing contains opposing characteristics: classic short examples include terms like 'malicious egalitarianism' or 'isolation through communication'). In some ways, this is the most annoying aspect of some of his writing, and other writers, like Benjamin, share his fondness for a deliberate obtuseness. It is particularly annoying if you want to process this work, as when writing a lecture on it, or constructing an essay about it, or summarising it so you can quickly go on and 'apply' it to something. But this is the whole point, of course: Adorno wants to make sure you cannot summarise, simplify or distort his work for these banal purposes. Theory is too important for that, and much too difficult to be simply rendered as a set of bullet points in some textbook (as I have just attempted to do!). Many readers have found him to be 'difficult', or even 'elitist', and there is certainly very little help given to the reader struggling to decode some of the slogans or aphorisms. For many commentators, advocates of 'plain speech', the style is deliberately mystifying, so that fairly simple observations can be accorded a great deal of intellectual importance. This may be so, but Adorno can also be defended – at least he sticks to his beliefs consistently in not only arguing but demonstrating that there are no easy answers. I can even feel sympathetic to this position, having been asked many times to summarise complex arguments in the form of six bullet points for people who cannot be bothered to try to grasp the full complexity. I was even asked once, by a busy manager, to summarise Habermas (just the first ten books, no doubt) on a side of A4.

Adorno therefore offers a relentless negative critique from a wide range of alternative positions. He has brought into the service of criticism sociologists like Durkheim or Weber, marxists, a range of philosophers, and even some empirical social psychology. He uses these negative resources to attack those positions that claim to have somehow grasped the essence or entirety of social life, usually by reducing it all to some simple process. Such approaches can only work through distortion, by leaving out contradictory sections or elements and by practising 'identity thinking', which, as we have seen, simply equates concepts with social processes. Adorno just has no easy answers himself as to what the social totality amounts to, but he can use it to argue against the claims the other philosophies make towards some universal applicability (especially positivism).

The result is a negative procedure, curiously incomplete, demanding and full of clever allusions to possibilities rather than clear statements. It is deliberately unspecific. It is based on a considerable admiration for the artistic avant garde, and those artists, including musicians, who are also attempting to put their work beyond the reach of simple summary, incorporation and use. It values those aspects of life that have remained incompletely incorporated, such as art and nature.

It is, as I say, a consistent approach, but a 'homeless' one. If you want to avoid incorporation in your own work and oppose it in others, you have to put yourself deliberately well outside the normal range of speech and thought, almost to the extent of having to work with a purely 'private language'. This is clearly at the opposite end from populist politics, and it becomes impossible to imagine an existing political group taking up this kind of approach for and by themselves. The only conceivable possible candidate for revolutionary politics was (and still is) the organised working class, but its members had become incorporated, which seemed to leave nowhere to go. Critical theorists had no choice but to see themselves as utopian thinkers, and perhaps as rather romantic ones, holding out the possibilities, as it were, while the rest of the world lived their one-dimensional lives.

There is much to value in the approach, despite its obvious scholasticism, and I have included a number of summaries in the form of online reading guides (a very un-Adornovian thing to do!), including one on the famous *Dialectic of Enlightenment* (Horkheimer and Adorno 1979), and some that revisit the key discussions on the 'culture industry' or on the paradoxes of 'free time'. I think this analysis is still highly pertinent to grasp the elements of phoney 'individualism' and 'freedom' in modern popular culture, and is necessary as a counterweight to some current work which uncritically celebrates it.

In Chapter 12 we also refer to one of the main exponents of a considerably revised Critical Theory, Jürgen Habermas. Overall, despite its paradoxes and oddities, Critical Theory still offers great promise, in my view, in the urgent task of analysing contemporary culture and politics.

# 8 Feminism(s)

I am hoping to begin, as usual, with a fairly simple story, to explain how people might get interested in politics. I suppose the classic route involves a series of experiences that people have in which they come to feel oppressed or dominated in some way. These experiences gradually become more and more politicised, that is, seen as political matters, to do with issues of power and authority, not personal ones or natural ones. The sort of revolutionary marxist politics we have examined in earlier chapters have a kind of 'escalation' mechanism of this kind, as individual members of the working class come to see that their experiences and interests are shared throughout the class as a whole.

There are a number of social conditions in which such escalation can take place. Marx himself suggests that individual proletarians have to be placed in identical social situations and allowed to communicate with each other, for example. The large-scale factory system of nineteenth-century Britain offered ideal conditions for this to take place, as workers were concentrated into large buildings at work, and large working-class housing areas outside, and were all exposed to very similar conditions of exploitation and economic domination. It was clear, purely from experience, that societies were divided into 'us' and 'them'. Workers saw members of 'them', the privileged class, enjoying very different social and work conditions. It was clearly in their interests to band together to try to overturn such an unequal system.

This would be at the last stage, however, when workers became conscious of themselves as members of a class, and started to take deliberate political action ending in a successful revolutionary overthrow. As we know, this sort of 'polarisation', which seemed likely to develop in the 1840s, did not persist. Social conditions seemed unlikely to generate this sort of automatic escalation after all, and we have pursued some reasons for this via the debate on marxist accounts of social class, and their rivals, in Chapter 5.

Turning away from class to gender, a similar sort of 'escalation' mechanism might lie beneath the emergence of feminist politics. According to some of those who were involved in it, for example (see the Introduction to Women's Study Group 1978), the women's liberation movement was initially grounded in the everyday experiences of women. Individual women might be inclined to believe, perhaps, that their low wages at work, or their excessive workload in the home, might be their fault, the result of an individual lack of merit, or, of some 'natural' or 'traditional' arrangements. However, sharing experiences with other women soon raises severe doubts about these explanations.

Some basic research can confirm this experience too, for example in demonstrating that women's wages are lower than those of their male counterparts, even where qualifications are equal. Household diaries seem to show that women still tend to do more domestic labour than men. There seems little doubt that this mere sharing of experience, including some based on sociological research, did lead to a raising of consciousness and to some support for feminist movements.

Issues like women's liberation seem to have sidestepped many of the problems that we have encountered in the earlier chapters with attempts to theorise politics. Indeed, from the account I have given, it seems as if experience alone is likely to be sufficient, and that social theories were not required to guide practice of this kind. Concentrating on a particular issue, one that looked as if it were a simple and single matter – one's gender – and building on experiences and spontaneous feelings of oppression generated by them, seemed to avoid the need for any theoretical complexity. The same might be said for other sorts of politics that might be most visible currently – protests about environmental pollution, vivisection, genetic modification of plants and animals, globalisation, and so on. In wait, however, is a paradox, pointed out best by Weber: once a movement escalates sufficiently to engage in struggle on a large public scale, it needs to become rational and organised to deal with rival 'parties'.

It is at this point, perhaps, that we find a perceived need to engage in some kind of social theory. Enthusiasm, propaganda, persuasion and other techniques designed to arouse consciousness might suffice for their early stages of recruitment, mobilisation and protest, but the more positive stage, the generation of actual policies and proposals for change, requires some understanding of the social mechanisms involved. Clearly, this means increasingly specialised academic labour again.

## Theory and experience

It is clear that any man attempting to discuss feminism critically has a particularly difficult problem to face. An important strand in feminism is clearly based upon women's experience, especially in terms of their relationships with men, and the way in which they experience forms of male domination. It is almost certainly impossible for any man to grasp this from the point of view of personal experience; although some of us with other irremovable and immediately visible 'spoiled' identities might have experienced some parallel forms of constant pressure to take on the values of dominant groups. Some of us have also experienced displays of power and even violence at their hands too. Nevertheless, these parallels can only take us so far into women's experience.

There is another problem too, in that if you have had a lengthy career in academic life, like me, you will almost certainly have a curiously deep-rooted view that sees feminist theory as a recent development. This is not an accurate view, but it is one that is hard to break with; it just so happens that most of the basic constituents of my (heavily institutionalised) knowledge of social theory have been produced by men. This has the unfortunate tendency of leaving feminist theory as a kind of additional option. It might still be possible to attempt to read feminist theory in as genuinely an open way as possible, doing one's best not to unpack it exclusively in the categories of conventional male theory, but this is likely to remain an intellectual commitment only, which is probably different from the more socially rooted commitments that some women feminist writers have developed.

There may be a methodological problem for men here too, in that they will be excluded from the experiential aspects of feminism, and thus unable to draw upon that shared knowledge that can act to validate feminist theory for women. For some women, the subjective feelings of relief and insight that feminist analysis has generated provides an ultimate and distinctively feminist test of validity. For others, it is simply that taking a woman's standpoint enables an acute and immediate perception of the gendering of concepts, even when reading the most reflexive theorists, such as Foucault or Habermas. Again, this is not entirely absent in a parallel way for males if they hail from a marginal social location – so much social theory struck me immediately, as a student, as somehow alien, as unconsciously reflecting a safe middle-class academic world, for example. Nevertheless this is not women's experience again.

Of course, some feminists would argue that feminism could be discussed, analysed and criticised in a manner similar to that pursued in any theoretical discussion. I do not think any feminist would dispute that there is an element of objective or public knowledge in feminism, which makes it as accessible to critique as any. Indeed, writers such as Walby (1990) suggest that relying too much on experience weakens the claims of feminism to be a perfectly adequate theory in the terms of conventional social science. There is clearly a danger that feminism might remain otherwise as another of these purely private languages, understood only by women (via some mysteriously biological mechanism only they possess, or particular kinds of contemporary experience?). Some uncomfortable assumptions underlie that position, of course, which could be questioned: apart from anything else, how far would such a restriction to experience extend? Could it be argued the other way round, so that only (Western European) men can fully understand Marx or Foucault, for example? It seems sensible to suggest instead that although men might not be able to adopt fully a woman's standpoint, they can at least do their best to understand aspects of it.

Nevertheless, there may well be important aspects of feminism that are permanently closed to a male commentator. It must simply be admitted that these limits may exist, and it would be foolish to imagine that unconscious perceptions, selections and interests can be overcome by an effort of will alone. I am saying this in order to explain to you the approach I have tried to adopt in this chapter. I am not going to pretend that I am some neutral commentator with the ability to develop some panoramic view of feminism. Instead, I am openly admitting that what follows is a particular gloss. This is always the case, of course, but it takes a particular form here: I am going to follow my own intellectual career, and discuss those feminist theorists and writers who have reacted to the sort of theory we have been or shall be discussing in the other chapters. This is, of course, largely written by males. Nevertheless, although I would like to begin the discussion by pursuing parallels between feminist theory and the accounts we have seen already in marxism and shall be seeing in Foucault, say, I have tried to discuss what is specific to feminism, to pursue, as far as I am able, what it is that makes feminism different, or 'other'.

Is the oppression of women located primarily in capitalist mechanisms, such as waged labour, or in social arrangements that pre-date, and will possibly post-date, capitalism, such as the family? It is important to know this in order to direct your political efforts at the main sources of oppression. Similar theoretical questions might well arise when considering cultural sources of oppression, such as unhelpful images of women in the mass media. If you think that these arise from male domination of the mass media, then one sort of feminist politics follows, such as attempting to recruit more women to the business of production. If you think these images arise from less personal cultural elements, such as cultural stereotypes, or practices of representation which have been deeply affected by gender in the past, then the main target for feminist politics should involve some cultural struggle with and replacement of these stereotypes and practices.

The need for some sort of theoretical explanation seems to arise in a most immediate sense: if you are working in a school and you want to raise the esteem of female pupils, it seems obvious that you have to try to analyse the main sources of low esteem in the first place. Is it the behaviour of the boys? Is it teacher expectations, the pattern of subject choices, the influence of cultural factors outside of the school altogether? Answers to these questions might lead to a wide variety of immediate political strategies designed to combat sexism – respectively, segregation of pupils by gender; campaigns to recruit more female teachers and to raise the expectations of male colleagues; curriculum redesign; or campaigns against popular culture, perhaps in the form of 'media literacy' sessions.

Some sort of theoretical effort seems unavoidable, just to help us prioritise, although it might well prove to be as frustrating and inconclusive as those we have examined already. It is completely understandable, in these circumstances, that some sort of pluralist account might be preferred instead. What I mean is that feminists might content themselves just to list the most important sites of sexist practice, and then to pursue a broad front campaign against all of them.

## Pluralist feminism

We might begin our discussion by looking at a popular textbook (in the UK at least) written by Walby (1990). Walby offers an interesting and rather typically sociological approach to the issue of 'theorising patriarchy', which is the title of her book. She offers a review of various 'theories', such as the familiar trio of varieties of feminism – marxist feminism (where the oppression of women is seen as integral to the functioning of capitalism), liberal feminism (rather like functionalism, where male oppression is seen as some kind of cultural lag to be challenged by more modern notions of equal rights) and radical feminism (where male oppression is universal and rooted in some ultimately biological difference that becomes a form of oppression, such as the ability to take advantage of women while they are pregnant). This trichotomy almost certainly originated in texts designed to simplify the debates for pedagogic reasons, and is thus as useful and as limiting as other familiar 'perspectives' in academic sociology (such as 'action' v. 'structure' approaches).

Walby summarises some of the main work in each of these perspectives, and finally lends support to a fourth variant, which she calls 'dual systems theory'. This approach elects not to decide between capitalism and some more universal patriarchy as a source of women's oppression, but allows both to have an effect. This tactic defers any choice that we have to make between different theories, of course. This offers a political advantage, in that it does not involve feminists in endless theoretical disputes, but there is a certain inconsistency in trying to hold both concepts together (see Adlam 1979, who pursues an argument based on the Althusserian approaches that we shall discuss in the next chapter).

Mostly, however, Walby operates in a manner that is not primarily determined by these different perspectives at all. Having acknowledged 'theoretical debates', what she tries to do is to establish that there are six key sites for patriarchy: 'paid work, housework, sexuality, culture, violence and the state' (Walby 1990: 16). This enables her to give due credit to the main emphases of the different perspectives, which tend to favour certain of these sites rather than others: listing all of them permits the kind of compromise we have noted above.

As important in this exercise to establish these key sites, however, is empirical work in sociology. Many studies are cited to show the existence of inequalities in the key areas: for example, an unequal burden of domestic labour in families, unequal wages at work, the persistence of personal violence against women and pressure towards 'compulsory heterosexuality', and so on. Again, one can see the political importance of doing this. Rather as we have argued above, the studies are useful in showing the broad extent, and the social political nature, of these inequalities. The existence and importance of these six sites therefore require very little in the way of tight theoretical justification. Where this is undertaken, Walby offers a discussion that shows how the various theories might comment on or interpret work in these privileged areas. This is probably the kind of 'incoherent' switching between levels that Hindess (1977) finds so unappealing.

Walby argues, for example, that the six sites are 'deep' structures and not just things that happen to cluster together empirically. It is important to argue this to overcome a common argument heard in sociology, but usually directed against class analysis – that class (or in this case gender) only exists because of the way that sociologists want to organise their research and group their data. There are, no doubt, many other relevant social groupings to research, like regional ones, more specific local market ones, groups based on various cultural allegiances, and so on. The argument goes that only a traditional or sentimental allegiance to the classic categories, usually class, provides their continued relevance. Maybe clusters of inequalities based on other factors are as significant as those based on gender. Indeed, Walby comes close to admitting that, as one would expect, ethnic origin is an equally important variable, one that cuts across gender differences. The example she gives turns on the role of the family – for white European women, the family offers another site of patriarchal domination, but for women of colour in non-European societies, the family can be a refuge against the oppression of society outside the walls of the home. She also admits that: 'Logically, there could be many forms [not just six structures], since I have identified six structures within patriarchy and two other major systems [capitalism and racism] with which it has been in articulation' (Walby 1990: 177).

While admitting the force of these other possibilities, Walby has to argue for the special importance of gender. One way to do this is to suggest that empirical research alone is not enough. Indeed, how could it be, since fellow feminists have often accused it of being dominated by male concerns? Citing such research in support of feminist claims must therefore be problematic. Of course, this is not an insuperable problem, and several options are available. First, it might be that empirical research techniques can be used, after all, by women in pursuit of their own goals, which implies that the sexism identified in such research lies in the purposes to which it is put, and not in the techniques themselves. Walby suggests something like this in her discussion of 'feminist standpoint' research methods, which advocate a special new set of qualitative and holistic techniques in order fully to uncover their positions. I am still not sure that this allows her to use official statistics to support her own arguments (about the unequal payments received by women in paid employment, for example), while offering standard objections to official statistics elsewhere (on the incidence of rape, for example).

The second option might be to suggest that there are certain elements of 'fact' which emerge despite the particular methods being used. If this is the argument, it would be a familiar but controversial one based on empiricism. Among the problems this could engender, it seems to allow that there might well be some other areas of 'fact' which could be studied objectively, even by 'male' methods.

The third option is that Walby is using empirical methods tactically, without any great faith in them, to make a primarily political point. She is using the results of official statistics to convince the reader of her political perspective, much as do party politicians, with their endless recitations of facts and figures. If so, there are clearly problems in doing this too, not least of which is that such a strategy looks just as propagandist.

This tactical note dominates parts of the discussion elsewhere as well. To finish the example above, Walby (1990: 20) insists that her six structures 'have causal effects upon one another, both reinforcing and blocking, but are relatively autonomous'. This could be an evasion like the one we have encountered in marxism earlier. However, they are also 'real deep structures and necessary to capture the variation in gender relations in westernised societies' (Walby 1990: 20), The word 'real' here indexes the 'realist' position of Bhaskar summarised briefly in Walby's Introduction (1990: 19), but never mentioned again. It is one possible resource to fight off the implicit drift to relativism in postmodern or deconstructionist accounts, including Foucault's work, such as those that argue that concepts like 'patriarchy', or even 'woman', are essentialist constructions, found as an effect of discourse. We have met the argument before and will do so again, but it might also be important at this point to suggest that such a 'realist' claim is available to almost anyone who wants to privilege his or her particular interests; probably it can never be used coherently and undogmatically.

Walby (1990: 19) sidesteps one obvious issue – the need to separate out necessary ('deep') and merely contingent ('empirically discovered') elements – by arguing that 'I do not think we need to make . . . [this] . . . distinction . . . since patriarchy is an open social system which can take a variety of forms'. However, she is content to dismiss some inconvenient elements of rival arguments – such as 'the base–superstructure model of causal relations' utilised by 'many of the grand theories of patriarchy' (1990: 16) – as 'contingent' after all. Other problems are dealt with equally briefly and cheerfully. Discourse theory is easily connected with marxism, for example, despite some of the problems that we shall see below, while empirical patterns are used to fight off relativism elsewhere: 'I think the postmodern critics have made some valuable points. . . . However, they go too far. . . . While gender relations could potentially take a number of forms, in actuality there are some widely repeated features' (1990: 15–16).

Leaving the argument after merely making a claim, without going on to use Bhaskar's work or arguments, looks suspiciously tactical. I was reminded of de Certeau's criticism of Bourdieu that we examine below (Chapter 11) – some empirical generalities are rendered as 'structures' with some peculiar qualities of their own, probably in order to make the whole argument work in a predictable way. Certainly, the argument seems to be 'asymmetric' in that empirical generalisations (supporting some critical reviews and summaries of earlier approaches) are used to establish regularities that then have to be claimed as 'structures' in some important sense. But this is the only role for Bhaskarian structures in the work, and Walby offers no way to derive her structures from Bhaskar independently or initially.

The same goes, probably, for the discussions of rival theories. Some familiar argument in favour of moderation and tolerance seems to inform the resolution of the debates. For example, a certain 'essentialism' is often diagnosed in some of the radical feminist approaches (curiously, less often in the others). To avoid this, we are told that the six structures help us to overcome some critics of earlier work – '[I want to] demonstrate that patriarchy is not an ahistoric universalistic concept' (Walby 1990: 177). Indeed, Walby goes on to argue that a major change has taken place in patriarchy, which has moved from 'private' to 'public' forms. Apparently, this shift can be traced in all six of the areas. However, there are further complications in that the public form can be further subdivided. Finally, while it is true that there may have been genuine reforms of patriarchy in individual areas, following the success of feminist resistance, the overall effect has been maintained by a kind of counterbalance strategy on the part of men: '. . . in response [to the success of first wave feminism] . . . patriarchy changed in form, incorporating some of the hard-won changes into new traps for women. . . . Women are no longer restricted to the domestic hearth, but have the whole society in which to roam and be exploited' (Walby 1990: 201). This is probably a 'radical feminist' position after all.

The mechanism that preserves patriarchy over time is also interesting but pretty straightforward. There is no necessary connection with capitalism or with biology, for example, but it is simply easier for men to take advantage of new social developments: 'The development of capitalism opened up new sites of power, and these were colonized by men because they were strategically placed to do so' (Walby 1990: 184). Whether this stems from the original world-historic advantage men gain over pregnant women or from their resources accumulated in other economic systems is unclear, though. There is a tautology in here somewhere too, possibly – we only know that men must and will always colonise new social developments because when we look, we find they have done so.

In dealing with the different theories, the advice seems to be the same in each case where this is found – not to 'go too far', but also not to abandon the 'usefulness' of the discussion, as in this example: 'Young has identified a key problem . . . but she overstates the strength of her argument' (1990: 7); '. . . criticisms . . . [of radical feminist accounts] . . . are often ferocious and I think overstated. In outline they have a point but they fail to deal with the rich nuances of the work' (1990: 102). We have already seen other examples too.

On a more abstract level, a spirit of moderation and compromise helps find a way through some complex debates. We discuss some of the problems with 'discourse theory' below, but here is Walby's resolution of one key issue: 'I want to draw upon the theoretical tools of discourse analysis, strengthened with a firmer account of patriarchal power, but tempered with a more thorough interconnection with economic relations . . .' (Walby 1990: 104). There seems to be no intention to do any more than cheerfully add several approaches together, with no consideration of the problems in doing so. Of course, perhaps this is precisely what we need to do to grasp the peculiarities of patriarchy, which do indeed cross over between several of the conventional (male) discourses.

With Walby, this permits some sort of evolutionary arrangement to structure the discussion, so that all of the earlier approaches can be given their due, as being somehow 'on the right lines' in heading towards a more adequate version of events, which is of course Walby's version of dual systems theory with its six privileged sites. Politically, as I have already suggested, the point is to marshal a number of arguments in order to persuade people to oppose patriarchy wherever it is found, and not to let any theoretical issues stand in the way for too long. Pedagogically, and this is an important implicit element in the argument too, student readers are advised to handle theoretical approaches in this way – to resist extreme positions, to apply 'common sense' and an approved form of 'critical analysis', in order to arrive at some sensible compromise.

## Early problems

Whatever the merits of Walby's specific arguments, some key issues have emerged already, and it might be worth summarising them before we proceed any further. One problem, for example, turns on what we described rather abstractly as 'essentialism'. This emerged in a political context for Walby, but it clearly has theoretical elements too: how unique and separate from the others is the particular struggle of women to liberate themselves from oppression? Politically, answers to this question lead to quite different sorts of liberation movement, it could be argued, which would range from separatist to 'broad-front' options. Theoretically, the answers run into an additional difficulty these days, since any form of essentialism is likely to be regarded as suspect. We shall be examining the arguments in more detail later on, but I have already hinted at them in my suggestions that Walby might be claiming some 'privilege' for her conceptions. It is obviously unsatisfactory to begin a rational theoretical account with an unfounded and mysterious claim that women are somehow united among themselves by an unknowable essence.

The options here emerge rather well in the discussion of Foucault's work, which follows in Chapter 10. Some feminists would want to see his arguments against essentialism as an unhelpful part of his work, which should be rejected as weakening the inherent solidarity of the women's movement. Others, on the contrary, both support and welcome anti-essentialism. Arguments by Foucault, for example, help feminists to insist that there is nothing essential in apparently 'natural' characteristics such as fixed sexual identities, a rigid sexual division of labour, and so on. Feminists can abandon them, and attempt to develop instead much more flexible notions of both identity and forms of solidarity between people. As the word 'solidarity' indicates, I sometimes find a rather Durkheimian undertone to these debates: some feminists seem to be advocating a kind of mechanical solidarity among women (which will keep them safely separate from the equally mechanical forms of solidarity of men), while others are more interested in forms of organic solidarity (which tolerates and defends differences between men and women in the name of some deeper unity).

Another main issue concerns the proposed relationship between feminism and far more conventional social sciences or social theories. If these are male-dominated, they may well be reproducing certain aspects of that domination in their very structure. For example, they may be operating with categories and concepts that reflect a typical dominant male view, one that fails to grasp the all-pervading nature of patriarchy, for example, but deals with certain aspects of the social structure, without ever seeing the whole picture. This is another kind of argument for 'object adequacy', which we have detected before in the works of Marx or Elias – other conventional social sciences operate too much 'on the surface', or with concepts that fail to grasp reality in enough complexity, such as economic or political descriptions of bourgeois society which involve the inter-actions of isolated individuals. As we shall see, feminist critics have pointed to the particular fallibilities of binary concepts like those that try to divide work from leisure, or the domestic from the economic: these also fail to grasp the deeper connections, by operating too much at the surface of a given form of social life.

The issue for feminists, then, becomes one of organising some critical rela-tionship with these conventional social sciences, just as Marx attempted to do. However, this relationship must take place against a very well-established con-ventional body of social theory, at least in 'second wave' feminism (Humm 1992; and see the online reading guide). Apart from anything else, this means that feminists often find themselves working as academics alongside their male col-leagues, and thus subject to the peculiar rules of academic argument, such as the one that relates to trying critically to appreciate the views of others and not rejecting them completely. Of course, feminist theorists might well believe that they have something to learn from those conventional theories. As I have argued with the work of Walby, a number of positions are open to them:

1   The tactical option suggests that they merely strip out aspects which might be useful to feminism, such as useful methodological or theoretical proce-dures.
2   A more theoretical option leads to an attempt to reread and then rewrite con-ventional social theory to bring it to bear upon the particular issues of feminism and patriarchy.
3   A final option involves working through conventional social theory, in order finally to engineer some decisive break with it, developing whole new the-oretical objects, and vocabularies of concepts and procedures to grasp them, on the basis of a thorough critical appreciation of what went before.

I am conscious that so far I have operated according to my own theoretical preferences, and tried to read off some of the problems of feminism by tracing them to well-known dilemmas in Durkheim and Marx. It is time to look in more depth at some actual feminist writings. It is helpful to begin with the work of some feminist students at the Birmingham Centre for Contemporary Cultural Studies (CCCS). We have examined some major works from this Centre, and from the Popular Culture Group at the Open University that succeeded it, in an earlier chapter (Chapter 6).

## CCCS feminism

The feminists who eventually organised themselves into the Women's Study Group clearly faced considerable problems in trying to articulate their position. They seem to have faced a certain amount of hostility, including some of a theoretical or academic nature. In fighting this hostility, the women not only risked disagreement with their colleagues, but faced the problem of incorporation and political neutering as well. It seemed they were worried about developing into yet another respectable academic option which could be somehow woven into overall (gramscian) frameworks. In other words, there was a view that feminist work should be different in more than one sense. The discussion in Chapter 1 of the subsequent book, *Women Take Issue* (Women's Study Group 1978; and see the online reading guide on the website) spells out the dilemmas really well, even at the most specific levels of whether to co-operate with the Centre and its practices at all, and whether this would restrict the group from doing more concrete and activist work.

The project the group wanted to develop seems acceptable enough – to pursue the issues of the articulation of gender with class, and thus to try to produce some kind of marxist feminism. As with their colleagues at CCCS, they began to examine media constructions of women, but then were forced to examine the relatively new area of domestic labour as a necessary extension of the inquiry into women's experience specifically. In this way, the project soon led into relatively uncharted territory, and into new theoretical work rather different from gramscian concerns and frameworks.

This trend towards novelty and innovation can be seen in several specific chapters in the book. For example Bland et al. in Chapter 3 began with classic work in Engels to explain the oppression of women through waged labour, heightened by their particular role in families that reproduce labour. However, they want to argue that the oppression of women rapidly took on additional dimensions, in culture as well as in the class system, as its particular forms became justified as 'biological' or 'natural'. Investigating these dimensions required new concepts, since they could not be logically derived from the requirements of capital and its reproduction. There was no necessity for *women* to be largely confined to unpaid domestic labour, and for *men* to waged labour. Pursuing these investigations led to an argument that the political and cultural dimensions actually pre-dated capitalism, and to the discovery that there were several other key areas of equal importance that had not been thoroughly investigated by marxism. The way in which social welfare works to make women into dependants is an obvious area which has largely developed since Marx's death, but there are other areas where the specifics of gender have not been theorised sufficiently, such as the deep involvement of women in consumption. Even Marx's classic work on the role of the 'reserve army of the unemployed' needs to be completed by a recognition that there are important subdivisions among female battalions in this army – between single and married women, or women with children and those without. These categories impact on women much more seriously in terms of employment than they do for men.

The apparent narrative of 'discovery' of the importance of gender in this account is presumably tactical, since other contributors, such as Brunsdon et al. (in Chapter 2 of *Women Take Issue*), argue that experience in the concrete struggles of the women's liberation movement had already delivered these insights, albeit in a slightly different form. The famous slogan that 'the personal is the political', for example, had pointed to ways in which the so-called 'natural' characteristics of women (closer to nature, better at caring, suited to domestic work) were really political ones. The realisation that these matters were part of political oppression led in turn to the need for a new kind of politics of emancipation. Brunsdon uses 'hegemony' to describe this new form of sexual politics, which is, as we noted in Chapter 6, the main theoretical concept of her male colleagues at the Centre, although she qualifies it by adding the term 'masculine'. Brunsdon also begins to raise another important issue bearing particularly on women, it seems, which is the reproduction of them as individuals.

Burniston et al. in Chapter 6 of *Women Take Issue* pursue this issue through re-examination of the work of Freud and Althusser. The internal politics of this move must have been quite interesting, as the Director of the Centre, Stuart Hall, had been involved in a minor academic feud with a rival perspective ('*Screen* theory') which had also used these works to develop quite a different theory of subjectivity (see Coward 1977). (We have already cited the online reading guides covering this piece and Hall's reply.) The overall conclusion of Burniston et al.'s exploration was that the work of Althusser offered the best kind of attempt to incorporate these concerns into marxism, but had not done enough to explain how women in particular are provided with sexualised social identities in material areas such as the media, education, work and family.

There are many other examples on offer (see my online reading guide to the book). Perhaps one more brief summary might be in order, this time of Chapter 8. Here, Bland et al. again attempt to argue that marxism fails to specify adequately the area of 'the social', and tends to over-emphasise its connections with the economic. Analyses of the family and kinship, clearly important areas for women, indicate the adverse consequences. Slightly esoterically, the authors begin with the critique of a famous attempt to spell out and test some marxist notions in the field of social relations. Hindess and Hirst analyse kinship in pre-capitalist societies as well as capitalist ones as an important element in the cycle of economic reproduction. However, they fail to grasp that the kinship system also assists specifically in the subordination of women, a theme better developed by non-marxist anthropologists such as Lévi-Strauss (a real blow here, as you might imagine, to those attempting to propose marxism as some universal theory). No conventional anthropologists are able fully to grasp the role of specific biological factors in the reproduction of social relations and the construction of sexual identities, however: feminist scholarship is better able to pursue this issue.

## Feminism and Foucault

Feminist reactions to Foucault's work have been equally critical in the academic sense of that word, and I have chosen two very interesting collections, Ramazanoğlu (1993) and Fraser (1989), to illustrate a useful range of possibilities. I have online reading guides on my website for both of these collections, where you might be able to find lengthier summaries. Slightly inconveniently, my chapter on Foucault himself in this book is Chapter 10, so you might find it easier to stop now and read that one first.

As you would expect, with a writer as complex and prolific as Foucault, feminist critics, like all his critics, react to different trends and emphases. As you would also expect by now, all feminist critics are going to argue that Foucault's treatment of gender is inadequate. They do differ in terms of where they locate the source of this inadequacy, and there are different opinions about what might be done, if anything, to develop Foucault's insights in the direction of informing feminist theory. As before, though, one of my main interests in these discussions is going to be whether such criticisms develop any distinctively new directions, and, if so, whether other more general implications, beyond feminist projects, might be detected and pursued as well.

It is not too difficult to see that Foucault's work is going to pose problems for those feminists who think there are some underlying essentialist interests that unite all women. Foucault is trying to develop a methodology, after all, which would suggest that essences are really an effect of discourses. He wants to criticise radically any notion of deep meanings or historical purposes in humanist views, but this would clearly apply also to similar meanings and purposes in any essentialist view. For some feminists, abandoning some essential links between women would be to abandon a strong form of solidarity that would guarantee feminist politics.

There seem to be several possibilities in responding to such an attack on essentialism. One is simply to reassert that there is some genuinely universal experience that does not just rely on feminist discourse: this sort of argument is expressed, for example, in Cain's contribution to Ramazanoğlu (1993). Cain wants to point to some of Foucault's own ambiguities about whether anything exists outside discourses, some of which we shall explore. She also wants to suggest that one major contribution of feminism is precisely to point out that patriarchy does underpin a number of important actual discourses, such as those of criminal courts in upholding a gendered version of legal equality. She also cites some work on sexual violence directed against women which offers an important context affecting discourse in a most obvious sense: it requires considerable work before the female victims can even begin to articulate in discourse what has happened to them – this is an example of an 'intransitive relationship [existing outside of discourse], pre-existing its possible utterance [in a discourse]' (in Ramazanoğlu 1993: 83).

MacCannell and MacCannell, in the same collection, make a similar point.

They accuse Foucault of only being interested in the discursive aspects of sexuality, which is far too abstract. The problem is seen in his analysis of power, which is famously treated 'neutrally', as a 'pure impartial drive to structure . . . open to all, even when it appears to be held by a few' (in Ramazanoğlu 1993: 204). Such an analysis omits any discussion of force or violence. Indeed, there is a curious notion that force and violence have become redundant in modern societies, and that people's consent is engineered in more discursive ways. There are few better examples of the continuing role of force and violence, however, than the relations between men and women. Those relations show that discursive forms of power are very commonly supported by the use of physical force or the threat of violence, and that victims respond to violence in very profound ways, affecting their entire lives.

No discussion of this is found in Foucault's work, and very extensive empirical investigation would be required. MacCannell and MacCannell begin to describe some of the areas such an investigation might research, and consider some quite disturbing examples of the effects of violence on victims. Worse still, Foucault's emphasis on discourse as a mechanism of power comes close to apologising for or rationalising away one of the major effects of force and violence. Both victims and perpetrators will often describe what has happened in a similarly abstract and neutral discursive manner, the former apparently as willing to legitimate violence as the latter.

This criticism is well founded. Without wishing to recapture it back for male-dominated analysis in any way, I suggest that it might well be generalised in at least two directions. In one direction, I think this discussion of violence towards women might well help restore the whole issue of violence in social relationships as a whole, in analysing the relationships between the social classes, for example. Secondly, in the other direction, I think it is not just Foucault who seems to have ignored violence in his discussions of power. For example, I have seen far too many commentaries on Althusser or Gramsci that focus so tightly on the ideological functions of government, trying to 'win consent' in some purely cultural struggle, that they seem to overlook completely the continuing use of repression. The use of military and paramilitary violence is a very common occurrence in many societies, however.

The MacCannells are quite right to suggest that a Foucauldian analysis of power, on the one hand, often combined with some token analysis of underdog cultural resistance, on the other, needs to be supplemented by a grasp of the use of force, or the threat of it, as a source of final compulsion. I think the whole analysis points to important problems with most abstract and scholasticised analyses of power, which tend to render the social world as it is experienced by academics. Such privileged people commonly do not experience force and violence and they are accustomed to a thoroughly discursive way of life. The astonishing lack of sustained analysis of the role of the military in sociology is another example of this abstractness (with some noble exceptions).

This problem returns to haunt many of the 'applied' works of social theory for feminists, as we shall demonstrate below. I have tried to suggest that many postmodernist writers would be open to the same sort of criticism. A witty recognition of relativism and purely discursive ways of overcoming it might be instantly recognisable to academic celebrities, but this practice is rarely found outside the confines of the university. There is little point in trying to explain to a policeman that you were hoping to join a picket line 'ironically', playfully or in a moment of philosophical schizophrenia, or in attempting to deconstruct the discourse of someone who is intent on beating you to the ground. Baudrillard might have claimed, notoriously, that 'the Gulf War did not happen' (see Norris 1992), since, in his world, media representations were all that were available, but in the world occupied by the military on both sides, and by many civilian victims, that war was a real event in quite a different way.

If these points suggest that there is something in everyday life that is obviously pre- or non-discursive, there are still difficulties in embracing some fully essentialist position for feminism. Perhaps the clearest ones arise from considering the political implications. For one thing, there is not always an obvious solidarity among women, who are also divided among themselves in terms of their other social allegiances, such as their ethnic origin. Important differences of this kind might be lost in an attempt to argue for some universal experiences. Bailey (in Ramazanoğlu 1993) raises another problem. In claiming that there is some essentialist divide between men and women, feminists can be seen as agreeing rather dangerously with a fundamental principle of patriarchy, which argues precisely the same thing. Feminism then becomes a kind of mirror image of patriarchy, and the contest between them gets reduced to that of a difference of opinion about which group is superior. Fighting off that option leaves the whole idea of essential underpinnings for feminism looking pretty tactical or pragmatic.

Another option for seeing off Foucault seems to involve a rethinking of the issue of pre- or non-discursive realities while avoiding a claim that these are somehow essentialist. One possibility here, mentioned by both Cain, and Walby, whose work we reviewed earlier, turns on an approach associated with the philosopher Roy Bhaskar, which is usually called 'realism'. We have met this sort of argument before (for example, when discussing Giddens in Chapter 4 – although there are considerable specific differences between Bhaskar and Giddens). To be very brief, realism of this kind operates with a deeper level of reality, somehow beneath or behind existing reality, where real objects in this sense are transformed and brought to the surface by routine social activities, including discourse. This level of reality cannot be directly observed, but it must exist, it is argued, as a necessary context and set of conditions for the observable social reality. Such a position would acknowledge the arguments of Foucault and others about the important role of discourse in constituting actual practices and theoretical objects, yet would insist that there is another level of reality 'behind' this, where his arguments are invalid. The full set of implications of this reference to Bhaskar in feminist thinking is still unclear to me, as I have indicated.

Quite a different approach altogether would be to accept what Foucault has to say about the crucial constitutive role of discourses, and to accept fully that this invalidates an essentialist feminist position. The great advantage, of course, is that feminism can still play an important political role in the everyday 'micro'-level struggles over power that Foucault predicts. It is a major opportunity for people such as Bailey (in Ramazanoğlu 1993) to reposition feminist politics in several ways:

(a) to use Foucault's arguments as a major support in the project to deny the fixed naturalistic categories of patriarchy;
(b) to develop his arguments about the important changes in the nature of discipline, especially the disciplining of bodies and populations (which impinges especially on women)
(c) to exploit fully the localised possibilities for struggle, to pursue projects such as the reclamation of 'Herstories ... forgotten and overlooked women's histories' (Bailey in Ramazanoğlu 1993: 103), and in general to press forward on a broad front, developing strategies which are 'myriad, local, institutional, political, scholarly, and metatheoretical' (in Ramazanoğlu 1993: 114).

Bailey advocates new forms of solidarity as 'loose, opportunistic coalitions which can embrace differences', including 'strategic essentialism ... a fictional essence deployed within very specific institutional settings where the terms of debate are already circumscribed' (in Ramazanoğlu 1993: 118–119). This position has problems too, of course, since it is doubtful whether such loose coalitions can ever be united by discourse alone, with no stronger forms of bonding between the members. Another problem is that rival political groups are equally capable of entering the fray, and offering a whole series of alternative and equally plausible coalitions, a point that gramscians were finally to recognise in their rather rueful recognition of the power of the articulating practices of fascist or conservative politicians and intellectuals.

I am conscious that in my discussion of the contributors to the Ramazanoğlu collection, I have not really mentioned any of the more substantial themes that feminists have found helpful in Foucault's work. I intend to leave this to be carried mostly by the online reading guides that accompany this book. However, I have already mentioned the work on discipline and bodies, and it is fairly easy to see that other themes seem to be particularly helpful as well, including the work on sexuality and its history.

I now want to review very briefly some of the main themes in Nancy Fraser's *Unruly Practices* (1989). This offers an excellent series of specific feminist critiques of a number of major social theorists, principally Foucault and Habermas as far as we are concerned. But I want to start with a general outline of Fraser's argument that runs throughout the much more detailed specific arguments.

In brief, Fraser is offering both a general and a particular argument about social theory. The general argument is that abstracted and intellectualised theory avoids 'unruly practices' at its peril. Mere theory can never generate an adequate politics without a close understanding of these concrete, complex and unpredictable activities. Thus even Foucault and Habermas exhibit rather dangerous omissions in their work when they come to consider actual practice. The particular argument is that feminist theory can supply a suitable grasp of unruly practices, that feminist activists are the ones actually working out there in the difficult areas, exploring the limits and constraints of political concepts such as power, autonomy and rights.

It seems to me that Fraser is operating with a particular form of critique that I actually first encountered when reading Colletti's (1975) accounts of the early work of Karl Marx. We have mentioned this critique once or twice before too. One major criticism that Marx had of Hegel, for example, seems to be making exactly these points about the dangers of pure theory. In Hegel's case, it was a theory of historical and political development, based upon some very abstract mechanisms involving Spirit, on the one hand, and embodiments of that Spirit, human society, on the other, and the dialectical progress that ensued from their interaction. (Again, readers of this book might want to consult my own brief online reading guide to aspects of Hegel's sociology to gain a quick overview.) The political error, according to Marx, was to return too uncritically from pure theory to actual societies. Hegel was prepared to 'apply' his theoretical work far too readily to the existing Prussian state in which he was located. He did not undertake a detailed political and social analysis of Prussia, and was forced to rely instead on the common-sense knowledge and assumptions common to the educated stratum to which he belonged. This absence of critical grasp made it all too easy to unite in thought his concept of the state as the embodiment of Reason, and the Prussian state of his day. No doubt the Prussian authorities would have been rather pleased by this philosophical endorsement of their actual policies, although, to be fair, followers of Hegel were able to point to obvious differences between a state based on Reason, and the horribly un-Reasonable activities of the Prussian government of the day.

This is a powerful criticism of abstract philosophy that operates well beyond the specific case of Hegel, and I have tried to put it to work myself when examining some of the more naïve sociological utterances in the work of Habermas, Hall, Barthes or Baudrillard (see Harris 1996). What interests me is why philosophers who are so rigorous, careful and explicit in their own fields seem to be compelled to blunder into crude 'applications' of their work involving messy and complex social and political issues. I can only conclude that it is because they wish to (re)acquire some social role as public spokespersons or analysts, as 'universal intellectuals' with the stern duty to speak for all on the things that concern us. Quite understandably, a scholastic perspective then gets generalised as a universal one. There might well be some impulses deriving from their position as public employees too, of course, at least with those currently or recently employed in universities. Whatever the reasons, such interventions are almost bound to end in generalisation about, and quite often apology for, the existing forms of social relations.

Fraser (1989) puts this critical approach to work in her excellent discussion of conventional (male) social theory. The book begins with an insightful reflexive account, which seems to be associated with feminist work in particular, of what it is like to try to be a critical and radical intellectual while working in a university. Then the main arguments are outlined: Foucault's actual politics are mysterious; Derrida's approach is far too abstract; Habermas's work turns out to be far too androcentric; and on her other target, the American philosopher Richard Rorty, whom we will not be discussing in any depth but see Hall (1994), she offers a useful critique, but fails to press it home sufficiently and thus naïvely reproduces central ideological values. All of these Great Men have provided us with useful critical and philosophical arguments, but all offer the same kind of flaw that limits their application to specific and concrete struggles. Fraser realises, of course, that her critique has problems of its own – perhaps it gives far too much weight to 'practical' politics at the expense of intellectual inquiry (and she says she knows only too well, as a university employee, how activism is not always an option, while intellectual inquiry can be an honourable and worthwhile pursuit). More abstractly, there are some obvious serious problems in attempting to strip off useful parts of philosophical projects, while rejecting the less useful.

Fraser begins her critique of Foucault by pointing out some aspects that we shall discuss further in his work. While insisting that his intention is to pursue a technical and rather analytic project of focusing on discourses, their emergence and consequences for practice, he cannot refrain from making normative judgements, even though this is strictly forbidden by his own approach. It is clear, for example, that he heartily disapproves of the spread of (self-)discipline into modern society, and he seems to be making the occasional political point as well about how dominant groups are able to harness discourses to meet their specific political ends.

It is these asides that can make Foucault look like a marxist, although Fraser detects liberal value positions in the analysis as well. Fraser's point, initially, is that Foucault should be able to discuss these value positions, instead of giving the naïve impression that he has somehow been able to deny their effects on his work. Had he been more explicit, a major flaw would have been avoided: Fraser agrees with the MacCannells' critique, as outlined above, and says that the concept of power just covers too many cases in Foucault's work, so that he is unable to distinguish between normative constraints, on the one hand, and actual coercion, on the other. She suggests that Foucault really needs something like Weber's work on different types of authority and legitimation in order to avoid this unfortunate generalisation.

The same kind of critique informs Fraser's discussion of Foucault's stance on modernity. In one reading of his work, Foucault begins to criticise modernity on the grounds that it has led to excessive surveillance and disciplining of human beings as subjects. Another account suggests that such developments arise from the self-defeating and limited nature of humanist resources to guard sub-jectivity against these trends (which makes him sound a bit like Weber on 'fate' – see Chapter 5). Indeed, as can be seen in *Discipline and Punish* (Foucault 1977; and see the online reading guide to this book), theoretical attempts to pin down the nature of individuals, no doubt with the best intentions initially, go hand in hand with practical attempts to confine and discipline them. Yet a third account summarised by Fraser suggests that this unfortunate development of humanism and subjectivity still has some way to go, suggesting an even gloomier view of a future social life suffused with surveillance and discipline, and offering a serious criticism of those who would want to reawaken subjec-tivity as a necessary check on social oppression. Fraser's point is that the whole discussion needs much more concrete investigation of what the status of sub-jectivity and freedom actually is in social life at the moment if these options are to become any more than abstract speculations. Feminist work happens to be a very important source of such concrete investigation, and social analysts ignore it at their peril.

The final argument takes up Foucault's work on emancipatory politics. It is clear that his own political interests turn on overcoming attempts to discipline bodies, and celebrating bodies and pleasure instead. He contrasts this kind of politics of the body favourably with liberal discourses about rights. However, Fraser argues that his own politics of the body seemed just as likely to become incorporated into modern capitalism as the discredited language of rights. The consumerist celebration of particular types of fit, slim, athletic bodies for young women would be an obvious example. The same general point is being made again, of course. Foucault is attempting to legislate about political activity from the point of view of an abstract intellectual, without bothering to investigate actual political struggles, whether based on dangerously limited notions such as 'rights', or focused on high street struggles over bodies and what they should look like.

It might be worth sketching in very briefly Fraser's criticisms of some other major social theorists, just to get at some of the general principles. There is an excellent criticism of Derrida and his followers, for example. Without going into any detail at this stage, the debates turned on whether Derrida's philosophical project, normally known as 'deconstruction', had any political implications, and, if so, what these might look like. We discuss deconstruction elsewhere (Chapter 13), but it is possible to rely on the common-sense understanding of this term to grasp the principles at stake. Without getting too technical, then, 'deconstruction' can be seen as a way of reading statements and arguments crit-ically, literally deconstructing them, taking them apart by exposing all the devices that writers use to try to develop a plausible argument or closed intel-lectual statement. Once we have exposed these construction techniques, we break the hold of the most carefully assembled attempts to fool, 'hail' or per-suade us, and we are in a position to learn something about language and how it works.

Now it is clear that, on the face of it, Derrida's version of deconstruction seems to have a lot in common with marxist or feminist criticisms of ideology: ideological arguments also typically try to confuse the reader by offering a closed and apparently self-sufficient account of what is a far more complex reality. Derrida himself was already suspected of harbouring such critical tendencies, although at the time, he had not actually published any work specifically on Marx (he has since – Derrida 1994; and see my online reading guide). However, participants at a conference on Derrida in France in 1980 argued that deconstruction involved a much more general project, patiently working away at deconstructing revolutionary politics and the accompanying series as well, especially in the name of opposing totalitarian tendencies and keeping a space for a politics of difference. Deconstruction therefore operates in a different space, beyond all existing politics, and all forms of existing politics are equally open to its critical approach.

According to Fraser, the whole discussion took a suspiciously scholastic, abstract and philosophical turn shortly after these alternatives were revealed, and before long, a whole new Centre for Philosophical Research on the Political was proposed in order to pursue these options. More analysis was clearly needed, or, as Fraser (1989: 82) puts it, politics was deferred in favour of 'a retreat into philosophy'. This philosophical turn was reflected in the actual debates as well, which featured ever more patient analysis, without even hints of a 'good old-fashioned political fight' (Fraser 1989: 82). Where the Centre did connect with actual politics, in the occasional discussion of totalitarianism or democracy, for example, a slide occurred away from rigorous analysis, into more familiar kinds of common-sense discussion, gestures towards the empirical level after all, and even (heavily 'constructed') political exhortation.

At no stage was there any attempt to link with any actual political movements or concrete political discussions about marxism or feminism, or to explore any of the sociological work on politics. 'Politics' seemed to be a matter of opting for a particular abstract political position 'decisionistically'. As Fraser puts it, the deconstructionists were looking for a new home, having lost faith in marxism, but did not think to explore various radical post-marxist possibilities (especially those in feminism). Instead they just oscillated from one end to the other, from marxism to neo-liberalism. I think this parallels the similar journey made by so many radicals in the UK too, and I take Fraser's view that this is because this kind of intellectualised politics is able to float free from any tangible commitments to any actual struggles.

As a final irony, Fraser notes that the Centre allowed its agenda to be hijacked by one fairly well-organised political group – the neo-liberals (rather like French Thatcherites or Reaganites) – and seemed powerless to resist! Nothing illustrates better the dilemma for philosophical positions of this level of generality and abstraction: politics can be easily abolished in thought, as it were, but only if someone else is prepared to take concrete action to organise programmes, control agendas, fight off take-overs, and so on. Again I take this as indicative of a more general point, that intellectual endeavour chronically depends on the much less reflective processes of everyday life (even in universities) for its material sustenance as well as for its stock of ideas.

Perhaps the most impressive criticism, however, arises when Fraser takes on Habermas (whom we discuss in Chapter 12). In the process, she makes some important points about the categories used in conventional sociology. These often turn on binary distinctions. Habermas's binaries include symbolic and material reproduction, social versus system integration, and system and life-world, for example. If these are based upon a picture of a world that fails to take into account gender, as Fraser alleges, these categories and their binary structure are going to be completely inadequate and one-sided. I think this is a very important point, with a much more general range of application, and one which covers many feminist critiques of many social theorists. Indeed, I think Habermas does so poorly here because he relies far too much on Parsonian sociology, which he has decided to incorporate into his own work in order to make it more sociologically concrete and relevant.

Without going into too much detail as to Habermas's specific project just now, Fraser is able to argue that these binaries are in fact combined in the experience of women. For example, when women do both paid and unpaid labour, as is common, it becomes impossible to confine them to either the symbolic or the material level of reproduction: in an important sense they belong to both. The same point can be made about the connections between the lifeworld and the social system. For males, Fraser (1989: 119) suggests, it might make sense to add further binary subdivisions so that people occupy either a private/family dimension, or a public/polity dimension, but, most unfortunately, this split '[uncritically and] faithfully mirrors the institutional separation in male-dominated capitalist societies of family and official economy, household and paid workplace'.

In essence, Habermas explores these dimensions and considers their interrelationship without once considering the importance of gender in the overall story of separation and integration, even despite his obvious sympathy for feminist politics. This renders his work both inadequate and deeply 'androcentric'. What we need instead is a new framework that sees the gendered aspects of these connections and places them centre-stage. Instead, there is the material link between male-dominated families and male-dominated states, and an ideological interest in keeping them separate, and a theoretical framework that unwittingly does the same. On another tack, it makes no sense to talk about the growth of the client relation as a major way in which citizens relate to states in modernity without apparently noticing that the client role is largely a female role at the same time.

Even Habermas's politics seems over-concerned with male values: men may indeed have found themselves increasingly silenced in the public sphere, but feminists have certainly not allowed the discussion of values to decline. In the course of this discussion, Fraser also comments in much more detail on splits and divisions between the various new social movements upon which Habermas does base some hope. He includes feminism here, although in a pretty unanalysed way. It is clear to Fraser that the social contradictions pressing on women have led to both feminist and anti-feminist struggles, for example.

This leads Fraser to reconceive the major axis of politics, in the remaining two chapters of her book, as a struggle to redefine and repoliticise 'needs', a struggle in which feminist intellectuals and experts have a particular role. This argument is difficult to summarise, but feminists should take the lead in contesting the (patriarchal) ways in which the State and its agencies define needs and institutionalise them so as to depoliticise the whole issue.

## Concluding comments

In conclusion to this chapter, it seems clear that feminist analyses have been developed which have the widest possible general relevance, as well as making their specific cases. At the same time, feminist perspectives have problems and limits of their own too. Some limits can arise from excessive commitments to political activism or to theoretical concepts, as with the other perspectives we have interrogated. Feminist 'Screen theory' (discussed in the next chapter) indicates the extent to which analyses can develop so scholastically that they can never be tested or evaluated against mere data or experience. They work, every bit as did some marxism, as a privileged and 'centred' reading.

Thus it is possible to see that feminist analyses may share deeper connections with 'male' theory than seem apparent at first. The critical apparatus that Fraser uses so well, for example, can be traced to a similar critical endeavour in the young Marx. Feminist work has not escaped all the flaws either. Fraser herself has a curious blindness when it comes to gramscian work, in my view. Gramscians are just as capable as deconstructionists in using theoretical couplets and binaries (such as 'pessimism of the intellect, optimism of the will', or 'hegemony' as both struggle and control) to flee from or defer endlessly any actual political engagements. While I am here, I think that Fraser and some of the contributors to Ramazanoğlu's collection also miss out the crucial issue of the professional politics of the university academic. Fraser is engagingly frank about her own professional politics, but we can see some of Foucault's or Derrida's avoidance of activism in the same light, perhaps. These writers escape everyday constraints and purely professional concerns not just because they are men, but also because they are in a privileged and insulated occupation. It would be a mistake to see male silences about the position of women as just due to male bias in the concepts, in other words. There are far more constraints at work than those of gender.

# 9 The Politics of Otherness

I intend to consider a number of recent important developments in analysing cultural politics, including the politics of identity. I shall then go on to consider in more depth the particular ways in which this approach has led to some interesting developments in feminism specifically. Again, I am not suggesting that feminist cultural politics has any more deep virtue than, say, the politics of racial differences, or struggles over the notion of disability, each of which could also be pursued here. I am prioritising feminist politics partly because I think it is an important case exemplifying the technical implications and difficulties.

As the consideration of those other examples shows, however, the politics of otherness is a widespread element of cultural analysis and cultural politics at a number of levels, including the micropolitical one. The basic principle can be stated fairly easily: somehow, a dominant group has taken advantage of the general cultural and linguistic tendency to divide the world into privileged categories and their 'others'. We know, for example, that words like 'black' are commonly encountered in ways that indicate some kind of inferiority – as in words like blackmail, or reference to black markets, or the black arts. In this way, 'whiteness' gets associated with the 'good' aspects of our culture. Slightly more subtly, 'whiteness' also becomes associated with the norm, what is normal or taken for granted, while its linguistic opposite is associated with the abnormal, the deviant, the stranger or outsider, that which does not belong, that which is problematic, dangerous, disruptive, and so on. I suppose the example of 'the disabled' is even clearer: here, a whole group of diverse people are defined entirely by what they are not – not normal, not able-bodied and thus not really belonging, or 'other'. Clearly, the same kind of argument is going to be used to explain the marginal status of women as the complementary 'other' to 'normal', that is male, societies and behaviour.

What gives this whole tendency its particular power is that language itself seems to operate with these simple binary divisions, at least according to that approach we have already discussed as 'structuralism'. Using the opposition between terms is an important way of conveying meaning, so that a whole explanatory narrative can be developed to clarify the meaning of the term by contrasting it with what it is not. Academics do this all the time, for example when they start their lectures or articles with common-sense definitions of, say, marxism, so as to demonstrate finally that real marxism is none of these.

If we take the structuralist argument at its most extensive, we can see that binary oppositions are used to develop the meaning of words in sentences or narratives, and also to act out meanings in social rituals. Thus kinship systems, for Lévi-Strauss (1977), are based around a system of similarities and differences – marriage, for example, is forbidden between men and women who are similar in important ways (like brother and sister), but must take place between strangers who are different in the sense of not being close kin (but who cease to be strangers once they are married). The difference between what we called relations of 'consanguinity' and 'affinity' (blood ties and marriage ties) is used to do important work of classification and organisation, to locate people in kinship systems. This allocation then brings with it social rights and obligations towards others. Lévi-Strauss was to argue that the same binary oppositions can be detected in cooking – oppositions between the raw and the cooked in cooking rituals are also used to stand for important social differences such as those between, say, children and adults, or men and women. Exponents of Lévi-Strauss's anthropology, such as Leach (1970), even suggest that the same mechanism of similarity and opposition explains the development of modern signalling systems such as traffic lights – having selected the colour red to indicate the need to stop, it makes perfect binary sense to choose its opposite in the spectrum – green – to indicate the opposite command.

This sort of recourse to the basic structures of language and culture is two-edged. On the one hand, we seem to have uncovered an important mechanism of cultural or linguistic differentiation to explain social differences. On the other, if binary divisions like this are as fixed in culture as they seem, there is a political problem. To expand this problem, it will be seen that certain social divisions are deep-rooted, so that any political activity to change them is likely to be unsuccessful. This sort of activity is found in liberal appeals to treat each other equally, or to attempt to grant some sort of basic equal rights. What is needed instead, it is argued, is a more culturally rooted form of politics. This can range from the familiar struggles over words which may or may not be used to describe various groups – usually referred to as a drive towards 'political correctness' (such as refusing to be called by the European colonial and usually derogatory name for your ethnic group) – to much more fundamental demands to recast cultural matters in completely different terms (to root out other legacies of colonialism too). Demanding the overthrow of literary, artistic or philosophical canons that enshrine only 'European dead white males' would be another example. The idea is to recover those 'subjugated knowledges', including 'Herstories', that we saw when we discussed Foucauldian feminism in the previous chapter.

Thinking of Foucault should also caution against the view that this cultural discrimination arises only because dominant groups managed to hijack particular terms, as we shall see in the next chapter. It is a more general process than that, dispersed throughout social life, in a 'capillary' kind of way, rather than monopolised by the state and its juridical apparatus. Reverting to structuralism, it becomes possible to say that language itself somehow develops these cultural and linguistic discriminations in the very way it works, and that only sometimes does this lead to social hijack by dominant groups. What this means is that a simple overthrow of the main dominant groups, even if it can be achieved, would not result in a kind of cultural or linguistic egalitarianism by itself. We also know that cultural discrimination cannot be simply legislated away, by banning particular words – the urge to discriminate simply finds other words. Perhaps my favourite example here turns on the use of 'ethnic minority'. This term was developed with the best of intentions, no doubt, to replace the highly dubious notion of 'race', but, as Sivanandan (1990) points out, the term still carries notions of inferiority: people in such minorities are seen as hopelessly 'ethnic', that is pre-modern, still dominated by religion and custom, still fundamentally other.

## Freud and Lacan

Turning to the example of feminist politics in particular, the linguistic roots of the politics of otherness were combined in a powerful way with a rereading of Freud in the works of the French philosopher Jacques Lacan (try the introduction to his work in Macey 1980; the section in May 1996; or the relevant section by Elliott in Turner 1996). Lacan is a particularly dense and impenetrable writer in my view, and so I will offer only a very basic account here. Lacan proposes to apply structuralist linguistics to Freud's work, especially Freud's relatively undeveloped theories of the unconscious. This can be done in a number of ways, such as reinterpreting Freudian terms like 'condensation' (how elements get condensed into symbols in dreams) as linguistic processes such as metonymy (the process whereby a part comes to stand for a whole). Most importantly, the whole unconscious in Freud can be seen as akin to the structure of language itself – both are unknown to the individual subject, and work in ways that are only revealed when you move outside of experience into theory. To take Merck's example (Merck 1987; see the online reading guide for a longer summary), the process of repression, whereby a subject manages to misinterpret and forget a traumatic experience, really involves a linguistic switch, in this case a metaphor. It is as if the mind makes a backup file but saves it under another name.

I want to pass hastily on to a more specific level of analysis. What Lacan's work did was to permit Freudian theory to round out and make concrete the formal possibilities offered by structural analysis of language and its capacity to make binary distinctions. There are two bits of Freudian theory specifically which have been very important for this project.

First, there is the work on the 'mirror phase'. Freud tells us this happens in early infancy, before the acquisition of language. Basically what happens is that infants come to recognise themselves in a mirror. For the first time, infants realise that there is an outside, so to speak, and that they live in one. It is a crucial moment in recognising oneself as some kind of unitary object, a necessary prelude to developing a sense of yourself as a subject. It is a paradoxical moment too, since this growing sense of oneself depends on outside objects (mirrors, both literal and social), and a recognition of some of the conventions of linguistic representation (you have to recognise the image as the image of yourself). Ironically, then, people become aware of themselves as individual subjects as a result of relationships that are objective, meaning both 'outside' and unknown to the subject.

This is not very dissimilar to the notion of 'interpellation' or 'hailing' in Althusser (1977) which we have discussed before (there is an online reading guide if you need a quick refresher). However, Williamson (1987) suggests that for Lacan, the sense of paradox, of having a split identity, of realising that subjectivity is incomplete, remains to haunt the subject for the rest of its life, so we are never fully and safely interpellated. It is this incompleteness, this sense of 'lack', that impels the subject to represent the world in 'the Imaginary', roughly a subjective set of experiences which act as a substitute for proper knowledge of the social and linguistic world.

Second, and with a much more obvious connection to sexual politics, there is the famous discussion of the Oedipal phase. Again the basics are well known. The male infant relates initially to his mother as the most significant other in his life, but this cosy dual relationship is interrupted by the reassertion of the authority of his father. In Freud, this crucial moment has very important psychological consequences, since it is through this little drama that male infants discover that they are not the centre of the universe, but are subject to authority relations to which they must submit. A new kind of adult personality needs to be developed to take this into account, although some of us may not have made it that far. As is also well known, this can lead to accusations of androcentricity in Freud, since the discussion seems to be based entirely upon the male personality, while the female personality was analysed largely as a kind of afterthought.

Lacan rereads the Oedipal phase to make it a key moment of discovery of the whole set of external symbolic constraints and regulations which the father represents. In the infantile mind, the power of the father depends on his possession of 'the phallus'. As Merck explains, some readers of Lacan have argued that this recognition of the power of the phallus is based on an empirical observation of the father's penis, and the mother's lack of it, but other exponents have denied this biological basis of the power of the phallus as a symbol. However, it is at this moment that the emerging infant subject experiences the first demonstration of crucial gender differences at the very level of the symbolic itself. Males have the power to wield the Symbolic (when spelled with a capital letter, this term refers to the whole area of culture and law), while females demonstrate only their otherness through 'lack'.

The Oedipal phase and the mirror phase both continue to haunt the activities of the subject, in an imaginary way. Much modern culture offers thinly disguised experiences traceable to these infantile dramas. Indeed, for a large number of film critics, allusions to Oedipal scenes are the main impulses driving forward many conventional films and stories, demonstrated, for example, in the 'coming of age' theme, found in countless westerns, war films, social commentaries, youth films and road movies.

## 'Screen theory'

The example I know best turns on a particular theoretical movement in film theory. We have already hinted at this movement, which is commonly known as 'Screen theory' because of its widespread dissemination in the influential British film journal Screen. One of the online reading guides discusses in some detail one general application of Screen theory in the influential debates about realism inaugurated by Colin MacCabe (in Bennett et al. 1981). We have summarised this debate before: the argument is that realist films help to construct a sense of subjectivity for the viewer that closely resembles the mechanisms of the mirror phase.

MacCabe explains that the turn towards psychoanalysis was prompted by a Screen editorial in 1974, which recommended that version of Freud which describes the construction of the subject: '. . . the entry of the small infant into language and society and the methods by which it learns what positions, as subject, it can take up' (MacCabe in Bennett et al. 1981: 226). The problem of sexual difference happens to be a decisive moment for the entry into the Symbolic – 'the whole cultural space which is structured, like language, through a set of differences and oppositions'. Such an entry must entail repression of the mechanisms that construct the subject in the first place.

There is a fundamental misrecognition involved in the successful use of language that makes it seem as if the subject constructs the discourse. The Freudian unconscious becomes an effect of language in which this happens, the process in which the subject objectifies him- or herself in language, moving from speaking subject to an objective presence. Verbal slips indicate cases where there is still a gap between 'what was said and what the conscious subject intended to say' (MacCabe in Bennett et al. 1981: 226), pointing to a wider distance between the subject that uses language and the subject experienced as an object. 'In this distance there is opened a gap which is the area of desire' (MacCabe in Bennett et al. 1981: 226).

What misrecognition about language amounts to is the tendency of the ego to try to read only one signified as present in the metaphor, and to try to end arbitrarily a signifying chain (to control and close down the flux of language, as it were, to aspire to impose unique meanings on signifiers). Lacan's 'function of desire' is found in those aspects of language that are beyond consciousness. 'It is clear that the classic realist text . . . guarantees the position of the subject exactly outside any articulation – the whole text works on the concealing of the dominant discourse as articulation – instead the dominant discourse presents itself exactly as the presentation of objects to the reading subject' (MacCabe in

Bennett et al. 1981: 227). In other words, the material presented in film looks as if it is just a series of 'objects' for the viewer to make sense of by imposing personal meanings, but this is an illusion and the meanings are 'structured in' all along. Some elements do manage to escape even this articulation, in the filmic equivalent of verbal slips. These are mere 'moments of subversion', and they usually offer no serious challenge to the overall structured meanings. What are needed instead, if you are into revolutionary politics, are whole strategies of subversion.

Realist films have a characteristic narrative structure for MacCabe (elaborated in the online reading guide to this article), where a number of plausible interpretations of events are demonstrated on screen, say through the speeches or activities of the central characters. Eventually, though, the narrative goes on to present a privileged view of events, sometimes through a demonstration of the limits of the characters' interpretations. This privileged view claims to depict reality itself, and is the only version of events that is not associated with a specific character (sometimes an all-powerful and off-screen narrator carries this view, at other times the combination of images and words triumphantly demonstrates it). In one example admired by MacCabe – the film *Klute* – the main characters are about to form a relationship, but we hear on the soundtrack what the female one 'really' thinks, as she confesses to her psychoanalyst that she is not ready for a long-term commitment. We knowledgeable viewers 'knew' or guessed that already from our privileged positions as all-seeing observers.

The actual specific views depicted as reality are usually the familiar elements of ideology – that 'human nature' cannot be denied, that sexy blondes are a disruptive influence, that the West is far superior to the East, and so on. However, the major effect of a realist film is to convince viewers that they are knowledgeable subjects who have somehow used 'their' experience to come to (or 'discover') the conclusions that the film itself has presented. We leave a realist film wisely nodding and congratulating ourselves on being right in our experience. It is some Lacanian 'lack' ('desire') which impels us to do so, to try to make sense of the film, and to experience pleasure when the film finally does it in a way which we can think of as 'ours'.

However, the main application of *Screen* theory that bears on feminist work concerns the famous article by Mulvey (1975; and again there is an online reading guide to this work and the most important subsequent modifications of it). Mulvey's analysis of mainstream Hollywood films offered a breakthrough in feminist work because it went beyond the usual demonstration of how women are stereotyped in film. Such stereotyping is easily detectable, of course, but its effects can be denied, or countered with (pretty frequent) examples of representations of non-stereotyped women. There is also a certain circularity and banality in endlessly demonstrating that women are stereotyped in Hollywood films: everyone is stereotyped, and probably has to be if popular films are to represent social reality in a way which viewers can recognise.

What Mulvey (1975) offered was a new form of analysis that looked not at representations as such, but at narratives and signifying systems. In her case, the particular Freudian theory that was used involved his analysis of scopophilia or 'peeping', the sexual pleasure gained from looking at people (mostly men looking at women), especially where the victims are unaware they are being watched. The very way the story was told reflected similar male pleasures and interests, Mulvey argued, and this is seen best in a system of 'looks' (rather similar to the Foucauldian notion of controlling 'gazes'). The way the camera looks at the characters, especially the females, clearly demonstrates this male control over storytelling. Less obviously, the way the characters look at each other indicates the same thing for Mulvey, delivering a central place to male characters, emotions, interests and narratives, adding the pleasures of identification to the scopophilic ones. As with MacCabe, much of this work is concealed from the viewer in realism. The obvious pleasures of involvement in the narrative absorb the viewer, while the less respectable scopophilic ones are smuggled in. The spectators (even female ones) have no choice but to adopt this male gaze, unconsciously adopting a fundamentally gendered system of visualising the world. Again, this whole process is taken as a model explaining how people come to use gendered forms of communication in applications that far exceed mainstream Hollywood films.

As Merck (1987) points out in the *Screen* 'special' on 'difference' (and see the online reading guide to this issue), this initial Mulvey analysis has also been heavily criticised, basically for attempting to reduce the many meanings and forms of signification in mainstream films to this single process of developing a male gaze. Both films and spectators' reactions to them are likely to be far more complex, it could be argued. Similar points are made against MacCabe's work on realism, and, indeed against the whole Lacanian project to reduce complex processes such as the emergence of subjectivity to particularly allegedly significant psychological moments or phases.

In Williamson's (1987) excellent critique, also in the *Screen* 'special', a major incoherence is identified in Lacan's work. We might illustrate this by considering problems arising when trying to explain how it is that actual viewers manage to experience what it is that films intend. The main problem is that viewers are supposed to be completely passive and unable to see the workings of the film that deliver effects of knowledge to them, but they are also credited with enough capacity to recognise the message of the film, to 'apply' it to their lives outside, and, indeed, to learn from it. I think this incoherence affects a great deal of cultural analysis, while I am here – Disney visitors are supposed to be complete 'cultural dopes', entirely manipulated by the narratives of the theme park, and yet at the same time to be capable of applying Disney values to their own experiences through some act of active interpretation.

Much subsequent work has gone into attempting to show how audiences may take up a number of other stances towards films. Mulvey herself, in a later piece (Mulvey 1999), suggested that it is possible for female spectators to take a more active stance in identifying with some of the more rebellious women depicted in films, but this was still a 'transgression', and such spectators felt out of place. Female characters who were allowed to break out of the passivity of the male gaze usually ended in being punished for their transgressions in some way. They were killed or left friendless, for example.

This kind of pessimism is characteristic, in fact, of the Lacanian perspective. After all, the tendency to categorise underdogs as 'other' is very deeply rooted indeed, both in language and other symbolic or cultural processes, and in universal psychological processes which play a major part in the formation of subjectivity. There is almost no space for anything other than deep and unconscious conformity to these processes. In this way, a familiar fate seems to have unfolded for political activists interested in trying to harness powerful social theory in order to achieve their goals. The conclusions that follow from theoretical pursuits seem to be ruling out the very activism that inspired the theoretical endeavours in the first place.

According to Merck (1987), there was yet a third position for Mulvey (see the online reading guide to Mulvey), which saw a space for feminist politics after all, since there was always a small but uncontrolled moment in the process of switching from one binary to another. The metaphorical equivalent is the day of misrule in medieval carnival, the day when values are inverted, and where there is some space for critical thinking, before the normal order resumes again. This ever-present space deployed in narratives (usually to add suspense) can permit women to seize a similar opportunity to create meanings of their own.

This final move has also had considerable echoes in feminist politics. Indeed, the invaluable Merck (1987) offers a number of solutions to the depressing conclusions apparently offered by Lacanian work. An obviously appealing one is to attempt to develop all-female utopias, or versions of them where males cease to hold any particular significance, even as providers of sperm (artificial reproduction techniques of various kinds might be welcomed here). This is associated with the work of the 'radical feminist' Shulemith Firestone, in particular, according to Merck. There are other possibilities too:

(a) to celebrate fully oppositional female difference;
(b) to concede full biological duality (but struggle for women nevertheless);
(c) to multiply the categories of difference, including differences between women, in order to diminish the significance of a single over-arching difference;
(d) to try to preserve difference, while criticising the inherent dualism of the position (attributed to Derrida – whom we discuss briefly in Chapter 13);
(e) to try to split the psychic process of sexual differentiation from the semiotic processes of identity and otherness. In this way the male/not-male distinction would be dethroned as the major one, permitting more positive notions of women as 'other than not-male', rather than 'other and not-male' (Merck 1987: 7). Merck mentions the work of Plaza here especially, but it is fair to say that many other feminists have seen this as the way forward, and have

developed projects to recapture the possibilities offered by language to multiply and celebrate other kinds of difference. We develop this option with Butler (below).

We might be able to trace some of these alternatives in the film work produced (and directed) by Mulvey. The film I know best is *Amy*, the account of the life of the famous woman flyer Amy Johnson, undertaken in collaboration with Peter Wollen. The piece starts with a discussion among 'ordinary women' about what is known about the life of Amy Johnson, and their reactions to Mulvey's film. When we move off into telling the story proper, the camera is not allowed to linger and gaze at the main character, who often appears off-centre or partially out of shot. The story is told mainly by reading (fictionalised?) pieces of Amy's own writing, such as letters and diaries, rather than by imposing some conventional male narrative of adventure and heroic death. Viewers are constantly aware that they are watching a film, signalled in the classic 'avant-garde' ways: the camera moves obtrusively, scenes are edited obtrusively, realism is abandoned, the mechanisms of film-making are exposed, viewers are encouraged to take an active role in discussing the film, and so on.

This style may be unpopular with viewers at first, but it is clearly necessary in any project that wants to break with male representations, distinctions and narratives, and is one example of the connections developed between feminists and the 'avant-garde' movements in film. Both seek to overthrow conventional ways of story-telling deliberately, for political reasons, and both try to develop alternative forms of expression. Both also attempt to break that comforting passivity that can grip viewers of a Hollywood film as they sit back and let the movie do all the work. It is this that probably causes most hostility from unprepared viewers exposed to this sort of work.

## Out of the Lacanian bind

Humm (1992; and see the online reading guide) has a useful section on similar attempts to celebrate difference and 'excess' in feminist writing and in exhortations to encourage women to speak out in various ways. If women are different, they should not apologise or be afraid to speak: their writings and speech should be seen not as inferior, but as just 'different'. Similarly, if they need to be contained so restrictively by the logic and binary categories of the symbolic order, this should lead to a celebration of their polymorphousness and power to threaten men and their control of the Symbolic. In the case of Kristeva (an example of her work is collected in Humm 1992), although she is by no means an orthodox 'feminist', the Lacanian argument that language is inherently combined with male domination, as in the description of the entry into the Symbolic, suggests a form of resistance after all. We should look instead for forms of expression that pre-date the mirror phase, suggests Kristeva, drawing upon a pre-lingual source of making meaning, the 'semiotic chora'. The power of this infantile form of signifying can often be tapped by poetry and avant-garde expressions.

Some excellent overall criticisms of the entire project to use Lacan and psychoanalysis to grasp otherness can be found also in a famous essay by Butler *Gender Trouble, Feminist Theory and Psychoanalytic Discourse* (published in several places – I read it in Nicholson 1990; there is an online reading guide as well). In what follows, I have condensed quite a few pages of close argument into some main points, and added some comments of my own.

Butler's work could well be described as a critical interrogation of the whole chain of argument involved in the psychoanalytic approaches. At each point in the chain, there are clear signs of a certain amount of manoeuvring and persuasion, a selectivity that is never fully justified, for example. The chain as a whole can best be seen as an entire narrative, where each individual link draws support from its neighbours. As Butler points out very neatly, feminists, of all people, ought to be particularly suspicious of narrative chains of argumentation like this, and demand to know which aspects of the overall text have been omitted by squashing it all into a neat story.

Let us begin with the privileged position given to the unconscious in psychoanalysis. Any sociologists among you might have already found the argument difficult to sustain that some infantile happenings, arising before the development of language, can have such a permanent effect on the rest of our adult lives. A great deal is claimed for rather limited infantile encounters like primal scenes, for example, which may only happen once: can the whole gradual development of sexuality, its pleasures and its cultural refinements really be explained by these allegedly powerfully determining events? What is worse, the Freudians themselves seem to disagree about what exactly are the determining events. It is the Oedipal scene for some, the mirror phase for others, the early bisexual phase, different versions of the female Oedipal trajectory, the work on fantasy, and so on.

In many cases, everything seems to turn upon what must be rather fleeting moments. It is really hard to know what to make of arguments about the differences between male and female sexual pleasures depending on female infants happening to glimpse male genitals, for example (a gloss on an argument in Stacey (1987) to explain the residual homosexual pleasures in women's unconscious minds). Feminists have turned to the unconscious, quite understandably, as offering a potential source of unity among women, and they have also been interested in bending powerful theoretical models to their particular interests, but this is hardly a sufficient justification for placing so much emphasis on such an elusive and much-debated concept.

The second such link in the particular chain we have been investigating, which is not particularly singled out in Butler's essay, is the choice of film to carry these major manipulative processes into everyday life. Again, it is quite understandable that film should be chosen, since it is with film that *Screen* primarily concerned itself, and there is quite an appealing similarity between watching a movie and having a dream, which permits connections to be made immediately with Freudian theory. But should the professional enthusiasms of feminist film theorists be given so much general weight in discussions of the entire field of gender, sexuality and pleasure? How important was the urge to make a theoretical contribution to long-standing debates in film theory itself, as an example of what I have insisted is the important 'academic' dimension to many of these theoretical and political interventions?

The arguments defending the central place of film are curiously circular, or based on rather dubious assumptions. Both (early) Mulvey and MacCabe simply assert that the existence of a major industry – Hollywood – guarantees the place of ideology in films. For that matter, unspecified wider ideological and social institutions in American capitalism simply must determine this role for Hollywood. It all makes sense, but in a rather self-justifying way: the existence of general ideologies somehow lends wider importance to the search for them through textual analysis of films, and, at the same time, the existence of ideologies in films helps support the general thesis that they saturate the whole of society.

A more 'applied' point can be made too, relating to academic politics again. Lacan's heavyweight and impressively Parisian general theory is used to under-pin particular analyses of films and to permit the rise to power of a faction within an important journal (*Screen*). This tendency manifested itself in several validating panels for academic courses too, as well as enabling the develop-ment of a profitable 'research programme'. Conversely, *Screen* theory, in its turn, revitalised and popularised Lacanian theory, especially in Britain, since *Screen* theorists simply insisted we read Lacan (by no means an easy task) if we wanted to be taken seriously.

Film is rather an odd choice of medium. To be fair, Mulvey comes to recognise this and moves to consider other forms of popular culture, carnivals in particu-lar, but these are also chosen because they happen to illustrate theoretical themes rather than because they are clearly widespread or popular. When one considers other dominant forms of mass media, such as television, or, above all, the Web, the possibilities arise of much more activism on the part of the subject, with many more chances to 'enter' the text. Indeed, the texts themselves are much more incoherent and complex, much less ordered by some underlying meta-narrative.

Cyberfeminists, especially Turkle (1995) and Haraway (1991), overflow with excess and optimism about the possibilities of electronic communication. It per-mits people to extend and manipulate their identities, to find common cause in electronic coalitions and associations (such as those constructing feminist e-zines), to reflect upon the many taken-for-granted and apparently naturalistic boundaries and divisions not only between men and women, but also between people and machines, or even people and animals. It is true, of course, that there is still a debate about whether gendered identities are quite as flexible as this (see Scott 1998 for a summary).

Another strange omission springs to mind. It seems curious to spend so much time analysing the rather refined and indirectly sexualised pleasures of watching films, and to ignore completely the studies of actual sexual conduct between people. Brake (1982) has a collection of some highly relevant sociological material, ranging from the rather comically positivist attempts by early sexologists like Kinsey, or Masters and Johnston, who were interested in measuring and quantifying the behaviours involved in sexual activity, to symbolic interactionist pieces. In a famous example of the latter, Plummer insists that actual sexual behaviour is affected mostly by cultural processes, performances and choices, and is hardly 'biological' at all. Everything can be sexualised, he argues, and, at the same time, everything can be de-sexualised, such is the power of sexual fantasy and cultural creativity. To take an actual example, a photograph of a football team can be sexualised if the spectator is also fantasising about having sex with the players. A male encountering a naked woman lying on a couch can be de-sexualised (and perhaps must be) by both parties if the encounter is a medical examination. This piece, it is worth pointing out, pre-dates by a couple of decades the discovery of sexuality as performance by Butler.

Of course, this work is about sexuality, which may not be the same thing as gender. The terms are connected together rather oddly in psychoanalytic feminism, according to Butler. Gender determines sexuality, usually in a binary way, and is itself determined by sex, even by genital difference, in the more biologistic versions. The whole thing turns, for Butler, on some model of interiority and exteriority, rather akin to the Christian notion of a division between bodies and souls. The Freudian unconscious is something inside, which determines what goes on outside. Butler herself wants to reverse this conception, arguing, with Foucault, that bodies are inscribed by disciplinary practices that are then internalised. In other words, the causal flows might work in quite a different direction to produce some coherent 'inner' personality in the first place.

As we have hinted already, this provides Butler with much more room for manoeuvre than is the case with the rather rigid options of psychoanalytic feminism and its major critics. It is not only sexual pleasure but also gender itself that might be considered as a performance, Butler insists. Like all cultural performances, gendered identities can be highly ambiguous, with much being made of surface appearances complementing or contradicting deeper identities. Butler chooses as an example the drag artist, pointing out that a number of identities are being played with here. Is the pleasure rooted in the confusion between the outward female appearance and the inner maleness of the performer, or in something deeper still, a person who really wants to be female but who is trapped in a male body?

I am reminded immediately of the famous study of the transsexual Agnes (Garfinkel 1967), which tends to make very similar points about gender as performance, detailing the ways in which Agnes learns to be 'a proper woman', initially in order to convince doctors that s/he qualifies for a sex-change operation. (There is an online reading guide to this study on the website.) Gender as a performance can easily be tracked through the work of Goffman too. I am not trying to steal feminists' thunder here, of course, but trying to point out that much of the abstract speculation about gender found in psychoanalytic theories might have profited by an encounter with some of the more detailed and applied work – much as Fraser (1989) argued in the case of male social theory earlier.

# 10　Foucault

We have considered the rival claims of marxist and Weberian conceptions of pol-itics in earlier chapters (such as Chapter 5). We can now move on by considering some of the work of Foucault, initially as a contribution to those debates too. Perhaps the best example for our purposes here is the famous work on the development of the prison system *Discipline and Punish* (Foucault 1977; there is an online reading guide on this piece too).

Briefly, Foucault argues that we cannot simply assume that the precise devel-opment of the prison system either follows the wishes of powerful groups in the judiciary and legislature or exhibits the unfolding of a process of rationalisation. Against both arguments, he insists that, additionally, there were important wide-ranging debates with a number of philosophers, commentators and reformers about the system of punishment developed in modern societies such as France. The system of punishment in France did indeed change radically around the beginning of the nineteenth century, and become much more focused on the use of prison. Formerly, a great deal was made of public spectacles of punishment instead, such as grotesque executions (which Foucault describes in some detail), or the public departure of convicted prisoners from Paris in a chain gang, an occasion for a kind of carnival, we are told. The new system offered instead imprisonment, and, for the first time, a policy of trying to reform the convict (or, later, rescue delinquents from their own criminality).

However, it would be a mistake to see that changes in the prison system simply followed changes in the more general conceptions of law and punish-ment, as a Weberian might suggest. There were general forces at work, including the rise to power of a rational bourgeoisie to replace the former hold of personal monarchy. That monarchy organised cruel and terroristic public punishment spectacles as a result of what was perceived as a direct challenge to royal and thus divine authority, but this did not appeal at all to the rational, calculating, individualistic morality of the bourgeoisie, who expected criminals literally to 'pay off their debts' to society.

Foucault wants to insist that the development of the prison system took place at its own level, as it were, and, far from being a mere consequence or effect of these general changes, it managed to generate its own effects on the whole debate about discipline and punishment. The arguments here are not too difficult. At the most obvious level, it would be pointless for any reformers to advocate a system of the gradual reform of convicts if there were no technology or machine to deliver these desired goods in the first place. As an aside, I am reminded of Kuhn's point in his history of natural science (1962), that scientific progress would not have been possible without a series of dedicated engineers and instrument makers designing bits of apparatus like balances or laboratory vessels, let alone optical lenses, that made accurate observation and experiment possible.

The real contribution of a number of reformers was not to argue about prison in a general sense, but to try to devise a practical prison system that would be cost-effective. In particular, reformers like the English utilitarian Jeremy Bentham, or the inventors of the US penitentiary system, or of similar models in France, were able to demonstrate that by the careful use of systems of punishment and reward, supported by a 24-hour surveillance system and the systematic use of observation and record-keeping, convicts could have their behaviour shaped towards reform of their characters. These principles were actually to be built into the design of the modern prison, such as Bentham's Panopticon, which featured a central observation tower enabling guards to look into each individual cell, while remaining invisible themselves. There was also a very detailed set of prescriptions of the sort of useful work the convicts might be asked to do. Rewards and punishments varied systematically according to whether they conformed. The detail extended even to the types of beds and mattresses that prisoners might be given, either if they made progress or slid back into criminal ways.

Foucault goes on to suggest that designs for prisons like this had a very widespread currency in the nineteenth century. For example, the people-processing technologies involved had several uses outside the prison system. They could be used to train soldiers, for example, or to educate children, and Bentham also became an early advocate of the UK Victorian 'monitorial system', expressed in his design for an ideal school, Chrestomathia (Bentham 1983). Foucault is not prepared to say which of these technologies and their applications came first, denying some simple cause and effect mechanism here as well.

The final basis for the claim that we need to look at institutions and how they work specifically and in detail is that they do actually create some new concepts of their own, arising from their practices. (Foucault wants to insist that these are new 'objects' rather than mere concepts.) In the case of prisons, a new conception of individuality was solidified. The internally disciplined subject emerged, someone who is aware that he or she might be seen at any time and who always acts accordingly, not relying on someone to tell him or her what to do, but anticipating what that invisible observer might make of his or her behaviour. This form of human subject makes the ideal student, worker, soldier or, indeed, hospital patient. To refer back to an earlier discussion of ours (in Chapter 1), this is how the general process of 'hailing' in state apparatuses really happens, only after someone has actually invented a social machine aimed deliberately at creating a type of person or subject.

More specifically, prisons are also responsible for creating an important category of criminality ('illegality' is Foucault's more general and interesting term). Try as it might, the most systematic set of laws and codes could never completely abolish types of illegality, of course, because people can always bend the rules. Indeed rule-bending was sometimes sanctified by custom and practice, or at least tolerated (smuggling, for example, or perhaps, these days, traffic offences). Some people in particular have sufficient power to do this systematically and mostly manage to escape punishment for it (such as powerful businesspeople who evade taxes).

Left unchecked, such illegality could come to form a glaring contradiction with the basic principle of the law, which is that it applies universally to everyone, and is only legitimate if it does so. It is clear that illegality has to be dealt with, by making certain aspects of it particularly worthy of punishment. Foucault is not the first to notice that this tends to be the illegality practised by the weak and powerless, like male working-class juveniles. This group can serve as a kind of scapegoat, a representative of all illegality, and their punishment can help uphold the legitimacy of the law, and thus conceal its weakness and contradictions elsewhere. At perhaps his most conspiratorial, Foucault suggests that this suppressed social function is the main reason why prisons persist: after all, everyone knows that their actual record in reforming convicts and preventing recidivism is pretty unimpressive.

Prison came to be seen as a particularly suitable punishment and corrective for these juvenile 'delinquents', people who had embarked upon criminal careers for a variety of social and psychological reasons, as well as moral ones. These were the clients who would be particularly likely to have their behaviour shaped in a positive direction by being removed from those social influences, subjected to various psychological tests (to sort out the 'imbeciles' from the morally corrupt, for example), and then exposed to a system of rewards and punishments to re-socialise them. Two important points follow from this specialism, according to Foucault:

1   It is clear that the prison system encouraged the growth of psychology and various social sciences such as sociology, and eventually criminology itself. I am using cautious words such as 'encouraged' deliberately, avoiding any simple notions of causes and effects. What prisons did was to reinforce these disciplines, lending them power and immediacy, because they were seen to be helpful not only in solving the problem of crime, but also by offering working laboratories, where researchers could observe human beings in detail and experiment on them.

2   At this point, the prison system was able to affect the system of law itself. Formerly, the law seemed to operate with fairly simple notions to explain criminality, but the prison regime showed the practical importance of psychological and sociological knowledge about the offender. Given that judges awarded sentences on the basis that imprisonment would cure people of their criminality, it soon became apparent that they should consider psychological and sociological elements themselves, by taking the advice of

experts before they handed down sentences. For Foucault, this was an important change which stripped judges and officials of large amounts of power, and redistributed it to other agencies – prisons, to be sure, but also social work agencies, educational agencies and what might be called the follow-up services dealing with ex-convicts.

## Foucault's theoretical object

We have looked at some of the more 'applied' analysis of Foucault, but we can now turn to some of his more general work. Our interest is in politics in this part of the book, and we have seen how institutions like a prison, hospital or school can be seen as undertaking important political tasks. In the most obvious sense of 'politics', they helped to produce docile, self-disciplined subjects, while in a more specialist sense developing an institution to bring those subjects into being. We have reason to be grateful that political forces have brought into being institutions like prisons, because without them, Foucault thinks, modern human sciences would not have developed in the way that they have.

Turning to a more general issue, where do the various intellectual and social resources come from before they get manipulated, fixed or condensed in specific institutions? We know, for example, from Foucault's work on the prison that that institution gave specific concrete emphasis to two academic disciplines, one based on the law (jurisprudence), and one rooted in the human sciences, especially psychology. In the case of the clinic, it is the disciplines of jurisprudence and medicine. In schooling, the human sciences combine in various ways to focus on the individual, and the social circumstances which affect education. We also know that these institutions helped to embody and thus to develop other academic disciplines: the prison led to an emphasis on juvenile delinquency, which eventually led to the creation of a special subject to study it, criminology; and the clinic similarly led to modern psychiatry. I have also suggested in my own homely criticisms of Foucault that he might well have paid attention to the role of the modern university, and its attendant publishing institutions and regulating mechanisms, in the creation of new academic disciplines like the familiar ones we see today.

The question to answer, though, is whether all academic disciplines arose like this, or just modern ones. If they all did arise from institutions like this, then there is nothing special about academic disciplines in this particular sense. However, if they arise in different circumstances, they must be exempt to some extent from the influence of institutional politics. In order to answer this question, we might well turn to one of Foucault's more general and abstract pieces on the 'archaeology' of knowledge (Foucault 1974; and see the online reading guide). Before we do so, however, we have to realise that this particular theoretical work probably represents only one stage in Foucault's overall thinking (see Dreyfus and Rabinow 1982).

We might well begin to grasp what this lengthy, complex and highly technical book is all about by pursuing the methodological issue hinted at in the title – how do you undertake an archaeology of knowledge, and why should you instead of, say, offering a more conventional history or a sociology or politics? One problem, clearly, is that these are disciplines themselves, and Foucault's project is to investigate how disciplines of all kinds happen to appear and to take the shape that they do, so that operating with these conventional disciplines would be too limited. Instead, we should proceed more or less as archaeologists do when they excavate, say, a buried city.

To pursue this in a common-sense way, an archaeologist is likely to find a number of bits and pieces, fragments of buildings and one or two other traces lying on the surface. Archaeological technique involves the careful excavation of those surface traces, to uncover what lies beneath. Imagine an archaeologist coming across the site of the pyramids in Egypt after they had been virtually buried in sand, leaving only the top layers above the surface. Careful archaeological investigation would uncover more and more of the structure of the pyramids until they were all revealed, together with the platform on which they stood, the quarries from which the stone was cut, other ancient monuments such as the Sphinx, and so on. It is this burrowing away to get at deeper and deeper levels that Foucault proposes we use as a method to uncover the structure of academic disciplines, using contemporary documents exactly as surface traces.

This is not just going to be an investigation of simple 'facts' lying around on the surface. The objects themselves are partially constructed by theories. Anyone excavating a site has to have some sort of model of the object that is lying beneath the surface. Indeed, theoretical ideas of what lies beneath may play as decisive a role as empirical discovery; if we wanted to emphasise this, we might well insist that theory 'constructs' the objects it investigates. Theoretical decisions also play a part in deciding where to stop excavation as well as where to start it: in deciding which objects, buildings and artefacts really do belong to each other, for example. Should the site be interpreted primarily as a religious one, a social one or an economic one? And, of course, politics is important, from the need to organise permission to excavate in the first place, to the need to fight off rival academic teams in order to be the first ones to discover something really important – in this sense politics also 'constructs', or perhaps at least empowers, permits or limits, archaeological activity.

There are indeed formations that lie at a 'deeper' level than the modern academic disciplines we know. There are discourses, for example. Those discourses have themselves been produced, however, by 'discursive formations'. At the most general level of all are entities called 'epistemes'. It is important to realise that these different objects can be connected in several ways, so that a single discourse might be shared by several disciplines, for example, but generally we can see this in simplified diagrammatic form as in Figure 10.1.

There are several other beasts in the Foucault bestiary that have defied my

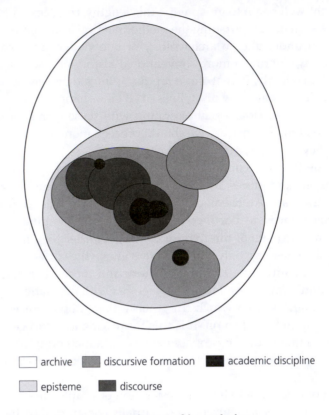

archive ◻︎  discursive formation ▦  academic discipline ■

episteme ▨  discourse ■

**Figure 10.1 Foucault – structures and forms of knowledge**

efforts to think of nice, simple ways to illustrate them, even though they play a crucial role in his work. There are, for example, various kinds of 'fields' or 'domains'. These are not easily drawn because they are implied, or referred to, quite often by an activity. Thus there is, for example, an 'enunciative field', to which an enunciation always refers. Similarly, a discourse relates or refers to various pre-discursive or even non-discursive fields. These fields are referred to by Foucault to make an important point, which is that neither enunciations nor discourses nor statements are simple linguistic objects. That is, they are not simply words relating to things, nor are they signs whose meaning derives solely from relations to other signs, as in structural linguistics. Enunciations, for example, refer not to simple referents but to much broader 'referentials', such as 'laws of possibility'. Discourses, similarly, always involve relations to objects, to subject positions, to other elements in a field, and to material institutions. This is not a simple relation, such as when words describe some existing reality or collection of objects; discourses are also 'practices that systematically form the objects of which they speak', they are practices with positive functions of their own (which have their own effects, offering transformations, linking or enunciation), and they are also focused by, and intertwined with, strategies, offering 'points of choice'.

Another term that crops up towards the end of Foucault's book is 'positivity' and even 'configurations of positivities'. The term 'positivity' seems to have a general meaning, referring to anything that is made positive or concrete, something that appears as a result of a strategy or practice. Foucault also uses the term, and flirts with its connection with positivism, to deny that any transcendental level of analysis (of 'human progress', for example) is required to explain the emergence of discourses of their objects. In this sense, any object more concrete than an archive is a positivity. The term is used in another discussion as well, this time to explain the difference between science and ideology: broadly, disciplines have to go through a number of stages, or cross a number of thresholds, which basically involves an increasing amount of formalisation, codification and abstraction. In this way they achieve a special kind of positivity – they become sciences.

Finally, my attempts to illustrate some of the possible combinations between the discrete objects at each level of positivity are also highly limited. I have tried to show how different discourses might coexist in the same discursive formation, for example, both semi-independently, and as a series of overlapping objects. Foucault's chosen preference throughout his work here is to show how difference and dispersion dominate the discussion of discourses, and perhaps I should have illustrated this more clearly, possibly by even using different shapes. It is clearly impossible to draw some of the other relationships between the objects concerned – how one might transform into the other, for example.

In other words, Figure 10.1 also sketches out what might be thought of as only the structure of academic disciplines, which are produced, as in structuralism generally, from deeper structures of knowledge. However, this is not entirely a structuralist analysis, because Foucault wants to add some important elements of dynamism. First we have to reject a number of simple conventional links to explain the shifts in level. Positivities do not appear as a result of the specific actions of a dominant class, for example, which would operate in the usual way in terms of taking all the possible discourses (say) that might be generated, and making sure that the ones that were actually generated somehow reflected their interest or their conceptions of the world. Humanist approaches might see the structures at the deeper levels as representing some sort of human potential, some general human quality, such as the need to know, and the specific discourses would simply be tangible products produced by this underlying need in certain circumstances. The model here might be the common view of the novelist as a person who articulates more general themes in human consciousness. Both of these are too simple, says Foucault.

The reasons for this criticism are really rather interesting for our purposes in this chapter. Foucault wants to suggest that discourses, for example, have an 'effectivity' of their own, that is, that they can develop autonomously. This is put at its strongest when he is discussing whether or not external events, such as economic pressures or evolutionary tendencies, determine the shape of discourses. He says that they do not, because the discourses themselves contain rules about how to interpret external events; indeed, how and whether to relate to them at all. This clearly seems to imply that discourses develop under their own momentum, and that you need to study these aspects of development without referring to any external economic or political processes. In another series of discussions, however, Foucault seems uncertain about the existence of anything outside of discourses, usually referred to as the pre- or non-discursive. On the one hand, these do seem to have a separate existence and are things to which discourses relate, but, on the other, we cannot understand anything about these levels except through discourse, so, in this sense, they fall within discourses.

Now this in turn sounds like Idealism, which grants ideas some sort of reality and force of their own. Foucault wants to deny this interpretation too, however. Discourses are not just ideas, but ideas that have been brought into being, that have been 'enunciated'. There is quite a substantial section in his book on the process of enunciation, much of which involves an attempt to preserve enunciation as some special function of language against other linguistic traditions (and which therefore need not detain us here, rather to my relief, because I do not claim to understand much of it). The basic idea of enunciation is an interesting one, though, in that it refers to the moments in which silence turns into speech, as Foucault puts it, the moment of creation, when a discourse or discipline actually begins, enters the public realm, takes on a social life. This is a material practice for Foucault, not just a simple form of expression of intangible ideas. As a material practice, it is clearly going to be affected by a complex of rules, resources and constraints, some of which stem from discourses themselves, and some of which arise from external factors and forces. Foucault insists that some sort of concrete investigation is required, and that one cannot find some all-purpose principle of creation and then 'read off' the development of discourses from its operation.

As another example of the importance of material practices, Foucault refers to the importance of the 'archive', the location of these various forms of knowledge and language. And this carries the implication that someone has actually collected things into an archive, that this is not a natural, obvious or self-organising collection. Archives are maintained by the activities of archivists. Foucault even wants to insist that history is an active material practice, involving the systematic extraction or excavation of archives.

One final warning to avoid simple readings of Foucault lies in the reminder that as a French social theorist he is unlikely to support the usual Anglo-Saxon view that individuals are somehow the active forces in these practices. We have already seen him arguing, in his book on the prison, that the modern individual is an artefact. The same argument runs throughout this general treatise on knowledge. Whoever the agents are who engage in the practices of collecting archives and then excavating them, they are not independent and autonomous agents as we usually think of them; their work and activity are also affected by the objects that they study. At one stage, Foucault is almost implying the standard structuralist view that agents are simply bearers of these traditions of knowledge and language, with no autonomy.

Now the way I have described this piece of work leaves a number of important issues unresolved, and it will be no surprise to learn that there are several readings of Foucault's work. We should restrict ourselves to the implications for what counts as politics.

## Foucault and politics

We have already seen in this account that Foucualt seems to have extended the concept of politics in an interesting direction. He wants to define modern politics as a matter of producing self-regulating persons, for example, and goes on to examine the sort of institutional machines (organisations and discourses) that are responsible. It is obvious that this leads to the need to examine organisations closely in order to see how they work 'politically' in this general sense. However, it is also clear that discourses are implicated as well, even academic disciplines. We need to operate at a much more specific and 'micro' level than we did before (and we discuss some examples of 'micropolitical 'analysis in the next chapter). We also need to bear in mind that politics (the deployment of power) is not always negative but that it enables us to do creative work as well, create new objects of analysis and new (social) technologies.

For some people, Foucault has simply extended the notion of politics back into the very issues of the formation of academic disciplines and other forms of knowledge themselves; this reading clearly attends to the discussions of material practice that I have tried to summarise. This sort of reading is expressed, for example, in the more 'applied' work of Hargreaves (1986), who uses Foucault to build on the basic gramscian account of politics to develop an 'elaborated politics' which investigates not only organisations but also discourses (about recreation, health and fitness in this case). It is worth adding that one of Foucault's postmodernist critics, Baudrillard, also sees him principally as a theorist of politics – the redundancy of this kind of politics is the main reason for simply forgetting him, he says (Baudrillard and Lotringer 1987).

Foucault also seems to have been an influence in some of the discussions about marxism, and its own 'discursive turn' (one version of which I have discussed at greater length in Harris 1992). Here we turn to the implications for academic politics. Roughly, one Foucauldian line is that marxism itself is to be seen as a discourse along with its rivals. Anyone familiar with postmodernism might expect that this would also relativise marxism, that is, making it no better and no worse than these other discourses, and certainly not some privileged 'science'. However, without going that far, there are enough serious political implications as it is – the class struggle, for example, can no longer be seen as some real external event which marxism describes and explains, but rather must be seen as an object constituted by marxism itself. If marxists stopped speaking and writing about social class and the class struggle, would they continue to have any political significance? As an extension, is there anything to stop analysts writing about other kinds of social struggles as well, such as those involving gender, ethnic identity or green politics? This sort of argument led to some very interesting exchanges between those wishing to retain marxism's original emphasis and a group calling themselves 'postmarxists'.

However, other writers (such as Dreyfus and Rabinow 1982) see Foucault as leaving behind marxist notions of politics, and conventional French theory as well, for that matter. He is operating with a set of new and controversial theoretical objects and processes which are quite different from marxism (and structuralism and hermeneutics too). This sort of reading clearly attends more to the sections where the conventional positions are seen as too limited – economic factors as not decisive, structuralism as lacking an account of dynamics, discourses taking on a force of their own, and so on. Not all of the critics agree that these are 'better' objects and processes, of course, but it puts Foucault in a relation of dispersion and difference with marxism, and possibly feminism, rather than as someone merely trying to complete those approaches. We have already seen, in Chapter 8, that this work has provided feminists with several quite distinct options (and similar ones are on offer with marxism too, although we have not discussed them here).

## A homely example

To summarise, let us return to the complex arguments Foucault presents, but consider a homely example to try to indicate some of the issues and complexities. I hope I have not milked this too much, but imagine we are interested in playing electronic games. For players, the interest might focus exclusively on how to play them, which strategies and moves are best for getting through the various stages, and so on. If you were Foucault, though, you might be more interested in asking where these specific strategies or moves came from – what 'constitutes' them. This is by no means a normal question to ask, but it is a typically theoretical question.

You could begin by thinking about the role of individual persons. The specific strategies or moves you use come from you as an individual, and might be explained using suitable terms such as individual consciousness, personality, ability, and so on. However, such an answer could be fairly easily refuted, I suspect, using the standard arguments. You have almost certainly not thought of the strategies or moves on your own, but have discussed them with others, observed others, talked to others, read about games and tips, and so on. Another way of demonstrating the limits of an individualistic analysis might be to demonstrate that there are social patterns (gender, age, social class, ethnic origins) in the strategies and moves, which is what a sociologist might suggest. However, a particular argument relating to the discussion here would be to suggest that individuals can only really ever choose options provided by the game itself – your strategies and moves are best thought of as options within a menu of strategies and moves made available by the designers of the game. It is in this sense that you could argue that games at least constrain individual strategies and moves. If you had a taste for French philosophy, you might want to think that the structure of the game in a way 'produced' or 'constructed' these apparently individual strategies too.

The next stage for a Foucauldian analysis would be to investigate the structure of the specific game itself, and how it came about. What does the program that controls the game actually permit? How many moves and strategies are allowed? How did these moves and strategies come to be chosen as permissible, and why are some preferred over others? We might want to classify these rules of design – rules about objects, about movements, about rewards, and so on.

Even at this stage, the relevance of institutional, social and commercial forces might be apparent. The game would be designed to permit moves that are especially popular and pleasurable, which would rely upon some knowledge of popular culture and of the commercial potential of the game itself. I have no idea about how electronic games are actually designed, but I imagine that the programmers themselves at some stage have to engage in some discussion with marketing people, advertisers, legal specialists and financiers in order to turn their game from a set of ideas into a concrete product, and at this stage the characters are designed to be appealing and what they do is designed to resonate with the values of the likely customers.

No doubt, to those in the business, these commercial or cultural factors are seen as genuine constraints again, which have to be followed, at least at first, although a really popular and innovative game is probably in a good position to change commercial and cultural conventions as well. Further, games themselves have an effect on other games. We could even try to trace out these effects in a list of terms of possible 'transformations' (some games would copy earlier ones, and some would differentiate themselves totally from earlier ones; some games would try to incorporate earlier ones; some would try to alter the values or improve the techniques following some technical innovation; some new games would try to combine two earlier ones – and so on).

Most players wouldn't think about these issues, perhaps, but they are clearly important in explaining how games appear and are put on the market before the players themselves get hold of them. At this level, knowledge is shared around all the games designers and games producers. To ask a specifically Foucauldian question – how does the same basis of knowledge produce such widely different games?

Further levels of analysis are clearly possible as well. How did computer programming begin and develop? This sort of programming clearly provides the techniques and the rules of application as a kind of collective body of knowledge which game designers draw upon when they turn to the business of designing characters, moves, landscapes, rewards and penalties and all the other characteristics of the electronic game. It might be possible to comment on the linguistic structure of programming rules, their vocabulary, structure and syntax, or on their linguistic functions (how you design a sprite and add characteristics to it, to draw on my own highly limited knowledge for a moment).

Knowledge about programming can be used to develop a wide range of business, military or technical applications as well as games, so how did a set of techniques aimed at producing games come into existence? Once more, there would be an interestingly complex relation between games software and programming principles in general. On the one hand, I imagine that you need to stick to the rules of programming when you are writing games software, but, on the other, I suspect that the needs of games software specifically have led a number of programmers to think again about what might be possible in their programming languages. As with all the other complexities, no single general explanation is going to suffice – there is no simple evolutionary trend, class conspiracy or mystical force of self-expression that will tell you what happened in each case.

Finally, we might imagine what might happen if an historian of the future wanted to research these topics. There would simply be various documents left around in a number of collections for the historian to study. Those that had been collected and stored would obviously be a selection from all the materials that could have been stored, and would reflect the practices of the archivists themselves, acting not just as individuals but responding to the series of constraints and rules too. Some of these archives would be more general than others, some would follow the specific interests of collectors or businesses, or perhaps even academics. Our historian would want to read at some stage some of the sociologies, psychologies and economics of electronic games, and perhaps even root around in other archives to try to find parallels with the development of films, business programmes, records of youth culture or whatever. The actual history produced would clearly result from the practice of the historian, but, again, this would not just be the result of his or her individual personality, but would depend on all the other archiving activities, which are practices themselves too.

## Concluding remarks

Let us return to the substantive issue by reminding ourselves that Foucault's analysis was devoted to rather unusual institutions – prisons and clinics – at a particularly interesting time of European history. Of course, institutions like these, able to marshal and focus total power over individuals, still exist in our society, as Goffman's analysis of 'total institutions' indicates (Goffman 1968). The state is still able to confine people in total institutions where the most minute detail of their behaviour and life can be inspected and controlled, and experiments performed on the self, as Goffman puts it.

However, there are rather different sorts of organisations and institutions that dominate modern life which are not capable of marshalling this degree of power. Most of us spend our lives in these institutions, such as (day) schools, voluntary educational institutions, families or work organisations. For many writers, even these institutions exercise some degree of (political) control, and are therefore seen as Ideological State Apparatuses, hailing us as individuals, or as exercising hegemonic functions, or as offering us some kind of patriarchal order. However, it is clear that the political power they exercise is likely to be much less focused, much less systematic, and therefore much more variable in its effects than that of the total institutions described by Foucault.

We have already examined the idea that some kind of resistance to political power is endemic in modern pluralistic societies, in the CCCS and feminist traditions at least. There is a range of sociological work on life in modern organisations which points in the same direction, especially if we allow 'resistance' to mean a wide range of activities, not confined to outright opposition to the boss or to management, but including a range of avoidance techniques, or taking advantage of opportunities to impose your own goals and pursue your own activities, irrespective of what the organisation officially demands. This is the area of micropolitics, which we explore in the next chapter.

# 11 Politics in the 'Everyday'

In pursuit of the intention in the previous chapter to investigate micropolitics in more detail, we are going to shift the level of analysis now to consider life in specific organisations. We might well begin with educational organisations, since we are all familiar with them.

The interest in micropolitics builds on some early work that challenges the idea of organisations as dominated by 'rationality', as in the classic definitions of bureaucracy in Weber, for example. Studies of actual organisations soon indicated that what we might call 'official rationality' could be found in the lists of technical procedures, rules, job descriptions, contracts and other devices to organise and limit the roles of personnel. Familiar devices like the organisational chart might represent such an officially rational picture. In my own organisation, for example, this is quite a large diagram with the Principal at the top, three Assistant Principals immediately beneath him, a number of Deans or Heads of Faculty beneath them, then Heads of Department inside each faculty, and so on. A great deal of management time seems to be spent on trying to clarify the abstract responsibilities of each post-holder, such as deciding who should be responsible for the research policy or the teaching quality in each unit. Particular problems, requiring even more time to resolve, arise in trying to integrate new individuals or new responsibilities into this structure. Nevertheless, the claim seems to be that the organisation could not function without such a complex diagram.

In practice, though, a whole series of unofficial organisational rules and procedures operate as well. For example, particular post-holders are clearly more capable than others and seem to be able to become more powerful, and have more influence than their official title would suggest. It is even true to say that some underlings, possessing very little official power and responsibility, nevertheless have a significant influence on decision-making: they might be able to cut through the layers, and get to talk to or influence the Principal directly, for example. Sometimes it helps if they have a particular authority, a special claim to expertise, or if they are able to marshal powerful friends, even some outside the organisation, perhaps, to support their views.

There is a range of additional 'subjective' behaviours that goes on besides, or underneath, the official structures of power and responsibility. Sometimes, senior managers exceed their formal powers and sponsor, campaign against or otherwise show some favouritism or bias towards an underling. Alongside the

official system of rules and responsibilities, there exists a whole area of subjective judgement, personal opinion and feelings. Officially, these should have no
place at all in decision-making, but, of course, in many cases they do. I should
say I am no longer just describing my particular organisation here.

It is almost inevitable that this should happen, since technical rules and procedures are most unlikely to be able to cover all eventualities. The 'wilder' and
more unstable the organisation, the more personal and subjective judgement
will be required to extend and apply the official rules. There are two elements of
instability in educational organisations in the UK in particular, for example.
First, we are taking on more and more students, including some who come from
unconventional backgrounds, and, secondly, we are increasingly under pressure
from the external environment, from the government and from 'business'. In
these circumstances, it is not surprising that the official rules and regulations
tend to lag behind actual changes, leaving a kind of organisational gap that
must be bridged by judgement.

To give a concrete example of the first area of instability, more and more of
our students are 'mature', that is, over the age of 25. Regulations based on the
conduct and behaviour of 18- to 21-year-olds often fail to cover the sorts of
'problems' that these older students bring with them: many of the mature students will have children, for example, which produces all sorts of problems for
existing rules and regulations about attendance, or extenuating circumstances
for late submission of work. Having to stay home to look after a sick child is a
typical problem for mature students, but it tends not to be mentioned in the official lists of extenuating circumstances for conventional students. Mature
students tend to bring different cultural expectations into the college as well in
that they have often developed careers already, or have settled into the local area
fairly permanently. Both of these might affect the ways in which such students
weigh up the vocational value of degree courses, or the careers advice they
require.

As a quick example of the second kind of instability, I have lived through a
series of UK government demands for accountability in higher education.
Leaving aside the political pros and cons for a moment, these have led to different sorts of demands upon staff at the organisational level. Take the recent
decision to encourage lecturers to gain teaching qualifications, for example,
which has led to a high expectation, especially among young lecturers, that they
should develop particular kinds of certificated teaching expertise. In some ways,
this contradicted an earlier pressure to develop a steady output of significant
research and publication, which would be funded after grading by government
bodies. The impact of these decisions has started to appear finally in the formal
contracts that lecturers are offered that specifically request teaching qualifications or a good research record, but for a long time there was a turbulent state of
uncertainty among colleagues at the unofficial level about which to specialise in.

My point is that while we are waiting for the official regulations to catch up
with these changes, there is organisational room for manoeuvre. Senior

management, for example, might have difficult decisions to make about whom to promote. Should they promote those with the old expertise, or those showing signs of the new kind that is required? Similarly, young and ambitious colleagues might have difficult choices to make in terms of preparing themselves for promotion: should they build up a profile as a traditional manager, as a professional and prolific researcher, or as a person who has enthusiastically embraced the 'new' pedagogies?

As this example illustrates, the gap left by lags in the old official rules and regulations tends to be filled by political activity, in this broad organisational sense. Individuals, working on their own and in groups of people with similar interests, realise that they can increase their power, prestige and rewards by a deliberate strategy. Anyone who has ever worked in an educational organisation will probably recognise this occurrence immediately. Some faculties organise themselves really effectively to claim more resources and bid for more students. Particular individuals, adopting management styles and arguing enthusiastically for management initiatives, indicate clearly that they are 'on the make'. These micropolitical activities are not just marginal ones, but are central to the organisation. As any young lecturer knows, to get on you need to know who the powerful figures are, and where the major organisational strategies are aiming.

Studying the official organisational chart is likely to be fairly unhelpful. At the most, the official organisation comes in handy only at particular stages of the strategy, when you are ready to go public, but it is of little use when you are mobilising behind the scenes. Sometimes, of course, the official version of events tries to catch up with reality, as I have indicated, and a working group goes off for several months to try to draft a new set of regulations, roles and responsibilities to fit the new circumstances. Sometimes there can be unintended and highly instructive consequences.

Take, for example, the vexed issue of extenuating circumstances. As I have indicated above, extenuating circumstances are those that explain, justify and condone the submission of late work. They have emerged as a particular administrative problem where there is extensive continuous assessment: if people missed the traditional unseen examinations, they would be permitted to sit them again only if they had one of a fairly small list of good reasons. The situation becomes more problematic with continuous assessment, especially where there are suspicions that students might be gaining some advantage by late submission. In the recent past, it was left to tutors to decide whether to accept the work or not, and, clearly, highly subjective judgements were involved. It is not surprising that various attempts have been made to systematise the whole process.

One such attempt consisted of trying to write binding regulations which specified permissible kinds of extenuating circumstances, and which excluded others. Thus, bereavement would be accepted as a reason for late work, but not the suspiciously common excuse of 'lack of books in the library', or 'computer failure'. However, this was clearly insufficient. What sort of bereavement is acceptable, and how recent should the bereavement have been? After some deliberation, acceptable bereavement was defined as 'the death of a close relative', but it is easy to see the problems that arise here – are grandparents close relatives, for example, or cousins? What about 'honorary relatives', like family friends, celebrities or family pets, for that matter? It is not enough for some body to legislate that the loss of the family pet should not have caused emotional disturbance; the question is, did it do so, and was performance affected as a result? What leads to a sense of bereavement for one person might lead only to a passing sadness, or even a sense of relief and new purpose, for another. Admitting that one set of circumstances should be acceptable but not the other is bound to look arbitrary, and punishing students who may have suffered a real sense of loss but whose case does not fit looks authoritarian as well.

Some working parties have plodded on gamely, getting deeper and deeper. Perhaps, they have mused, we should attempt to measure emotional distress caused by bereavements? Perhaps we should only accept as valid those cases where there seems to be a demonstrable fall-off in performance? Should students be allowed to claim extenuating circumstances from bereavement only once in their career? Each of these extensions involves more and more problems and risks more and more arbitrary outcomes, until the suspicion dawns that this is the sort of problem that can never really be addressed by attempting to formulate abstract rules at all, since the whole point about emotional loss and its effects is that it is a subjective business. What we have here is a problem that can be identified technically as akin to positivism in social theory: the technical rules and definitions begin by claiming to represent reality, but end by having to dominate it.

Any large and complex organisation that divides people into task-oriented groups runs the risk of this kind of breakdown of organisational systems. There are different names to describe what happens. Gouldner (cited in Lockwood 1992) found that particular departments or divisions in a company tried to develop 'functional autonomy', to gain more resources for themselves, regardless of the aims of the organisation as a whole. Weick (in Westoby 1988) describes the phenomenon as 'loose coupling' between the elements of an organisation. The phenomenon seems to be recognised in those discussions of management style that stress the need to tolerate or even encourage such 'structural looseness'. It is easy to see that, in some circumstances, a flexible, rather 'flat' structure, with wide areas of initiatives devolved down towards underlings, might be more effective than the traditional bureaucratic hierarchy. However, there is always the risk that the powers of initiative might be 'misused', or at least used in directions away from the organisation's main task.

## Everyday tactics

This kind of activity could be widespread in our society. Everyday life itself, for some writers, notably de Certeau (1988; and see the online reading guide to this work), shows individuals and collections of people endlessly engaged in strategic and tactical behaviour, taking advantage of the same sort of gaps in the power structure that we have seen at the level of organisations. In a way, this is inevitable, and takes place for the same reasons. No matter how far the surveillance society spreads, it can never cover every eventuality, and in the gaps it leaves, the initiative shifts to the relatively weak and powerless. We shall return to de Certeau and his general argument later on, but first let us examine some more concrete examples.

Take the example of censorship. Not long ago, the state in the UK had a battery of institutions and legal powers which it used to censor the media in particular, including the theatre. These powers were spread around a number of non-government organisations, such as the British Board of Film Censorship (now Classification), and they were also diffused down to local authority level (so that local committees could refuse to grant licences to films or performances of which they disapproved). However, without taking sides on the pros and cons of censorship as such, it is relatively easy to see the problems that beset this effort to censor.

Can we define offensive, pornographic or obscene material, for example, in such a way that it will become clear and acceptable to ban it? This just is not easy to do, since so much depends on subjective opinions and tastes, as well as the particular circumstances in which material is collected and used. To cite one famous example, a collection of controversial photographs by Robert Mapplethorpe was seized by the police from a university library in Birmingham, UK, and the Vice Chancellor of the University faced the prospect of being charged under the Obscene Publications Act! The point is that someone had to decide whether or not the photographs were 'likely to deprave and corrupt', in the words of the Obscene Publications Act, even though they were 'art', and even though they were housed in a university library, which presumably restricted access not only to responsible adults, but also to academics who might be studying pornography or art. In this case, the harassed police vice squad had to take the decision, and risk being seen either as ineffectual or as punitive philistines. They chose to use their discretionary powers and not to prosecute in the end.

Despite amassing these powers, there is simply no way that the state can effectively ban undesirable material. People can defy the law, and many UK citizens do so. People can now acquire all sorts of material on the Web, and although doing so can be illegal, the chances of being detected and prosecuted are very low. For this reason, some groups are now advocating that censorship be eliminated altogether, and that instead members of the public should be made informed about pornography and left to choose for themselves. Exactly parallel arguments are also currently in progress in the UK concerning the legalisation of soft recreational drugs.

To put these debates in a rather abstract framework, what the state faces is a crisis in its authority. Authority is not the same as power, I am arguing, although the two may be combined. Authority, classically, involves a willingness to obey on the part of the underdog. To take responsibility oneself, to initiate, to do more than just follow orders, involves some element of belief or commitment, some belief in the rights of a person to instruct or advise. People who exercise authority do not often need to use actual raw power to get their way, but can gain it through compliance or apparent consensus. This might involve some deep or subtle exercise of power, as we have seen, but regardless of that issue, authority is generally seen as more effective if people carry it around inside themselves, just as they do as self-disciplined subjects in Foucault's work. They can therefore act without close supervision, knowing what is required of them, and being willing to deliver it.

Increasingly, the authority of the state is diminishing, perhaps, so it no longer acts to fill in the gaps left by the exercise of power. The decline of this authority has been much discussed in sociology, and we have already seen a number of possibilities. Thus Durkheim saw the problem in terms of a shift from mechanical to organic solidarity and talked about the changes in 'moral density' of social groups arising from social and cultural change. We might need to remember this analysis, and perhaps start to look for reasons for the decline of authority in three general directions:

1   One issue has become familiar to us from discussions of modernity and postmodernism. There has been a considerable change in the direction of cultural pluralism. No longer are we tied, in matters of culture and identity, to the old social structures, such as those affected by social class, gender or ethnic identity. At a time when more choice is possible, the mass media in particular offer us more choice than has ever been available before: we know far more about alternative lifestyles, for example, and it has never been easier to adopt them. In consequence, the authority of traditional cultural patterns has been substantially undermined.

2   This cultural instability takes the special form captured in the well-known remarks of Lyotard about the 'scepticism towards narratives' (see Lyotard 1984; and the online reading guide to this work). No-one believes the great promises of modernism any more, whether it is the claim that socialism will lead to liberty, that psychoanalysis will make you happy, that town planners can design a harmonious city environment, or that physics and chemistry will help us produce clean and inexhaustible energy. A part of the reason for scepticism is provided by another major spokesperson – Baudrillard – who points out that most of us have been so bombarded by forms of strategic communication, such as sermons, spin-doctoring or surveys, that we have become permanently apathetic. We automatically engage in what used to be called a 'hermeneutics of suspicion', immediately suspecting some ulterior motive, and rooting around for it, behind any claims to make us healthier, wealthier or happier. We do not believe in any of it any more, but we cannot even be bothered to reject it openly, since that would

only bring even more ideas salespeople to our doors, ready to go through their sad little routines to persuade us to buy. A knowing kind of apathy is what results, where people become 'black holes', with an almost infinite capacity patiently to absorb strategic communication, while emitting back no information of any kind.

3   Of course, there is a material base for these changes too, for marxist writers such as Jameson (1991). Relentless economic pressures on a global scale, for example, have led to unprecedented rates of casualisation in employment (higher education in the UK is one of the best examples), and this obviously weakens commitment and authority. Who could get seriously committed to a profession, with all that is entailed, if it were radically uncertain that the profession was committed to you? Releasing excessive market forces in social life has the same effects, it could be argued: if everything becomes a commodity, then merely a 'cash nexus' connects people to these commodities, so that if you can get better value (in education, religion, therapy, marital arrangements, family life), you will go elsewhere. The old sentiments, loyalties, beliefs and hopes have finally been squeezed out of the system. Cynicism and narcissism dominate our lives instead.

Let us ask a typical theorist's question about these events, assuming we have outlined them accurately. What does all this apathy, evasion and resistance tell us in general about social life? To put it slightly more crudely, what is the main source of people's ability to resist and evade, where does it lie in our society, and, bearing in mind our specific interest in politics in this part of the book, can this residual ability to evade and resist ever finally be controlled, made subject to power?

De Certeau can appear as a champion of popular resistance and creativity, the person who reminded us that even the powerless have certain resources available to evade the system, to trick it, to 'poach' (de Certeau 1988; see the online reading guide for more details). However, Buchanan (2000) says there are quite different interpretations of de Certeau's project. To take a specific example, it looks as if de Certeau in his 1988 book is pursuing a fairly familiar idea of life as a text. Following this analogy, walking in the city can be seen as a way of writing your own text with the signs provided by the urban environment. This is a suggestive idea, and one that might well illuminate the power of the everyday to resist even the most sophisticated and complex intentions of designing or 'theming' the urban environment 'from above'.

I certainly borrowed this idea myself in some work I did on the heritage industry. I wanted to argue that, despite the intentions of the town planners, and the local and international muscle they were able to apply, the inhabitants of my home town largely lived in a pre-themed environment. Whereas the planners referred to areas of the city under their new 'heritagised' names such as King Richard III Street, instead of Commercial Road, the locals insisted on using the earlier version. Indeed, some inhabitants, including my parents and in-laws,

continued to use names for parts of the city that ceased to have any concrete referent after the bombing raids of World War II. For example, they would try to
direct me around the city by inviting me to turn left at the site of the cinema that
had been bombed in 1942, had been rebuilt as a series of local shops, and had
been a supermarket for the last twenty years. This sort of naming was done for
a number of cultural and political reasons, from what I can tell, all of them
grounded on some claim to have a privileged knowledge of the city, confined
only to those of a particular age. This knowledge and these names were used as
a kind of private language among themselves, and also to exclude outsiders,
whether the younger generation or the alien town planners who had done more
to change their city for the worse (in their view) than had the Luftwaffe.

## Power and resistance

When looking at gramscian approaches to revolutionary politics, for example (in
Chapter 6), we noticed that the concept of hegemony implied a source of resistance to it. Domination of oppressed groups was never total, and could never be
complete. The everyday experience of these groups continually generated
sources of opposition and resistance, it might be suggested. In the early stages of
the work, it is likely that some rather classical notion of the working class as the
group destined to smash capitalism lay behind some of these points. Certainly,
in some of the more specific studies, working-class experience offered a series of
historical and cultural resources, alternative ways of organising your life, which
could be used very effectively to challenge attempts by schools to impose their
visions on working-class students (in Willis's 1977 study, for example, the subject of an online reading guide), or to counter proposals by the state for an
educational system with demands for 'really useful knowledge' (in Johnson
1981).

   Later, as faith in the revolutionary potential of the working class diminished,
the histories and cultural traditions of other groups were seen to provide a basis
for opposition to the dominant order as well. The history of slavery and oppression was somehow carried around by black immigrants to the UK, and by black
people born and raised in the UK as well, for example, and this again provided
a set of resources and alternatives to white conceptions of social life: the
Rastafarian version of Christianity, the traditions of 'slave' music and the rejection of the work ethic have all been seen in this way (CCCS 1982 – see the online
reading guide). We have already seen in Chapter 6 how the cultural experience
and traditions of the parent culture assisted a number of youth cultures to
develop a form of symbolic politics too. We also noted in Chapter 8 how the
everyday life and experience of women became a source of opposition to patriarchy.

   Of course, relying on this historical cultural tradition can cause problems, as
the tradition fades over the years, and as the culture industries and disciplinary

institutions of the present society increasingly dominate the consciousness of its members. To become parochial for a moment, the UK of the 1970s did display enough industrial and social unrest to preserve this notion of continuing rebellious undercurrents, but the conservatism of the 1980s and 1990s, the demise of socialism as a political force, the collapse of the Berlin Wall, and so on, 'bent the twig' away from this view.

The new politics that ensued took a slightly different tack, one that had been developed first as 'Eurocommunism'. Here, more direct, local and immediate interests were to be addressed, such as the local resentments of the unemployed and the marginalised, small businesses, single-interest pressure groups who objected to the expansion of the military, or to increasing pollution of the environment, and so on. The trick was to try to articulate these interests, to line them up so that they came to be directed at the system as a whole. Since these dissatisfied and marginalised groups would always be present, as monopoly capitalism dominated official state politics, there would be a constant need to organise such a popular front. However, clear risks arise here too, as capitalism shows itself flexible enough to respond to some of these specific demands, and apparently to satisfy them, much as Critical Theory had predicted (see Chapter 7). Some cuts in military expenditure, and some greater powers to regulate the discharge of waste, and the anti-capitalist coalition can fall to bits.

Given the success of modern capitalism in this direction, it is not surprising to find the analysis of the sources of resistance being refocused in a much more abstract and theoretical way. Capitalism and the cultural institutions it has engendered, it could be argued, have been almost completely successful in mopping up these residual sources of resistance, and in adjusting themselves to placate and defuse the localised oppositional groups that remain. Is there any area of human life that cannot be managed and domesticated in this way, and if so, could we possibly base a politics on it?

Those at the bottom of social hierarchies, the oppressed, the powerless, the weak or the underdogs, may be forced to comply with the wishes of the powerful, or at least appear to comply with them, but they do not have to believe in the rights of the powerful to control them. And as soon as surveillance is removed, the underdogs are free to pursue their own projects.

## Active consumers

Many examples are provided by the turn towards the 'active consumer' in cultural studies. Initially, consumer activity was seen in terms of 'resistance', as we have seen, since cultural studies itself tended to be dominated by gramscian notions such as 'hegemony'. That concept presupposes cultural and political resistance, as we have argued, since the whole point of hegemonic power is to incorporate such resistance, or otherwise modify it, so as to serve dominant interests. But the forms that resistance actually took needed to be described.

Some classic work was undertaken by Fiske (1989). In a series of studies of popular cultural activities, he showed that cultural resistance was alive and well. To take a few of the more spectacular examples, shoppers were resisting all the pressures put on them to buy goods and were shopping for recreational purposes instead, trying on all the clothes in the clothes shop, say, and then leaving without buying anything. Young women were buying music videos (inevitably Madonna videos), and then using them to make statements about their own femininity. When the world of the video games player was analysed sympathetically, players were seen to be symbolically opposing capitalist regimes, and joyfully and creatively playing with the signs provided for them. Knowledgeable viewers of television news delighted in the occasional technical glitch that revealed how the news was constructed. Surfers were engaged in a kind of philosophical meditation about nature and culture – and so on.

Some analysts, such as Nava (1991), saw in these forms of consumer resistance and revolt the basis of a whole new form of politics, taking the form of the consumer boycott, like those against the fur trade. Indeed, there were several large-scale and successful consumer revolts in the early 1990s and some of them are still around; it is still possible to see demonstrators protesting about various policies of supermarkets or local defence industries. It remains debatable, however, whether such movements have been successful in seriously modifying international capitalism, or whether they have acted only as a kind of advance warning of changing consumer preferences.

In media studies, the 'active viewer' had also been discovered. In the early stages, viewers were seen as entirely dominated by ideology, and the pleasures they reported in watching melodramas in the cinema, or soap operas on television, were simply seen as ways of luring them even deeper into the embrace of capitalism. At the most, a small minority of viewers might be able to 'decode' critically the cunningly constructed ideological messages (Hall in Hall et al. 1980; and see the online reading guide to his article on 'coding and decoding'), but most of the public would simply go along innocently. When they watched football on television, for example, they would unconsciously be acquiring ideological notions of 'the nation'. They would come out of Bond movies deeply affected by racist, sexist and imperialistic 'codes' (Bennett in Open University 1982).

All that was to change, probably more under the influence of feminist analysis than anything else. Feminists could hardly believe that their sisters could be so stupid and powerless, and began to think in terms of 'recuperative' readings of films and television programmes. Ang (1985) discovered ironic women viewers of the American soap opera *Dallas* who found pleasure in the caricatures of women devised for male pleasure. Gledhill (1987) found women 'reading' melodramas in ways that rewarded their own skills in understanding the subtleties of emotionally charged looks and glances. Crucial to many of these discoveries was the notion of intertextuality, even in Bond films, according to Bennett and Woollacott (1987), where a viewer was able to draw upon remembered knowledge of other texts. These included other films, critical reviews in news-papers, even books on media theory, and this knowledge helped to interrupt the careful narratives of the pieces being watched at the time.

## Resistance at work

It is worth reminding ourselves of many other examples of such resistance as well, including some in the sociology of work. One classic account of work in a then socialist country (Hungary) was provided by Haraszti (1977). The workers he describes were not at all impressed by the official ideology of the tractor fac-tory in which they worked, which extolled the virtues of manual labour, and tried to persuade them to follow various rational plans. Instead, they would impose their own work practices as soon as the supervisors' backs were turned. This included making their own goods for their own amusement ('homers') using the firm's machinery and time, and 'cheating the norm' or 'looting', where machines were run faster than they should have been, in order to produce larger quantities of goods and thus earn more money (workers were paid on a piece-rate). There was even malicious sabotage. These activities were sustained by a thoroughly sarcastic and scurrilous workplace humour aimed at the supervisors and their official rationalities.This work is interesting, and helps make up for the relative neglect of workplaces in this sort of cultural sociology, although Willis's (1977) study of working-class kids included a visit to a local factory, and is the possible exception here (see the online reading guide).

There is a long tradition of the discovery of resistance in the equally recently neglected sociology of education as well. In fact, formal education systems are probably the most likely places to find 'resistance' by the students. You will almost certainly know of cases for yourself, as students at school, where teach-ers have been run ragged by skilled and unco-operative pupils who have taken every opportunity available to challenge the teacher's authority. When I did teaching practice myself, as a trainee school teacher, more than thirty years ago, I encountered a 12-year-old whom I still remember vividly: he had a particularly effective mocking and resilient style that offered constant challenge to me, to my insecure knowledge of the subject, and to my weakly developed sense of author-ity. He had an excellent sense of humour, which he used to great effect to turn the tables on me: appeals to his better nature were mockingly rejected, and he seemed completely impervious to any punishment I could level. I will admit that he got the better of me, and I was very relieved to leave.

There are some classic examples of such pupil resistance in studies such as that by Willis (1977), which we have mentioned before. Another famous piece, building on Willis's insight, has been written by Riseborough (in Ball and Goodson 1985; see the online reading guide) who describes some extremely unpleasant encounters that teachers have had with pupils, sometimes ending in physical violence, more often in activity that can only be described as bullying.

The results have often been devastating for teachers, who sometimes responded by leaving the profession after a series of these encounters, occasionally accompanied by a nervous breakdown. For those who survived, a very tough skin was rapidly acquired, together with an equally tough style of teaching. In this way, Riseborough suggests, pupils themselves create the kind of authoritarian teachers that you see in schools. The pupils' role in this respect has been little researched in theory. After all, officially, they are simply there to be dominated – a picture that most teachers in my experience will readily tell you is far too simplistic.

This sort of work has been largely influenced by marxist conceptions of domination and resistance, and it is possible to see that this has led to some rather dubious conclusions from the empirical data that have been gathered. As we have argued above, the concept of 'resistance' has to be made pretty flexible to cover the kinds of things that school students or factory workers actually do. To take the most obvious and controversial examples, is the sexist badinage found in both Willis and Riseborough best seen as a form of class resistance? Willis does attempt to see it like this, arguing that the conception of tough manly labour that enables a confrontational worker identity to be maintained against the bosses also has the unfortunate side-effect of leading to a very negative view of women. However, it is quite possible, of course, that sexism has its own origins and effects. Similarly, as a study of pupil humour by Woods (in Hammersley and Woods 1976) indicates, not all mockery and laughter can be seen as a disguised form of class conflict. Riseborough simply asserts the class dimensions of his work, but his own theoretical and political convictions seem to have pre-dated his actual fieldwork.

I have also included an online reading guide to some of the pieces in Westoby (1988), which contain further examples of micropolitics in educational settings and some further discussion of the theoretical arguments stressing the importance of the micropolitical level to explain organisational life.

Before we leave this analysis of work and education, though, one thing that a class conflict perspective has produced is a good analysis of the micropolitical strategies of bosses and supervisors. This tends to be lacking in some of the more cultural work, where the infernal arts of capitalism tend to be taken for granted. Thus Roy (in Nichols 1980) describes management strategies against unionisation as taking the form of 'fear stuff', 'sweet stuff' and 'evil stuff'. 'Fear stuff' involves the obvious threats of redundancy or shop closure, but also campaigns of pressure and bullying ('riding'):

> [The supervisor] done most of the riding. It was a patrol job . . . I'd [have to] quit whatever I was doing and do what he told me to do . . . [He would] have me pick [things] up off the floor when there [were] a lot of more important things to do. He tried to get my attention off my business so I'd make [mistakes with my work]. (Roy in Nichols 1980: 402)

'Evil stuff' consists of some sort of sermonising campaign, for example to persuade workers that striking is evil. As for 'sweet stuff', Nichols describes this as follows:

> One tactic of this sort is the 'Dad's back' speech, usually delivered from a prepared manuscript by a leading member of local management. . . . The gist of the speech is: 'Dad has been busy, unintentionally neglectful; but he is back with you now, to stay, and things will get lots better.' (Nichols 1980: 407)

## Theorising the everyday

I feel strangely reluctant to turn from this kind of concrete and detailed material towards the work of de Certeau, who, in cultural studies, is usually seen as one of the main advocates of close attention to 'the everyday'. Indeed, he was a major inspiration for Fiske's work, which we have examined briefly above. According to Buchanan (2000), de Certeau became interested in the enormous potential of the everyday to challenge the power and authority of dominant groups after the famous 'events' of May 1968 in France, a period of considerable cultural and political turbulence that initially defied the efforts of theoretical analysts who struggled to define and evaluate them. We have mentioned 'the events' of 1968 in Chapter 6. A series of student occupations of universities, large street demonstrations, including some opposing the USA in the conduct of the Vietnam War, and some industrial unrest (especially in France) seemed to offer an entirely new form of cultural politics. Perhaps the most famous strand in these cultural politics was situationism, as we saw. As an indication of the conception of politics:

> The closest English translation of [the key term] *détournement* lies somewhere between 'diversion' and 'subversion'. . . . It is plagiaristic . . . and subversive, since its tactics are those of the 'reversal of perspective', a challenge to meaning aimed at the context in which it arises. . . . [Some] methods were essentially reworkings of those employed by the Dadaists and Surrealists. . . . Buildings were appropriated by graffiti; a plethora of texts, graphics, and images were incorporated into . . . films. (Plant 1992: 86–9)

In more specific terms, street politics could also develop, as in the following extract:

> Orange Alternative brought a kind of Dada provocation to Poland. . . . [In 1987] Poland's Official Day of the Police and Security Service . . . was marked by an enthusiastic march in Wroclaw to 'thank' the police, in which they were showered with flowers and embraced by the participants who were later arrested. The streets 'were flooded with Santa Clauses' at Christmas 1987, leading to the arrest of both bogus and 'real' Santa Clauses and a 2000-strong demonstration calling for 'the release of Santa'. (Plant 1992: 149).

The appearance of street protests against globalisation in 2001 shows a last legacy of situationism, perhaps. Contingents at a London demonstration included 'fluffies' (probably a media term originally, but reappropriated in the classic manner) who dressed in a variety of carnivalesque ways and organised events such as a slow bicycle race in London. The WOMBLES (White Overalls Movement Building Libertarian Effective Struggles) dressed themselves in a parody of police riot uniforms, complete with (white) overalls, cardboard shields and balloons for batons and marched forward to line up against the police. Of course, in these events, as indeed in the student events of 1964–69, real power was soon marshalled against these cultural provocations, and arrests and arbitrary beatings ensued.

De Certeau (1988) cites rather strange examples to illustrate his own insistence that everyday life displays frequent use of tactics by the weak to overcome the strong. We have already seen his views on walking in the city. Other examples in the work include the art of story-telling, or reading, and these have been particularly influential in the discovery of the 'active' cultural subject described above. However, there is also some important theoretical work in the book as well, and we should really explore this in our quest for some theoretical account of everyday life to complement the descriptions we have cited. One person criticised by de Certeau is Foucault, for example, and we have met his work already. The other major theorist is Bourdieu, and before we can get into de Certeau's critique, we probably need a short summary of the offending piece.

Bourdieu begins his work, promisingly entitled *Outline of a Theory of Practice* (Bourdieu 1977), by insisting that practice needs to be accorded its own place in sociological understanding. It is mistaken to think that sociological theory objectively describes practice: usually what happens when sociologists do research is that participants agree to theorise about it themselves. These home-grown theoretical statements are then taken as 'data', and further elaborated into more rigorous theoretical descriptions. Since practice is driven by unconscious impulses, it can never be simply innocently described.

Similarly, it is a mistake to assume that people act as a result of the impulses described by theory: activity is not rule-governed in this way. Practitioners do not remember rules, and, indeed, have to be reminded of their own conventions and traditions and other social circumstances. Furthermore, practitioners are able to act tactically, to selectively interpret traditions, to take advantage of situations that are not covered by social rules. As might be expected, the most powerful groups principally use such tactics, but Bourdieu seems to be at one with the other authors we have cited in arguing that everyday life is effectively constituted by these tactical manoeuvres.

I have refrained from giving any specific examples of Bourdieu's work here, since they are based entirely on his own early anthropological studies of Kabylia (Algeria). Bourdieu describes a number of occasions when the people of Kabylia resort to tactical manoeuvres over matters such as marriage rules or the interpretation of their calendar as guidance for agricultural practices. It is clearly pretty unproductive to pursue these examples here, since they are so rich in detail and rely so much on context, although Bourdieu clearly intends them to be used to make more general points about everyday life in modern societies like ours.

Perhaps the most famous arguments in Bourdieu's book concern the 'habitus(es)' in Kabylian society. Like many readers of Bourdieu, I was familiar with this concept in some of his work on education, and we have met it before. 'Habitus' in Bourdieu (1988) seems to refer to a set of unconsciously held judgements and preferences, organised into an aesthetic, which is self-reproducing. People like university professors and school teachers draw upon these preferences and predispositions to make judgements about students' work. We are told that this habitus forms in a fairly conventional way, as a result of upbringing, where particular cultural experiences are introduced to children and they just automatically become a 'way of life'. Cultural experiences depend on cultural capital, which is passed on from generation to generation, and is as unevenly distributed as economic capital.

In the study of Kabylia, however, a different mechanism is described. Here, the family dwelling itself provides the cultural capital for the new generation. Briefly, the social arrangements in the home, and the very spatial arrangements of the rooms and interiors, indicate to the child how he or she should relate to members of the family, and thus to the wider society and the world 'outside'. An habitus is learned via the body, Bourdieu tells us. It takes the form of a few generative principles, usually oppositions such as male/female, inside/outside, wet/dry, and so on. Once learned, it can be applied to a range of cases. It is learned in the earliest interactions between children and their families – who stands where in the house, who goes out first, or who does what for whom.

I suppose that the domestic arrangements in contemporary societies still do some of this work. My own house in England was built during the Victorian era, and still features a series of large rooms for the use of the owners, and a set of discreet stairs and small rooms for the use of the servants; domestic spaces are clearly designed according to a gendered division of labour too, of course.

This work by Bourdieu seems to agree exactly with the themes of the importance and the political significance of everyday life that we have been discussing, but de Certeau subjects the work (and Foucault's) to a searching critique. To be brief, he accuses both Bourdieu and Foucault of insufficient attention to the complexity and 'otherness' of everyday life. In both cases, the detailed description of everyday life is very rapidly made to fit with theoretical concerns and allegiances to academic disciplines (sociology for Bourdieu), although this is heavily disguised. Indeed, the very foreignness and complexity of the case studies – Kabylian social life, or the massive detail of historical examples of punishment regimes – enables both authors to pursue a clever tactical manoeuvre themselves. Both write their accounts as if their theoretical generalisations somehow 'emerged' from this mass of detail, but de Certeau insists that the usual processes of selection and abstraction have taken place, just like the ones we have criticised in positivism. The detail of everyday life has been managed to make it fit theory, sometimes by the Kabylians themselves. Examples are chosen to fit theories, while others have been neglected; the form of the examples has taken precedence over the detailed content, and so on. It is a skilled and detailed critique, and I summarise it much more fully in the online reading guide to de Certeau. Incidentally, I think the critique has a much wider potential target too, and have been inspired by it in offering criticisms of ethnomethodology's procedures in Chapter 12.

This is also close to what we have been arguing, of course, with the marxist analysis we have just examined. The ethnographic material, assembled so convincingly by Riseborough or Haraszti (or Willis), seems to lead us towards marxism, but we are entitled to suspect that it would have done so in any circumstances whatsoever, since marxist categories were used to select, construct and interpret it in the first place.

## Concluding thoughts

It is fair to point out that Bourdieu (2000) has flatly denied that his work is so crude and reductive. He maintains that he has always seen the Kabilyian habitus as split and complex, for example, and that no-one has done more to oppose sociologism. In responding to de Certeau and other critics, he has also produced some thoughtful asides about methodology in his highly detailed study of everyday suffering (Bourdieu et al. 1999; and see the online reading guide). The actual accounts in this collection are described with particular care, aiming to acknowledge the influence of theory, but not let it dominate the stories of the suffering people.

The debate really raises a more general methodological and theoretical problem: how can we describe everyday life and its politics in ways that do not lose its complexity and its strangeness? De Certeau talks of the tendency for theory to domesticate and reduce the very stuff it is trying to explain. We might be familiar with a limited form of this argument, which is usually levelled against the methods of positivism, but it is meant to apply far more generally. Theorists impose narratives on what they observe, it is argued, and this cuts across the narratives that people construct, far less systematically, and perhaps more tactically, in everyday life.

This kind of thing can be detected in 'action sociology' too, of course, which tends to assume that the relevant theories and methods describe action without imposing any particular form on it. Doubts about this assumption surface in the more recent critiques of ethnographic method, by Clough (1992), for example. Clough suggests that the styles of ethnographic writing in the American interactionist tradition (which we examined in Chapter 4) are best understood as pursuing variants of realist narrative. As we have explained before, such narratives deliver a powerful 'knowledge effect' in the reader, who thinks what has been read is independently acquired 'knowledge'. I have used this sort of critique myself, incidentally, to explain the plausibility of gramscian work as a result of the skilled deployment of 'academic realist' narratives.

As we have seen, understanding the illusory neatness produced by academic accounts that use conventional narratives has led feminist writers to attempt to develop alternatives. Bourdieu et al. (1999) do not go so far as to offer 'avant-garde' broken narratives, yet there is certainly an 'episodic' and diary-like quality to the pieces in the collection, and a good deal of caution to alert the reader to narrative effects.

This may not be enough, of course. De Certeau wants 'the everyday' to be placed beyond any kind of academic apprehension if it is to be a genuinely 'other' level of experience. It is an elusive domain which loses its qualities as soon as any attempt is made to describe or theorise about it, he argues. It is the ultimate area of 'emergence', to refer back to the themes of Chapter 3. It is that which is not captured by concepts, to cite the work of Adorno in Chapter 7. De Certeau even plays with the idea that it may feature some mysterious 'pre-social' survival instincts. However conceived, it takes on that quality of necessary opposition to self-sufficient theory and to thought itself.

Of course, this may be an appealing idea, especially if you are interested in the more challenging forms of cultural politics, and it is necessary occasionally to point out that some things may never be capable of being theorised, especially to those researchers who believe they have discovered some universal and infallible method. But this leaves us in a dilemma too – we can never know about 'the everyday', except in the most abstract sense as something that theory and thought cannot grasp. Here we have the most ironic consequences of theorising about the everyday, in other words – the eventual realisation that we cannot theorise about it at all!

# PART IV

# 12  Language Games and Linguistic Turns

It is not surprising that many social theorists should be interested in language and how it works, but there are quite different ways of thinking about the role of language in social action. I suppose the most obvious and conventional way to think of language is as a neutral medium to transmit thoughts and meanings formed in our consciousness. This leads theorists to examine the ways in which consciousness works to create meanings and to receive them from others, as in many varieties of action sociology, including Weber's work, and American interactionism. These activities are detectable through the important public 'symbols' (including words) that are produced, received and exchanged.

There is another way, however, of thinking about language that gives it a much more central and important role. This approach sees language as far more than just a medium used by consciousness to express itself. Language becomes something that creates and constrains meaning in its own right. Before we get technical, let's just think about this in terms of the customary homely examples.

To take an example of the problems faced by professionals in this area, Bennett and Woollacott (1987) describe how the company that made James Bond films encountered some of these creative and artistic problems when trying to develop cinematic versions of the Bond novels. In the novels, much is made of the creative flexibility of James Bond, who can adapt very rapidly to emerging situations, and use his initiative, because he is, after all, British(!). The novelistic convention of writing inner dialogues, where characters reveal their thoughts to the reader, conveys this quite well in print, but endless verbal speculation does not translate well to the cinema screen, especially for 'action' movies, according to Hollywood conventions at least. One solution to this problem is instead to have Bond use a number of highly visual gadgets to illustrate his ingenuity and flexibility. This led to a much-enlarged role for gadgetry and the character 'Q'. There are many other examples of innovation in the shift from novel to film. The point is that the conventions (or 'language') of film quite clearly affect what 'looks good', and the conventions of the novel have similar effects on 'what works' in print.

The same points apply to anyone attempting to master some of the new technologies associated with computers. In the discipline of educational technology, it becomes a problem first to master the conventions of, say, basic web design, often involving trimming intentions to what can be achieved easily. If all goes well, there is a later stage, when constraints become opportunities, so to speak.

The issue then becomes one of asking how the new possibilities offered by electronic text can be fully exploited. For example, web-based materials can be linked together conveniently using hyperlinks, offering new possibilities of writing. Instead of just thinking how writing develops linearly, from the start to the ending of a piece of text, the writer now has another dimension to play with. There is now a layer of text 'behind' the discussion, so to speak, perhaps offering additional examples, or some debates about an aspect of the original text, made available to readers if they choose to click the hyperlink. If you refer to some of my online reading guides (Harris 2002), especially to the one on Stuart Hall on the 'ideology effect', you will see what I mean. There are also possibilities which arise from using images or sound, of course, which are much more convenient to exploit with electronic text. Although I use graphics overwhelmingly just for tables, and I have no sound files at present, there are some interesting examples in Lomax and Casey (1998).

So far, I have considered rather strange examples of 'languages', perhaps. My examples have been linked to the mastery of various technologies and their conventions of use. We are likely to learn these in later life, and we can become more consciously aware of constraints and possibilities offered by them. It requires more of a leap to appreciate the argument that natural languages, the ones we speak from birth, also offer patterns of constraint and opportunity. We are not so aware of these, of course, but for some writers they are so important that they become prominent in the study of social life itself. Studying social life means studying language, its rules, its uses or its formal structures (depending on which particular conception of language is being deployed).

If this is so, there are some important implications. For example, human beings ('subjects') cease to be creatures with consciousnesses that provide them with meaning which is then expressed in language, and become instead mouthpieces for (or 'bearers' of) language, so to speak. The point of investigation of social life shifts from exploring consciousness, and any social or economic forces that affect it, towards one which tries to explore the linguistic rules that people are using in order to construct some meaningful patterns of social interaction. For some researchers, this is a particularly welcome shift from something unobservable (consciousness) to something that can be recorded and studied with some precision (language use). This is clearly going to have some implications primarily for the kinds of action sociology we have been investigating in earlier chapters. There are more far-reaching consequences as well, as we shall see.

We have hinted at the arguments launched by structuralism in this area already. We saw from Chapter 2 that the mystery of what 'the social' was, and how it actually affected action, was to be pursued through the notion of a virtual structure of language, a set of potentials or resources. This structure had its own rules for creating meaning, often involving the establishment of a series of differences between signs, either over time (as in narratives), or 'across' time (as in the use of metaphors). These formal relations between signs provided meanings, and actual individuals operated and realised these relations in speech. Social analysis became increasingly a matter of analysing texts. I have explored the problems with this 'textual' approach in my own 1996 work if you are interested: basically, it runs the risk of over-emphasising textual aspects of social life at the expense of non-textual forms. We have discussed this point in Chapter 10, when we looked at the accusations that Foucault had over-emphasised discursive forms of power at the expense of the more physically coercive kinds.

## Winch and the challenge to sociology

However, I first encountered this argument for language, so to speak, when I first began to study sociology and read the work of Winch (1958; and see the relevant online reading guide). Winch was heavily influenced by the work of Wittgenstein, which (eventually) came to see language use as rule-governed, as in a game. He was to explore the implications and develop radical consequences for all those sociological attempts to study meaning that had gone before. I think the implications are as important for 'action sociology' as for positivism, although the latter is the target for Winch's critique initially.

To summarise the main points very briefly, Winch began by suggesting that sociological methods of inquiry were really reducible to linguistic inquiries and explanations. There has been a long discussion in social sciences about whether a scientific method of empirical inquiry ought to be adopted. Such a method would attempt to find causes, regularities and laws that specify what is likely to happen under certain conditions. These parallel the investigations of the natural sciences, which try to explain observable regularities like the relationship between the temperature and the state (solid, liquid or gas) of a particular substance (such as water). Social scientists also engage in what Winch calls 'conceptual inquiry', trying to clarify the meanings of concepts used to explain and account for social action. His point is that only this form of inquiry can be suitable for a social science, since social action, uniquely, depends on meaning. The activities of specialist social scientists are best described as a kind of applied philosophy (conceptual inquiry), and the activities of ordinary social actors offer a kind of equivalent to philosophy, less rigorous, but still devoted to clarifying meaning. Thus philosophy becomes queen of the sciences, and everyday life becomes a kind of philosophy as well.

We can see how this argument works in a bit more detail by considering how it is that actions come to have a meaning. As you might expect from the above, meaning does not arise from the consciousness of individuals, but from concepts, found in language. Winch wants to extend the notion of language to include non-verbal communication, symbols, gestures and the rest. These will convey meaning because they also operate within systems of linguistic rules. To understand a gesture or word is to be able to follow a rule in the use of language, which may be done unconsciously or implicitly as well as consciously. Of course, we can make mistakes in this process, and often do. The rule in use is often not clear, and we need social support in our interpretive activities. Thus, as with Wittgenstein, clarifying what is meant by 'meaning' (*sic*) leads us to focus on rule usage, which leads to our appreciating the social support for these rules in linguistic communities or, as Wittgenstein calls them, 'forms of life'.

Turning to social relations, we can now grasp them as expressions of collective ideas about reality. 'Forms of life', social patterns clustered around rule use, become the starting point for social analysis. All social life is rule-governed, including dissent or disobedience. The rules for language use provide us with stocks of meaning (and not some transcendental consciousness, as in, say, Schütz – see Chapter 4 or the online reading guide).

The implications for conventional social science are clear. Causal analysis is misplaced (and J. S. Mill is the target here – see the online reading guide to a well-known account of aspects of his work). The regularities displayed in social life arise because rules tend to be followed, not because of underlying causes. There are no causes as such, and that extends to Mill's attempts to render motives as special kinds of mental cause. To the extent that social life is predictable, this is because it conforms to accepted rules, including those that suggest that past and present events might be connected. It is acceptable for social scientists to theorise about these regularities, as long as they realise that their specialist meanings can only be based on the common-sense meanings of actors.

There is another notorious implication of this argument. Since meanings are rooted in the rules of language use, which are themselves rooted in separate communities or 'forms of life', meaning and truth must be relative matters: both will vary according to the rules established by different communities. We can only study them in different communities – a further problem for any sociological theory that attempts to generalise across different local communities. Even social science itself is only a kind of linguistic community, with its own notions of 'truth'.

The attempts in the social sciences to argue that these common-sense meanings are superficial, effects of some deeper structure or whatever, depend on conceptual distinctions being made, but these are not well clarified, and tend to be imposed arbitrarily. Thus expert meanings are acceptable initially, to suggest analogies, but they cannot be taken seriously as an attempt to replace common-sense meanings or rigorous conceptual analysis. These points are obviously likely to undermine marxism and functionalism, but there are also some critical implications for Weber. While Weber certainly directs attentions to the meanings of actors, as in the whole discussion about meaning adequacy, he wants to see subjective meaning as involving more than rule-following. (Schütz argues that Weber needs an explicit model of consciousness as providing these meanings.) The notion of causal adequacy is simply a mistake, argues Winch, and sociology should be doing conceptual analysis as the only way to try to grasp forms of life and the meanings they express.

## An aside on ethnomethodology

In my view, some of the elements in ethnomethodology and its critiques of sociology bear a remarkable similarity to the arguments of Winch. This is hardly surprising, since ethnomethodology has also been heavily influenced by Wittgenstein's philosophy, and, specifically, the work of Winch. There are a number of useful accounts of the development of ethnomethodology that spell this out in more detail, especially the one in May (1996). I have an online reading guide to a more extensive (and rather favourable) account by Heritage ( in Giddens and Turner 1987). As we saw with American interactionism in Chapter 4, however, much of the development in ethnomethodology and conversation analysis is found embodied in the large number of concrete studies. You will have to explore these for yourself, although I have online reading guides to some initiated by Garfinkel, and some included in the classic collection by Atkinson and Heritage (1984).

To sketch in May's argument here, ethnomethodology clearly reflects a number of inputs as well as that provided by Wittgensteinian philosophy – including the influence of Schütz and Parsons (the role of the latter in the formation of ethnomethodology is spelled out slightly better by Heritage, perhaps). To be very schematic, ethnomethodology borrowed from Schütz the idea of the constituting consciousness as lying at the heart of social meaning. It is consciousness and its characteristic activities which make sense of the world, as we saw in Chapter 4, and the precise mechanisms of subjective intentions, motives and syntheses need to be clarified. This can also be used to critique much conventional sociology which tries to overlook these activities and operate at some 'second-order' stage, making sense of action only after the individual has made sense. The worst sort of confusion arises when sociologists try to impose their specialist meanings on the meanings of the actors themselves, when they try to develop 'scientific' accounts of action on this basis, and when they fail to realise that they too use the same subjective processes to develop their specialist understandings of the world. (The online reading guide to Schütz's work picks up the implications for Weber especially.)

However, Schütz is not in a position to offer much comfort to those who wish to continue doing sociology. We are urged to explore our own consciousnesses for an answer to a particularly vexing question – how exactly are sociological explanations linked to common-sense ones? Schütz says the two sorts of explanation differ in terms of the level of generality at which they operate, the explicitness with which they are formed, and the worlds to which they refer (the common-sense 'paramount reality' or the specialised sociological realities).

If I understand the argument correctly, May suggests that ethnomethodology proposed to solve this problem by invoking a Winchian argument. The focus of research should be at the common-sense level of making meaning, and should proceed by the careful analysis of language use. The later stage, sociologising about this level, can be postponed, or even abolished altogether (depending on whom you read). Garfinkel's experiment involving some students and a tape recording masquerading as a counsellor (Garfinkel 1967; and see the online reading guide) reveals the ways in which people make sense of random answers to their questions. They use a version of the 'documentary method' (a term borrowed from Mannheim), where, roughly, isolated answers are interpreted as examples of some underlying sensible and continuous 'document'. Garfinkel goes on to say that this interpretation accompanies 'ordinary' responses to sociological inquiry too, and, for that matter, sociologists also use it to make sense of those responses when they get back to their laboratories. He proceeds to isolate aspects of conversations that had been neglected before, including the way they 'index' shared understandings of context (see May 1996 on this). In general, conversations show us how 'ordinary' actors make sense of each other and construct some orderly patterns of interaction among themselves – these are neglected aspects of social order and offer concrete examples of 'nomic' (the opposite of 'anomic') activity.

The Winchian turn is more apparent, perhaps, with conversation analysis, which developed subsequently. This consists of the very detailed and elaborate transcription of conversations, classically in 'naturally occurring' settings (but more recently in organisational settings too). I have online reading guides to some studies from Atkinson and Heritage's (1984) collection, such as the one developed by Button and Casey based on telephone conversations. To be brief, these often feature what normal usage would call open-ended questions (such as 'What's happening with you?' – technically described as 'topic initial elicitors') or prompts ('So . . . what happened yesterday? – 'retopicalisations'). The point of the article seems to be how participants ('members') manage these operations skilfully to prolong conversations, another example of how social order emerges at the common-sense level, even in the most mundane and routine sort of activities.

There is no time to illustrate further, but conversation analysts have also studied: political speeches and 'applause generating' strategies (Heritage in Atkinson and Heritage 1984); the peculiarities of speech in classrooms, especially the use of questions where the teacher already knows the answer (Mehan in Hammersley 1986); the sales pitch of market traders (Pinch and Clark 1986); and the nature of polite talk at awards ceremonies (Manning 1989). These pieces vary, but they are claiming to be able to offer concrete empirical study of conversations as a method to understand how individual meanings can be articulated together to generate some local social order. The extraordinary range of examples helps to show how widespread and thus 'normal' order-maintaining activities are – and it also serves to mark a significant departure or 'break' from the older concerns of classical sociology.

This is a controversial claim of course, and this kind of study has generated considerable debate. We shall return to the general problems with Winch below, which can be applied nicely to Conversation Analysis too in my view. I should say here that ethnomethodologists have their own responses, of course, but some of them do look rather 'tactical'. There can be a claimed innocent 'discovery' of elaborate rules in conversations, for example (see below), following from some studies which one just happens to have undertaken (see Sacks in Atkinson and Heritage 1984, or the online reading guide). In addition, I have doubts about the claim that ethnomethodology has been able to leave behind the problems encountered by conventional sociology just by announcing that it intends a new departure. There is probably a 'university dimension' to relate in the story of the emergence of ethnomethodology too, specifically in pointing to the early close professional connections between the founders, their subsequent need to separate themselves from earlier traditions, and their ability to recruit keen newcomers to what almost looked like a 'mission' in the early days. Be that as it may, more detailed criticisms follow.

### Ethnomethodology – some common-sense objections

(1) You cannot keep discovering the same thing. What I mean is that once Garfinkel has suggested the use of the documentary method to understand common sense, no-one else can 'discover' that ordinary people use it. Once Sacks or Schegloff has identified the use of 'adjacency pairs' in everyday conversations, no subsequent disciple can claim to have discovered them purely from detailed empirical studies of turn-taking in telephone conversations. All subsequent work will be more than just empirical discovery. It will also involve some attempt to apply theoretical work developed by the founding members, and it is disingenuous to render subsequent studies as purely empirical, as a series of 'discoveries'.

(2) Ethnomethodology may try to be 'indifferent' to the substance of the topics it investigates, but this is no easier than, and no different from, earlier attempts to be 'value-free' or 'detached'. It is not clear if this claimed ability is a matter of 'methods', or 'values'. A focus on methods seems to imply a positivist position, whereby the deployment of suitable methodological rituals will somehow conjure up 'the facts' – the arduousness of the ritual, such as using laborious recording and transcription methods, serves mostly to reassure the magician and any sceptical observers. The positivist tone of some analyses extends to a refusal to consider different interpretations of the conversations taking place – despite all the transcription codes and symbols, I am not sure if ethnomethodologists could or would want to distinguish between a sincere inquiry for accounts of newsworthy events and a tactical one in a telephone conversation. These matters probably require an attention to social contexts and other matters well beyond the formal properties of language in use.

If 'indifference' arises from value commitments, however, the effects and the sources of these need to be clarified. There might be a claim involved that we have met before: that the ethnomethodologist is operating with unconsciously held values – in an habitus – that just seem to be 'the way to do things'. We might be talking about the cultural capital of the modern Californian academic, as others have suggested (see Gouldner 1971 and the online reading guide). Whatever the case, as feminists and others have argued, no-one can wish away the effects of such values merely by trying to deny that they exist. Incidentally, the reference to an habitus calls to mind Bourdieu's objection (Bourdieu 2000): ethnomethodologists need the concept unless they really think that people discover order literally each time they meet and talk with no past experience to guide them. However, the concept of habitus also implies more conventional sociological concerns again such as social distancing, stratification and power.

(3) Ethnomethodologists may believe that the methods they use are essentially the same as the methods used by any 'members', but they are members of a special professional and academic faction. Ethnomethodology always had a special purpose in professional terms – to critique academic sociology, possibly to replace it, and certainly to establish a whole tradition of its own, with all that goes with that in the form of chairs, research programmes, publications, institutes, and the like. Garfinkel's own lack of institutional ambition seems to be the exception here. As a result, the 'indifference' of the approach needs to be overhauled – behind all those laborious empirical investigations are recognisable academic and professional motives. They need to tell us how important these were in the great attempt to proselytise and to expand ethnomethodological work: when indifferently investigating 'normal' conversations, how did they manage to control their own ambitions to gain PhDs, research grants or lecturing posts? How important were these professional motives in 'guiding' empirical studies towards recognisably academic ends?

Underneath some of these arguments, it might be possible to detect some more technical ones as well. We know from Schütz, for example, that it is impossible fully to know the meaning of the activities of other people, and all that sociologists can really do is to develop ideal types of varying levels of detail and concreteness. Ethnomethodology therefore seems to be involved in the construction of extremely detailed types, but of ideal types nevertheless. Incidentally, to deepen our scepticism, we might add some of the arguments about the intentionality of 'everyday' life that we discussed earlier. It follows that ethnomethodologists' attempts to generalise between different studies involve the same kind of syntheses of levels of typifications within the same professional consciousness. It is not surprising that a series of empirical studies confirm the use of the documentary method, or the 'rule' about adjacency pairing – that is the way that professional consciousness works to construct a coherent synthetic view of the world. What this means, of course, is that ethnomethodology proceeds in the curious way that it does only after a highly selective reading of the social phenomenological work that it claims as inspirational.

## Problems with Winch

We might return to the general level again, and summarise quickly some of the main criticisms that have been directed at Winch's position. Many of them turn on the notion of the 'forms of life' that play so crucial a part in the argument. As you might expect, marxist theorists, and we shall use Benton (1977) as our example, will want to say that these forms of life need to be investigated in much more detail. Such an investigation would rapidly reveal that definite social relations and particular economic conditions are responsible for those forms of life in the first place. The same theme is pursued by Giddens (1976), who says that actual forms of life do not exist just as pools of linguistic rules and resources in some abstract sense, but reveal a whole set of processes whereby certain ideas become institutionalised, supported by the use of power, and subjected to the results of subsequent action. Giddens also has serious general reservations about linguistic analogies for social action in that they tend to be functionalist, and thus overstress conformity, reciprocity and co-operation.

I think this is a major weakness, which we have identified in abstract philosophy before. It is one thing to posit some ideal community and award it the functions of providing linguistic resources, but quite another then carelessly to identify this ideal community with actual communities. This is certainly one of the points made in Gellner's (1968) waspish and highly entertaining critique of 'linguistic philosophy' as developed out of the work of the later Wittgenstein. (I have offered a brief online reading guide to this critique on my website.) There is an important general argument in this piece for a separation between philosophy and sociology: it may be true to argue that the rules of language are established in social collectivities, but it is a mistake to argue that social collectivities are merely and nothing but embodiments of rules of language.

In practice, communities exist in states of some complexity, and they even overlap on a global scale these days. The possibilities of highly localised relativism simply do not exist any more. Marxists and feminists, of course, have always hoped that localism would diminish as a result of political consciousness-raising. Gellner suggests that holding to some advanced relativism is an absurdity, which only philosophers actually believe in. As we shall see in the next chapter, this 'aversion against the universal' (Honneth 1985) persisted in 'postmodern' forms of Wittgensteinian linguistic philosophy too.

Instead of studying actual communities and discovering this universality, linguistic philosophers have simply incorporated characteristics of the only community they really know anything about – their own, as academics based largely at various elite universities. As several other critics have noticed too, Winch's own philosophical investigations seem exempt from the criticisms he wants to make about everyone else's. He does far more than just describe ordinary speech himself, but wants to make judgements about it, and, indeed, translate it into more abstract philosophical categories, while all the time forbidding any other discipline the same route. Presumably, he would quite like us to believe that his arguments have a far wider currency than that found among the strange linguistic community of abstract philsosophers.

Winch's arguments derive most of their force from a philosophical struggle with other philosophers. Why sociology should be singled out as a target remains a mystery, says Gellner – some irrational dislike of sociology by linguistic philosophers is the reason he gives. My own view, for what it is worth, is that this dislike arises because philosophers, and many other commentators, feel obliged to make some remarks about existing social events in order to lend their work some social relevance: sociology has to be driven off first, though. Doubtless, the usual entanglements of academic and political rivalries and differences are also involved.

Winch attempts to replace transcendental philosophy with a search for the social roots of language, and finally to repel positivism with his stress on the irreducibility of meaning. But he never closely interrogates actual sociological approaches such as the ones in modern marxism (and there has been some discussion of Winch in the work of Habermas and his associates, not all of it negative) or structuration, as outlined in Giddens' commentary.

## Habermas

In discussing Habermas, we are encountering the usual problems for a writer of a mere textbook. Habermas is a very prolific author, and his work has been much discussed, applied and criticised. Only a very quick sketch can be attempted here, supplemented with some online reading guides to a few of the main works. As always, the themes I have selected omit a lot of detail and many equally worthy discussions. There are additional commentaries, of course, ranging from the systematic but rather preliminary Waters (1994), to the more extensive and generally excellent McCarthy (1984).

Habermas began his academic career as one of Adorno's research assistants, and we can begin to see how the themes prominent in the early Critical Theory are pursued. Habermas can be seen to continue the project, sometimes defined as developing a 'philosophy of history (an attempt to both explain and analyse the characteristic forms of capitalism especially and how they have developed), but with 'empirical intent' (that is, taking on what was known about society from a range of social sciences). The initial statements on Critical Theory by Horkheimer and Marcuse flesh out this intention into something approaching a programme, as we saw in Chapter 7.

However, we have already seen when looking at Adorno that there is a danger of excessive criticism and negation inherent in this project. We are to subject all accounts and ideas, including Marx's, to a thorough critique, arguing that they all prematurely identify themselves with some empirical reality, or reify one aspect of a complex and dynamic (and unspecified) 'totality'. This is a pretty unappealing project for political activists, and it makes the idea of liberation into a very abstract and philosophical possibility almost bound to be confined to thought alone. Habermas can be seen as offering one way out of this impasse, by trying to ground the notion of critique and liberation in something much more positive and material, some aspects of human nature.

If we want to make social criticism a concrete practical activity, not one just confined to philosophers, we can suggest that particular activities, such as the social relations of capitalism, are not as free or as emancipated as they might be. They do not sufficiently express or reflect some natural tendency towards critique and liberation. I am using terms here that Habermas himself would not be using, in fact. We shall see how he tries to suggest that this tendency towards critique and liberation is not grounded in anything dubious like 'human nature', but is found instead in the very practices of human language.

Here we are entering some familiar ground, perhaps. It is really difficult to sustain the traditional view of the human subject as having a 'consciousness' or a 'nature', for reasons we have met already. Subjects are already constituted or constructed by social processes, including their immersion in social practices or in language. There is also a growing awareness of the embarrassment of having based an entire analysis on something inherently speculative like what it is that human consciousness or nature reveals. This field is often colonised by liberals or conservatives too, of course, and we want to share as little ground as possible with them. Relying on human subjectivity used to offer some political hopes for leftists, however – an inherently 'rebellious subjectivity' would always strain against the impositions of capitalist rationality and discipline, meaning that there was always a potential for emancipation and revolt. Echoes of this notion can be found in the work of de Certeau in Chapter 11. Habermas broke with this conception too (see Bernstein 1984 and the online reading guide).

However, Habermas's first attempts to pursue this project operated with different philosophical baggage. In one work (Habermas in Adorno et al. 1976; and see the online reading guide), we find Habermas criticising positivism as offering far too limited a perspective on the world. What it ignores or banishes as irrelevant are perhaps the most important aspects of human life, such as the attempts to communicate and interact. Positivism and scientific rationality can be traced to important human activities too, however, and thus have their place. Habermas was to refer later to the notion of 'work' to encompass these activities directed at manipulating physical objects in the world. However, it would be quite wrong to suggest that this interest in work encompassed all human activities, which is the tendency in positivism at its most aggressive.

Habermas (in Adorno et al. 1976) was to go on to make two points specifically from this insistence that there are more interests in human activity than just work. One relates specifically to the debate about positivism. Scientists, when they argue about theories and evidence, use the full range of human interaction and communication, and do not confine themselves just to scientific rationality. It is quite right that they do so, and it shows the importance of the separate intent to communicate and interact, even in what seems to be a cold logical and objective process. Habermas (1984) later expanded these insights into a whole discussion on the 'theory of argumentation', pointing to the free-ranging (and fundamentally democratic) nature of human conversations and arguments.

The second point is more political. A number of other social theories have simply tried to install an interest in work as somehow essential to human activity, downplaying the equally important interests in communication and interaction. They can also be criticised for advocating a premature closure, a too-easy identification of some central key to human social relations. These theories include marxism, because Marx himself failed to give enough attention to communication and interaction as activities in their own right. So did some other marxists, including those who embrace the central concept of 'alienation', which once more tends to blame some central process located in consciousness and originating in work. Habermas's approaches open up possibilities for this approach in two directions: first, an interest in work has to be given its due, as something central to human activity that cannot be abolished by some playful socialism; but, second, work is only one interest, and must not be over-emphasised. Socialist politics should really be aimed at controlling the interest in work, preventing it from becoming dominant and from 'colonising' communication and interaction. The process of colonisation in question looks very much like Weber on rationalisation, at first: social life itself becomes increasingly rationalised, organised and 'work-like', although Habermas (1984) was to suggest that Weber did not get it quite right either, and thus new terms, such as 'system' and 'lifeworld', were required to grasp fully what was happening to social life.

Habermas did not entirely support those existing cultural and social sciences that were devoted to understanding interaction. His 1984 work includes an excellent criticism of some of the central tendencies in 'action sociology', which, very basically, argues that even these have a limited view of human interaction and of the possibilities for it escaping social constraint, as we hinted in Chapter 4. Indeed, this has produced an intriguing classification or taxonomy of theories of human interaction, which might well be useful in trying to order the field and classify the various approaches one learns about as a beginner, such as Parsons' notion of communication, symbolic interactionism, Goffman's interactionism, ethnomethodology, and so on.

The same kind of point is made about linguistic and cultural sciences. Here, Habermas turned to Freud (and to Gadamer). Again, to be very brief, Freudian psychoanalysis is indeed a reflective analytical method which spans both positivism and cultural sciences. It has liberatory intentions as well, aiming to dissolve the 'blocks' to emancipation which have been produced by various cultural and symbolic processes, and which prevent individuals from adequately expressing and pursuing routes to full self-understanding. Indeed, the earlier generation of critical theorists read Freud with the same interests, albeit in rather different ways. It is possible to see a critical social theory as offering some kind of parallel analysis, where ideologies are a kind of social neurosis, requiring analysis to be directed against symbolic and more material 'blocks' to understanding at the social and cultural levels. Freudian analysis was much discussed, but finally rejected as inadequate on the grounds that it failed to provide sufficiently critical materials to pursue social and political emancipation.

Gadamer became famous as an advocate of hermeneutics of a particular kind (I have a web file, not an online reading guide this time, which sketches the basic ideas), and the argument again turned on whether this was adequate to explain human action fully. Hermeneutics could be critical, it was finally accepted, but still in a rather particular way. It is possible to use it as a technique to show how particular linguistic traditions, sedimented in cultural traditions, affect and constrain our present cultural and social activities. However, this is only one kind of 'block', and there are others that arise not from linguistic and cultural traditions alone, but from material practices. Hermeneutics cannot grasp these, partly because it has argued itself into a corner, so to speak: it becomes impossible to grasp the effects of past cultural traditions 'from the outside', its main advocates argue. We shall be returning later on to this argument that 'nothing exists outside of language', but it is clear already, I hope, that Habermas will want to reject this, on political grounds alone. The approach has an in-built conservatism, suggesting that traditions can only be endlessly recycled, tweaked and repeated, and never be decisively left behind.

There are more technical objections too, but we will content ourselves by repeating Habermas's argument that we should not be assuming that human social life can be explained exclusively in terms of any interest in 'work' or in 'symbolic interaction' alone. Both are needed, and it would be particularly convenient if we could identify a third one as well – an interest in 'emancipation'. This would suggest that human beings are capable of doing far more than just dominating their environments, or endlessly recycling cultural traditions, no matter how dynamic that might be. They are also capable of, and profoundly interested in, attempting to emancipate themselves from constraints and blocks, engaging in self-reflection, utopian thought and political action to enlarge their freedoms.

What we have described here is a model developed in the middle stage of Habermas's work, in fact, and it is known in the trade as the 'quasi-transcendental human interests' (QTHI) model. In *Knowledge and Human Interests* (Habermas 1972), the general argument is intended to show that theory can never be 'pure'. (I have an online reading guide to the Appendix to this work which outlines the central ideas.) Habermas argues that theoretical 'purity' is a rather modern concern anyway, and that the Greeks always imagined that theorising was intimately connected to the idea of achieving a good life, expressed as achieving unity with the rhythms of nature and the cosmos. Since that time, there has been an attempt to abstract theory from this idea, and turn it into some self-sufficient body of propositions, stripped of any reference to values. Habermas sometimes describes this best in his criticisms of obsessions with methodology.

Theories always imply some set of presuppositions about the world. These implicit understandings actually lead to certain matters being given the status of 'fact' or 'proper knowledge' in the first place. Abandoning reflection on how this happens leads to that typical self-misunderstanding of positivism. When we do reflect on how 'facts' and 'objects' are derived from everyday understandings, we encounter the key role played by interests. It is a continuing and common interest that produces common views of the world which are taken as objective facts in such a way that we can then do 'work' on them.

Habermas wants to describe interests in a very general way, rather than list those specific interests that have affected actual theorists. He talks of a 'technical cognitive interest', expressed in empirical sciences, a 'practical' interest expressed in historical and social sciences, and an 'emancipatory cognitive interest' found in the 'critically oriented sciences'. Roughly, the first is concerned with trying to establish laws and make predictions about the world in order to exploit it in the form of a technology. It is this universal interest in dominating nature that has produced consistent sciences, since it has affected the very ways in which we experience the world and thus attempt to explain it. This helps us dispense with scientism, the belief that science is some pure self-sufficient theory offering us some neutral and optimal (and thus universally applicable) way to apprehend the world.

The second interest involves understanding meaning. There are some approaches to the understanding of meaning that also fool themselves that they are dealing with mental facts which can be experienced directly, 'but here, too, the facts are first constituted in relation to the standards that establish them' (Habermas 1972: 309). In other words, interpreters of meaning bring their own pre-understandings to the task. What they actually do is best described by the discipline of hermeneutics. They attempt to communicate with the subjective world of a writer or speaker, bringing their own understandings, but also modifying those understandings in the light of what they have learned about the subjective world of the other. The process goes on in a spiral fashion, which enables Habermas to offer his first argument about the transcendental nature of these interests. He says that processes of interpretation expose a 'constitutive interest in the preservation and expansion of the intersubjectivity of possible . . . mutual understanding . . . [aimed] . . . toward the attainment of possible consensus among actors' (Habermas 1972: 310). In this sense, the intention to understand must transcend purely individual interests, and is designed to uncover layers of some shared intersubjectivity among human beings.

The third interest is one of special concern to a critic. If we are going to change social organisation in a progressive direction, we need to know whether the 'laws' of capitalism are really necessary, or whether they 'express ideologically frozen relations of dependence that can in principle be transformed' (Habermas 1972: 310). Here we have quite a different intent from that expressed in the other interests. We want to critique cultural and natural laws, not just to use them. Self-reflection of a particular kind is the methodological technique here, but it would be a mistake to see this as some abstract philosophical analysis, since it is really driven by some shared interest in emancipation from unnecessary social constraint. Analytic philosophy needs to reconnect its critical techniques with this emancipatory interest. (We could also direct some of these critiques at Winch.)

However, all thinking needs to reconnect with interests. These interests explain why we see reality in the way that we do (a more technical sense in which they are 'transcendental'). We cannot know the world in any other way, Habermas argues, in the strongest sense of 'transcendental' this time: we can only become aware of this essential connection between knowledge and interest. Of course, Habermas is aware of the misunderstandings that he risks by using terms like 'transcendental' or 'essence' – it seems he is using old philosophical terms which have been much debated, instead of trying to develop some new approach. He uses terms such as 'quasi-transcendental' to help avoid this, but still complains he has been misunderstood (see the online reading guide to his Postscript to Knowledge and Human Interests. Habermas (1972: 312) goes on to suggest that these interests 'have their bases in the Natural History of the human species', but denies that he has a simple evolutionary explanation here. The three interests emerge when human beings decisively break with nature, and try to overcome its constraints, heading towards some notion of 'the good life'.

Human interests manifest themselves in social institutions, devoted to 'work, language, and power' (Habermas 1972: 313), but language also appears as common to all social institutions: 'Through its structure, autonomy and responsibility are posited for us' (Habermas 1972: 314). Since language is the common element, and permits both pure and applied 'reason', it reveals the connections between knowledge and interest. It also permits us to perform the necessary self-reflection that leads to emancipation, to 'unblock' distorted dialogues and constrained communication that are apparent in our current society.

Similarly 'blocked' self-misunderstandings arise from positivism. In the case of the natural sciences, this leads to a focus on methodology and technology, but also a dangerous tendency to accommodate to the existing political order. In the human sciences, knowledge gets 'sterilised', the past banished into a museum, and life 'squeez[ed] . . . into the behavioural system of instrumental action' (Habermas 1972: 316). The realm of values is reduced to a mere matter of choosing one set or the other ('decisionism' is the term sometimes deployed to describe this arbitrary sort of choice and commitment): values seem arbitrary, and can even then become things to be explained by some positivistic history. In both cases, the 'illusion of objectivism' (Habermas 1972: 316) has to be critiqued, and the role of interests restored to a central position.

Exponents of this model were able to do some extremely useful work with it, criticising positivism and interactionism alike (as being based in only one of these interests, as above). The model was used in another attempt to classify human sciences in terms of their recognition of all three QTHIs (see, for example, Apel in Brown 1979). There is even an influential book attempting to spell out some of the implications of this general view for something as specific as curriculum design, or research methods (Carr and Kemmis 1986). The argument is that these areas too should feature all three QTHIs if they are to cover the full human experience, as a kind of philosophical recognition of a 'Holy Trinity', as it was sometimes irreverently described. The adequacy of this threefold model is at the heart of the debate between Winch and Apel (also in Brown 1979).

However, Habermas was to change his mind yet again about the adequacy of this model. Instead, he finally came to see that all these necessary tendencies, including an emancipatory one, could be grounded in language, more or less as he had implied. In this, Habermas is following a general 'linguistic turn' in social theory (see Bernstein 1984), moving away from seeing human consciousness as the source and origin of language and culture, and turning instead to the actual uses and practices of language as something far more concrete and far less speculative.

It is clear how this might work, I hope. Language is a crucial dimension in all three 'interests' mentioned above. A particular type of language is used to integrate the activities involved in 'work' while another set of linguistic practices permits symbolic interaction. Indeed, language is inseparable from these important areas of human activities. I suppose the real trick is to demonstrate that language use is fundamental to the progress towards emancipation as well. Habermas demonstrates this by first showing how the language we use permits, maybe even constitutes, the all-important reflection. Until we have expressed our understandings and feelings about events, activities and symbols in language, in discourses, we cannot begin to reflect upon them in a suitably objective and analytical way, free from context. As societies progress, the reflective power of discourses grows. Here especially, incidentally, it is possible to see some links with the sort of philosophical pragmatism associated with American interactionism, which we reviewed in Chapter 4.

All human beings can use language in this way, to analyse, question and reflect. Language offers a kind of constantly subversive possibility in capitalist culture, always threatening to enable people to reflect on and analyse what seems to be natural, real, inevitable and permanent.

Habermas had already analysed dominant forms of communication in capitalist cultures in his analyses of political legitimacy and the crises that threaten it (Habermas 1976; and see the online reading guide). In order to secure political legitimacy, the state and its functionaries often resorted to 'strategic communication', communication which is designed to persuade, to manipulate people, to present one-sided analyses of events which convince us that the state is pursuing the only correct action. Anyone interested in modern politics can think of scores of examples of this kind of thing. The strange works of 'spin doctors' represent the most blatant forms of strategic communication, I suppose. Their attempts to hide embarrassing information, to release it to the press during a quiet period, to stress only some aspects of the story, to resort to euphemism or linguistic camouflage, to hide behind dubious statistics, to spread stories about the opposition, to strategically leak the intentions of the government (or a version of them), are all well-known features of current politics. At my most cynical, I imagine that managers, advertisers and PR consultants devote their entire time to strategic communication too, although colleagues who teach those disciplines assure me that they attempt to clarify communication as well (and sometimes cite Habermas, of all people, as an inspiration).

Because the state in modern societies faces a particular difficulty, there is another kind of communication which is dominant: 'distorted communication'. Modern states needs to engineer the consent of a majority of the voting public, and they also rely on the voting public seeing them as following the 'interests of all'. In fact, Habermas argues, the state must really privilege the interests of particular powerful sectors of the public, including the interests of capital. This tension, between acting in the interests of all, and acting in the interests of a powerful minority, is the main source of a whole series of crises which Habermas and his colleague Offe (1984) were to predict, providing their readers with some hope for political change, at last. Desperate attempts to manage this tension can also take a form familiar to us from Marx himself in his account of ideology: statements are issued which represent minority interests as the interests of everyone. Examples here include slogans such as 'What is good for Ford is good for the country', or, perhaps, 'We are taking this military action to defend civilisation'.

Luckily, anyone who speaks the language is capable of challenging the claims inherent in such forms of communication. It is probably routine to do so when considering party political statements, manifestos or broadcasts. Most people faced with a politician will immediately begin thinking about the claims made to sincerity, for example: is the speaker sincere, does what he or she says come 'from the heart', from some consistent set of personal beliefs, or is it all written down by a spin doctor? Then there are questions that can be asked about truthfulness: do the statements bear a proper relationship to knowledge about outside events (in ways which would attract a broad consensus)? And, finally, there are questions about social appropriateness: the UK Prime Minister encountered a challenge on this dimension when he addressed a meeting of the Women's Institute and began outlining his political commitments, much against the conventions that demand a non-political address. He was slow-handclapped. Mr Blair is also famous for hijacking national events and trying to gain political capital out of them, but then they all do it, turning up at football finals, the Olympics, funerals of the famous, church services, spectacular accidents and scenes of crime, and so on. Incidentally, thinking of politicians also reminds me of the fourth area of challenge, which I am prone to overlook because it is normally rarely problematic – intelligibility. Most people can speak a well-formed sentence as a matter of routine, but it is true that some politicians and executives have developed a remarkably impenetrable jargon.

The areas of intelligibility, sincerity, truthfulness and social appropriateness are justified as crucial in a suitably technical if abstract manner. Habermas thinks of them as claims related to linguistic competence, to the inner, psychological world, the objective world and the social world, respectively.

These are fairly harmless and trivial examples, of course, but I hope it is clear that these main claims to validity are implicit in any actual form of communication, and, crucially, questions about these claims can be raised by any participant in that communication. It is always open to me, in principle at least, to stop dead a politician, manager, colleague or close friend, and demand that they justify their claims to intelligibility, sincerity, truthfulness and social appropriateness. If they cannot do so, I can accuse them of dealing in strategic communication, and demand to know why they are manipulating me and what they hope to get from me. No specialist philosophical or social science concepts are required. Anyone can ask these questions of anyone else. We can now see the radical democratic and emancipatory potential in everyday language, or at least in a particularly abstract communicative act – the 'ideal speech act', as it has become known, which permits all the claims and questions, and is dominated only by the search for the best argument. We seem to have at last an adequate description of the full potentialities of human language, and a triumphantly emancipatory potential. Of course, there will be a struggle if we are to preserve this potential, and to keep language free from those strong colonising tendencies that try to turn it back into a mere co-ordinating mechanism for work-based activities.

Perhaps we should round off this section by pointing out what Habermas himself uses this model to achieve, apart from the project of grounding emancipatory interests. He wants to offer yet another classification of sciences, including social sciences, and the type of language that predominates in them, according to whether they are 'praxis-dominated' or 'reflection-dominated', or various combinations of the two. He also wants to connect up a lot of theorising about human progress. This includes the work of Piaget and Kohlberg on the development of reflexive powers in children as well. Habermas's perspective on language at the social level takes on evolutionary undertones: our linguistic powers are not given to us already formed, but have to develop. The key part in this development is played by a number of social institutions that provide learning mechanisms (rather reminiscent of Hegel here, some critics think). The most famous of these, perhaps, helped to develop a 'public sphere'; the fate of this public sphere in modern societies, and how it might be represented in political institutions, has been much discussed since. In many ways, the political task can be summarised as defending what remains of the public sphere, and trying to extend it as a home for the exercise of the 'ideal speech act' by all citizens.

## Some criticisms

Perhaps the best collections of such criticisms are Thompson and Held (1982), or McCarthy (1984). It is obviously impossible to do justice to all of these criticisms, so I am going to divide them into two types of general criticism, and then illus-trate these types with some specific examples.

With a piece of work like Habermas's, which attempts to synthesise, order and classify a number of other famous philosophical and sociological positions, one sort of criticism is going to come from those who have been synthesised: they are going to argue that their positions have been misconstrued, reduced in some way in order to be a part of Habermas's grand scheme, and that they are perfectly adequate on their own anyway. Habermas can be accused of either reductionism or incoherence here, and we might briefly examine the work of some rival philosophers, such as Bubner or Heller. One variant is going to come from people with their own rival grand interpretive schemes, and here we might include Giddens, who obviously wants to press the case of his own synthesising effort ('structuration theory'), which has already appeared once or twice in ear-lier chapters.

The second sort of criticism is a familiar one, applied to many general theo-retical schemes. It is that they have not pursued sufficiently concrete analysis of states (Held or Arato), of social reproduction (Giddens), or of speech (Thompson) (all in Thompson and Held 1982). We have also met Fraser's excel-lent feminist critique (1989) in Chapter 8, which accuses Habermas of failing to notice the concrete effects of gender in matters such as linking systems and life-world, and thus of operating with unreflected androcentric binary concepts.

There has also been a third controversy, which I am going to postpone for Chapter 13, turning on the celebrated disputes between Habermas and Lyotard on postmodernism, and especially relativism versus universality.

Let us proceed with the first kind of criticism. Is it really going to be possible to incorporate so many things into one coherent account, based on the universal capacities and competences associated with language? Partly, this is going to depend very much on a close reading of Habermas's texts, which will take quite some time. We would need to ask whether he has really rendered Marx's posi-tion accurately, for example, in a way that fully justifies his own attempt to press the cause of communication as an area of life separate from work and labour. Is he right in his characterisation of the various sociological theories and approaches that are organised so neatly in the various works, according to the models of communicative competence that they attribute to actors?

What we can do, instead of pursuing this detailed level of analysis, is briefly to outline some more general criticisms to illustrate the problems. At the heart of Habermas's project is this insistence that there is something transcendental about language, something universal, in the later work. This argument is used again and again to do critical analysis of other social theories that do not realise the full potential of human language, and that operate by trying to privilege par-ticularly restricted versions of it (such as positivism, but also a wide range of action theories, marxism, hermeneutics, Freudian analysis and the rest). Not only that, the potentials of human language in the 'ideal speech act' can also be used to found some universally democratic alternative to existing social and political practices. You might have already found this sort of argument a bit over-general, and, if you are a sociologist, a bit abstract and 'philosophical' too.

Let us take the idea of 'quasi-transcendental human interests' in the earlier models. How exactly do we get to discover these? Where did they come from? The answer is still not clear. Habermas seems to have arrived at these in advance of any empirical analysis, although he does assure us that such analysis is needed to demonstrate that everything can ultimately be explained in terms of the three interests. However, he seems to have taken a few philosophical short-cuts to get to this quasi-transcendental level. He wants to argue, first, that this level is presupposed, somehow, since something is needed to establish the more specific kinds of theories and activities that we can observe. Critics like Bubner (in Thompson and Held 1982) suggest that this is a version of a Kantian analy-sis, trying to establish, by conceptual analysis, what is presupposed in activities such as language use based on work or communication. Much will depend, therefore, on the philosophical rigour of the analysis. I am not really competent to discuss this myself, but I am impressed by those critics who argue that evi-dence is lacking for the emancipatory interest in particular as something that underpins human evolution. Indeed, my sociological training would probably lead me to want to investigate the whole notion of social evolution in the first place: it has a number of well-known problems, such as operating with some presupposed notion of progress which it then claims to demonstrate in the course of human history. I also feel slightly alarmed to see such an emphasis placed on the work of Piaget, a rather controversial figure to put it mildly. Finally, I suspect that in skilled hands, a number of alternative, but probably equally plausible, transcendental interests can be detected in human history – an interest in domination, perhaps.

Bubner goes on to claim that another kind of transcendental argument is also present when Habermas turns to political criticism. This is not so much some formal analysis of what is presupposed, but more a matter of asserting what could be achieved politically, what is implicit or potential in human interaction. Some critics find this utopian or idealistic anyway, of course, but Bubner's point is that, technically, this kind of transcendental argument is not the same as the Kantian one, and so the project to unite them must be incoherent. Social criticism is based on practical reason, Bubner argues, and this is quite a different matter from attempting to establish undoubted premises that underpin knowledge. There are other incoherences too: an ideal society can only be linked to some pure ideal speech act if you see social life as being determined by language. The emancipatory interest in particular tends to run together philosophical and political criticism. This supposed connection between the two crops up in a number of criticisms, in fact, and we shall return to it.

Several critics have also pointed to the difficulty of claiming that Habermas has detected something genuinely universal, and is not just choosing his own general synthesising scheme. If all the other major theorists have fallen prey to unperceived limits on their thought, what confidence can we really have that

Habermas's scheme has escaped, and has somehow projected itself on to a position free from constraint? We seem to be offered a number of arguments again. Habermas demonstrates the superiority of his critique by being able to incorporate and progress beyond everyone else's theoretical schemes, or he argues that he has discovered something really universal by claiming to recognise common universal elements in those schemes, and, for that matter, in everyday speech as well. Again, however, as McCarthy argues, this is either a philosophical assertion (a claim to a priori status in his words, one of many such claims apparent in the Western tradition of philosophy), or something that needs to be checked against data 'conforming in a mass of crucial and clear cases to the intuitions of competent subjects' (in Thompson and Held 1982: 62). Habermas offers us no clues at all about how to proceed to gain such empirical data. Ideally, we would particularly need to know what sort of evidence would count against his views, so we could test them rigorously.

Of course, the real reason to suppose that this whole substructure of quasi-transcendental human interests is suspect is that not long after having persuaded us that it was crucial and well founded, Habermas promptly accepted that it was flawed and abandoned it in favour of an emphasis on universal pragmatics! There is also a whole new battery of concepts required as a result, such as the differences between action and discourse (see the online reading guide to the Postscript to *Knowledge and Human Interests*). However, the full turn to language still involves some problems, according to Thompson (in Thompson and Held 1982). The problem of relativism persists: why should we accept Habermas's view of language as describing some universal characteristics, and not just his own preferred approach? Thompson finds other things equally puzzling. We are told, for example, that only unconstrained communication can properly reproduce social relations, and this is why the lifeworld is ultimately under threat from colonisation. But what exactly are the arguments to support this view?

Similar problems relate to the ideal speech act, where it is not at all clear why we should accept this as some kind of archetype of democracy, as Lyotard is going to argue (in the next chapter). At times, I must say, I have seen in the advocacy of the ideal speech act the personal and professional values of the university seminar – unconstrained discussion, the pursuit of the better argument, a meeting of minds irrespective of status, and so on. I am sceptical about the right for a majority(?) to deny a question its social appropriateness in particular (and see the criticism below). In all these cases, Habermas seems to be making a claim that his position is somehow 'value-free', to put it in sociologists' terms.

Of course, Habermas, rather like the other general theorists we have seen and will see below, is forced to become a kind of amateur sociologist. He does rely on some sociological studies to support his arguments, best of all, perhaps, in *Legitimation Crisis* (Habermas 1976; and see the online reading guide). He has also increasingly turned to proposals (never actually carried out) to pursue

empirical investigations of social life, language and politics, instead of the 'philosophical detour', as he calls it himself (Habermas 1984), which has occupied so
much of his time up to now. However, his sociological discussions seem abstract
and one-sided: I have already noted the strange preference for functionalism,
and for functionalist analyses of political culture and subcultural revolt, say, in
*Legitimation Crisis.*

A number of critics line up to confirm this in Thompson and Held's collection.
Thompson argues that real speech acts, and, for that matter, real theoretical discussions, seem quite different from the ideal speech act. They are not always
aimed at consensus, and often conceal hidden kinds of coercion, including
experts trying to baffle or mislead the other participants. I am sure that most
feminists would want to argue that these are typical of conversations between
men and women. Habermas himself has accepted this point and has rather late
and lamely come to the conclusion that unconstrained discussion pursuing only
the better argument might not be socially appropriate in all social institutions
anyway: 'Now . . . Habermas acknowledges that the content of particular life-
forms depends on traditions, no matter how reflexively appropriated, and that
"socialised individuals cannot relate hypothetically to the form of life or to the
life-history through which their own identity has been formed"' (Dews 1992: 17).
Finally, educational institutions are the obvious case where it might be appropriate to postpone unconstrained communication to a fairly late stage in order to
permit initial learning to take place.

Heller (in Thompson and Held 1982) has observed, rather as MacCannell and
McCannell do for Foucault (in Ramazanoğlu 1993; and in the online reading
guide), that force is barely discussed, even though it is frequently impossible to
disconnect it from actual discourse. Lukes (in Thompson and Held 1982) notes
that Habermas operates with ideal actors as well as ideal speech acts, asks
whether real actors could ever be expected to escape their prejudices (as admitted above), and suggests that the whole model is circular (ideal speech acts can
only really be engaged in by ideal actors, who are then capable of ideal speech,
and so on). He also asks who will actually be invited to participate in a real politics established on this basis – everyone? Representatives of relevant groups?
Which groups? The whole scheme is but a 'rationalist illusion' until economic
and social changes provide the kind of actors capable of this kind of discourse.

Finally, Giddens (also in Thompson and Held 1982, and elsewhere) suggests
that Habermas needs to look at real examples of interaction, which probably
cannot be reduced so easily to communicative action. For Giddens, interaction
always has a dual structure, as in his general 'structuration' approach, so
Habermas's attempt to reduce it just to something driven by a communicative
intent is precisely the kind of reduction that Habermas has criticised in others.
Giddens also objects to the connections between psychology and sociology,
which he finds abstract again. What we really need instead is some more concrete account of how people develop the values that they do, instead of some
abstract analogy between individual and social development. Further, there is no

proper account of the production and reproduction of the social level. Instead, Habermas just borrows this from functionalism, and he is surprisingly uncritical about the normative biases in that approach, such as its tendency to over-emphasise integration, to see all struggle as arising from functional problems, and so on.

Of course, there is a political difference lurking here, in that Giddens argues for a necessary connection between analysis and action, leading to a pleasantly optimistic and activist feel to his work. Habermas, on the other hand, wants to separate social theory and political action. Not only is the former much less driven by practical concerns, but he also wants to raise some doubts about a strong claim among social theorists that theory can somehow be used even to guide action. Action, being strategic, involves much more risk than does theory, and politicians should largely be expected and encouraged to bear those risks for themselves, without getting the approval of theorists first, so to speak.

Habermas actually replies to these criticisms in his own right, and to his own satisfaction at least, in the same Thompson and Held collection. I will leave it to you to read his response, but I must say I found it both variable and rather tactical, admitting problems in some areas, denying them in others, suggesting that some issues can only be resolved by empirical analysis yet to be done, and so on. Of course, there are some excellent points in reply as well. However, I want to leave Habermas at this point, although we will return to him later, and go on to discuss one final famous case of the linguistic turn – postmodernism.

# 13 Hitting the 'Posts'

Perhaps the most relevant writer to pursue in slightly more depth here initially is Lyotard, especially via his argument in *The Postmodern Condition* (Lyotard 1984; and see the online reading guide). As the Foreword by Jameson points out, this is an argument that attempts to illustrate what might be called the theoretical impact of the postmodern, and which directs several arguments specifically at Habermas. Habermas had himself by then already written a couple of pieces challenging the direction in French philosophy towards postmodernism (see the online reading guides on Habermas). (An excellent summary of the debate overall is provided by Dews 1992, and there is an online reading guide to this work too).

To be brief, Lyotard takes up two major themes. First he offers an account of social changes that have drastically affected the basis of legitimation in social life. This seems to me to be rather speculatively based on an account of traditional knowledge, folk tales and myths, and their narrative structure (with shades of de Certeau again – see Chapter 11). The basic idea is that these traditional narratives expressed the collective folk wisdom of the community, concerning how to act in different social circumstances, for example. More than that, however, they offered a basis for social solidarity, since in a traditional narrative, both the teller of the narrative and the listeners are acting out a social relationship. The narrator him- or herself does not own the story, but claims to be relating some social piece of wisdom, owned by the collective. Narrators make it clear that they have listened to these narratives themselves, and listeners are able to imagine themselves in the place of the narrator. Narratives therefore create a kind of organic solidarity between speakers and listeners. The whole argument sounds a bit like Durkheim on the social functions of religion, but Lyotard differs from him in a number of respects.

Organic solidarity changes into a more complex form, and, for a while at least, these more complex industrial societies are themselves split into two by the formation of social classes and the ensuing conflict. Lyotard wants to argue that forms of narrative also change, and that this is just as important a factor as the external causal factors (population growth and so on) identified by Durkheim behind the shift in types of solidarity. Traditional narrative ceases to act as a legitimating myth and collective ritual, because it no longer has a monopoly on legitimation. Among the challengers to traditional knowledge, the growth of science is destined for a particular role.

This is Lyotard's second major theme. He offers us a summary of some recent trends in the sociology and philosophy of science to begin with. Originally, science might be understood as challenging the legitimating function of traditional narratives, and substituting for it the legitimating function of 'performativity', that is, the ability to produce both cognitive and technical progress. The emergence of such a successful way of understanding as science produces problems for intellectuals as well, who have either to attempt to integrate science into some universal quest for truth, or to operate with an awkward dualism that sees two ways of understanding the world. The latter is expressed by the familiar splits between perspectives in sociology, but it is also the position attributed to Habermas in his attempts to operate with two (then three) knowledge-generating human interests.

Things have moved on, argues Lyotard. Science itself has become split and subdivided into quite different understandings, and the belief in some underlying objective reality that is being described by science has long been abandoned. Lyotard here draws upon some famous work like that of Thomas Kuhn (1962), who argued that science progressed by the fundamentally irrational process of choosing successive 'paradigms'. (I have an online reading guide to this work.) These operate with different worldviews, based on particular conceptions of problems and key examples, their own research programmes and their own passionate adherents. Many other philosophers and historians have taken up this insight, and argued that there are different sorts of responses to it, some arguing that some common logic persists across different paradigms, while others suggest that there is now a kind of free-floating anarchy in science, with no consensus about the objects or the methods which characterise the discipline.

Lyotard is one of those who emphasise the proliferation of differences in modern science. These are now so well advanced that science is best seen as a series of different 'language games', more or less as Winch has described them in the earlier section of Chapter 12. In line with Wittgenstein, Lyotard wants to suggest that these different language games bear little relation to external notions, but contain their own definitions of truth, validity, scientific procedure, and the like. Even a common interest in performativity has now disappeared, although scientists still maintain that this is one of their goals, more or less cynically, to persuade funding bodies to finance their research, says Lyotard. The state also wants to develop the myth of science as a coherent pursuit of truth and progress, to justify its own huge expenditure on the activity. But in practice, scientists themselves are interested in language games, and are driven primarily by a desire to think up a new move in the games they happen to be playing. The way they think up new moves is often by rethinking what is known, and trying to place what is known in a new theoretical framework. I think this is what Lyotard means by 'paralogy'.

This argument is an interesting one in locating the much-publicised emergence of relativism in serious science, instead of in the more obvious locations, such as popular culture. It shows that considerable intellectual effort is required to develop relativism as a commitment, and to overcome the pressures towards conformity that dominate less abstract modes of thought. I think Gellner was quite right to rebuke Winch for the quaint view of isolated linguistic communities he held (see the previous chapter), but Lyotard has an important counter, enabling us to criticise Gellner in turn for assuming the universality of science.

Universities and university departments are arguably indispensable locations for this sort of protected endeavour in the conduct of science, however, even though Lyotard is perfectly correct in pointing out that scientific research goes on in a large number of alternative commercial companies, research institutes, and the like. Competition between these institutions for funding and for prestige seems to be an important factor in scientific change and progress as well. A curiously under-cited commentator on scientific progress in Lyotard's review, Lakatos (1979), makes this general point, suggesting that scientists get together in teams, with institutional backing, and try to launch and maintain 'research programmes'. Particular scientific theories and metatheories are often chosen because they seem to be likely to yield a productive and prolonged research programme, as we have already argued.

Perhaps Lyotard overlooks this point as a part of his general scepticism about the future role of universities (one of the more entertaining sections of the book). The great universities (Lyotard chooses the University of Berlin) were trying to police all the differences that were emerging in knowledge, and to tie them back in again to some underlying philosophical project. Alternatively (and here Lyotard chooses French universities), they were in the business of harnessing the separate and various knowledges to some universal interest in the pursuit of the popular good. Both integrating projects fail, the first because even German speculative philosophy cannot in the end integrate the different knowledges under some grand philosophical project, and the second because the public get isolated from the specialist knowledge required to do academic work, and even science begins the drift already described from performativity into language games. I think there are profitable connections here too with the drift towards scholasticism, as Bourdieu (2000) calls it, which is not only a response to external crises in knowledge and legitimation, but also a distancing trend with its own determinants and effects.

Together, these trends lead to an irreversible combination of changes in knowledge and in society. In fact, Lyotard is sensible enough not to insist that social changes *cause* changes in knowledge, or even that they emanate from some underlying similar trend; more research is needed, he argues. We can rescue him from the charge of sociological naïvety that it is possible to level against other commentators in this field (such as Barthes, for assuming that his own scholastic project to found a 'new semiology' of free-floating intertextuality expresses some irreversible world-historic social movement away from the old forms of social bonding). As a result, though, a quest to reintegrate the knowledges back together into some universal form of knowledge is in vain.

Differences between language games, in science at least, are now so well established that the project is impossible. Attempts at reintegration are only possible through some policy of 'terroristic' suppression of differences.

The last two points apply pretty directly to Habermas and his project, which we have outlined in the previous chapter, to see 'universal pragmatics' as somehow lying behind, or constituting, all the different variants of natural and human sciences. The ideal speech act should not be celebrated as some fundamental universal way to question validity, for Lyotard, but rather as a form of thought policing, demanding that differences in knowledge may not be pursued, even playfully, without being subjected to some stern people's tribunal ready to launch a barrage of questions about validity.

Habermas and his defenders have launched their own rejoinders, and some of them look rather similar to the attacks on Winch, which we have seen in the previous chapter. For example, Habermas himself points to the tendency of the notion of language games to leave the world as it is. Not only is this an abandonment of the whole heritage of critical thinking, but it also lends itself to dangerous conservative trends trying to oppose the whole heritage of modernism (Habermas 1981). Other criticisms have been more 'philosophical' or methodological. A number of commentators, including Benhabib (1984; and I have an online reading guide to this piece) have pointed to the obscure philosophical foundations of these views of irreconcilable differences. Postmodernists seemed pretty sure about these differences for others, but this implies that somehow their own discourse has risen above the status of a mere language game.

The strongest version of the preference for difference has certainly led to some political embarrassment, and has even placed Lyotard dangerously close to the dubious company of Holocaust deniers. Norris (1992) tells the full story, albeit in a pretty partisan way, but we can follow the bones of it easily enough. There are no universal forms of legitimation, but only a series of self-contained language games, Lyotard tells us. So does that mean that there can be no universal condemnation of the Nazi 'Final Solution', and that we should tolerate Holocaust denial as an expression of 'difference'? The mass slaughter of people made sense inside the Nazi language game, no doubt, because Jews were genuinely perceived as a threat to the racial community, and so it made sense to exterminate them. Should we not condemn the Nazis? Worse, how can we be sure that our own moral outrage and indignation are not just effects of our own language games? Do we even agree what happened, given that history is only a language game after all, and recognising that a liberal version was clearly imposed on the events by the victors? Is there any real difference between the Nazi language game and the liberal one, or are both equally valid? Lyotard was forced into some rather delicate manouevring to avoid that particular and politically disastrous implication of his work.

It is tempting to extend Gellner's mock sociology of knowledge here and argue that postmodernism reflects the values of the community that spawns and develops it, not the gentlemen of north Oxford, in this case, but the professors of

Paris. More seriously, Bourdieu (1986) has suggested that there is a peculiar affinity between the critical/conservative tendencies of postmodernism and the class position of the 'new petit-bourgeois', who wish to criticise groups both above and beneath them, both traditionalists and social scientists, in order to confirm their own social position. Of course, there is a dangerous tendency to reduce philosophical argument to the worldviews of particular social groups here, as if people were not capable of thinking beyond the horizons of their experience, more or less as we saw some marxists arguing in Chapter 1. This kind of sociological critique also seems dangerously likely to rebound. It should be perfectly possible, in theory, to trace the views of Gellner or Bourdieu back to the (gloriously marginal) social status of both of these thinkers, if one wished to devalue their criticisms in turn.

A particularly appealing criticism of Lyotard is offered by Honneth (1985; I have an online reading guide). If we might make his defence of critical theory more academically neutral than it really is, it might be possible to rephrase it as the demand for some kind of further research or investigation of the central claim to both positions. Habermas's critics accuse him of ignoring or trying to suppress difference, but it is quite possible to accuse Lyotard of an equal but opposite fault: ignoring any tendency towards universality. Again, we might have seen this before with the Gellner–Winch debate: Gellner there was asserting that the local folkish differences between isolated communities playing their own language games were themselves 'nostalgic', invoking some pre-industrial or pre-global society, before we all got to know much more about each other, and before we found we had considerable collective interests after all. What exactly such research would look like is an intriguing question, and if Lyotard and the other Wittgensteinians are right, it could never finally arbitrate between the two positions.

Perhaps there is in the work of Honneth, and Gellner before him, some revived hope for the old critical project after all. Perhaps genuinely collective interests will emerge again, and might even take some social or political form as a 'public sphere'. Perhaps we should also add a pessimistic view to balance this, following our stern duty as a pedagogue.

Baudrillard's views (1983) on the saturation of life by mass media, and of the retreat from the social, suggest that we are far more likely to get some kind of 'bad' universality instead. For him, the dizzy relativism produced by the collapse of traditional narratives and the emergence of hyperreality is replaced by a new form of practical knowledge, found best in the media. All the media will produce in the end is a kind of knowing apathy directed towards all forms of strategic communication, a fatalism in the usual sense, describing an attitude where nothing can be done and nothing much matters. There is even a hint that this will produce systems crisis, rather like Habermas's motivation crisis. At least in the short term, knowing apathy seems to triumph against all the black arts of the persuaders, the manipulators, those who would wish to discipline us. As we have hinted, it means we can simply 'forget Foucault' and all his gloomy predictions about a carceral society, to cite the title of a wonderful polemic (Baudrillard and Lotringer 1987).

Before we end this already rather long chapter in this rather long book, I just want to sketch briefly two further well-known contributions to debates about social theory, the way they use language, and the issues of legitimacy that are involved.

## British post-structuralism

The first contribution is associated with the names of Hindess and Hirst. It is possible to explain their concerns with what they call 'discourse' by seeing it as originally connected to the work of Louis Althusser. Again, we can only be extremely brief, although there is a much lengthier discussion in Crook (1991).

In his attempts to define Marxist science, Althusser was keen to dismiss rival approaches as error, including 'empiricism'. This was not just the usual and much-criticised approach that asserts that there are facts out there, and the job of science is simply to describe and generalise about them. Althusser wanted to deny any role at all to independent empirical facts in the validation of different theories. Instead, and with a recognisable link back to French structuralism, he wanted to consider validity in terms of internal relations between levels of knowledge. The role of marxist theory in particular was to transform the concepts of common-sense or more scientific ideologies into more adequate theoretical concepts (actually via some intellectual 'mode of production'). The adequacy of fully theoretical concepts could not be judged according to their ability to describe some external reality, but must be established internally – briefly, did they relate in a consistent manner to each other, to the knowledge they had produced, and to the concepts that they had transformed?

Equipped with this notion of adequate theorising, Hindess and Hirst began a substantial programme to critique rival explanations to marxism. Most interestingly, for our purposes, they chose to critique much classic sociological theory particularly. Again we cannot do justice to these critiques here, although there is an online reading guide to some of their work (such as Hindess 1977). Basically, they found that most conventional social scientists, including the greats such as Weber and Durkheim, deployed their core concepts extremely inconsistently. This meant they could not qualify for the prestigious title of science, of course. What made these accounts look plausible were what might be called linguistic manoeuvres, aimed at either concealing the inconsistencies, or attempting to solve them by a quiet use of dogmatism glossed with persuasiveness.

I must say this provides a fascinating critical technique for anyone interested in close and detailed reading of the arguments of sociologists (or historians, for that matter). Even complete beginners can sometimes develop an intuitive grasp of inconsistency, I find, which they frequently and characteristically report as being unable to understand the particular tricks, manoeuvres or sequences of argument. Much specialist criticism has followed a similar path too, pointing to a convenient combination of different things, say in Giddens' discussion of 'rules' and 'resources' (as we have seen), or in feminist critiques of Foucault for trying to squeeze too many different things into one concept (in his case, the concept of 'discipline'). Critics have pointed out considerable inconsistencies and variation in the use of key terms, such as 'hegemony' in the work of Stuart Hall (see Harris 1992 for some examples). Then there are the simple assertions that rival approaches are flawed or wrong – we see plenty of examples throughout this book, most recently in the Habermas–Lyotard debates. There are evasive metaphors scattered throughout the works of the great thinkers, and we have noted some. There are fairly simple and uncritical borrowings from the research of people in different fields, so that, as we have seen, much sociology is imported uncritically into the work of the more abstract theorists.

Having said that, there are one or two oddities with the work of Hindess and Hirst that also need to be pointed out. No-one seems exempt from the charge of incoherence and dogmatism, not Marx and, eventually, not even Althusser (Hindess 1977). The suspicion grows that this whole project has turned into one of those corrosive and eventually rather pointless scholastic arguments that have long ago lost their original purpose. The critique also tends to look rather trivial – so what if people are not using theoretical concepts consistently enough? As we know from Habermas, real arguments use a large variety of argumentational techniques, including assertiveness, rhetoric, analogy and metaphor, and it is not clear why all this should be reduced either to the dull logic of positivism or to the rigorous notion of discourse employed by Hindess and Hirst. We are left with the old problem of 'decisionism' – should we just choose a particular version of discourse without justification?

## Derrida

If Hindess and Hirst seemed to run riot particularly in British social theory, my last example has a much more lustrous international stature – Jacques Derrida. Even the usual apologies for brevity seem unconvincing here, and I can only admit that I have squeezed this great thinker into the last section of my last chapter. The deferral of a proper discussion to a series of online reading guides looks thin and tactical even to me. All I can do is to give a quick account of some of the basic implications of adopting Derrida's view of 'writing' as 'deconstruction'. It fits into this chapter only in terms of forming the basis of another claim to attend very carefully to the mechanisms of language if one wants to do social theory. There is, of course, far more to it than that.

Nevertheless, according to Kamuf (1991), we can see Derrida's work as tracking out of French structuralist linguistics. We have explored this approach several times, and referred now and then to the claims that 'signs' take their meaning mostly, or even exclusively, from their relationship to other signs. This is one basis for arguing that 'nothing exists outside the text'. This argument can be seen as a perfectly defensible view that meanings arise from these relationships with signs inside the text, and not primarily from their relations to some external referent. Of course, this point has also escalated into an extraordinary claim that structural linguistics alone heads towards sufficiency and universality, as some queen of the sciences. We have seen a similar escalation in the work of Winch too, where language games expand to become the entirety of social relations themselves.

One response to this approach has been to attempt to reintroduce some notion of the external, and our discussion on Foucault, and whether anything exists outside of discourses, represents one such attempt (in Chapter 10). In some traditions, attempting to isolate a human subject outside of the text has assumed a particular urgency. Our own common-sense conception of ourselves is as unique objects that have a separate and special existence, regardless of the influence of all the texts that have affected us. Critics like Giddens (1979) have advanced a slightly more technical argument, that a reader is logically required to make the text work, so to speak, especially once it came to be realised that there were no simple central meanings to texts. Textual enthusiasts such as Barthes might want to insist that texts themselves play with meaning, disclosing themselves and the various meanings that are formed in them; but Giddens would argue that a far simpler approach is to reintroduce the notion of a reader who is able to focus and thematise particular meanings offered by texts. I find Barthes ambiguous on this myself. In particular it is never entirely clear whether the poetry that Barthes describes as a feature of some of the texts he cites can only be seen by skilled semiologists such as himself, acting as a particularly systematic reader, or whether it is somehow there waiting to be discovered by anybody.

Derrida insists that there is a creative moment not only in the reading of texts, but also in the writing of them, although again he is ambiguous about whether poetic writing is located intertextually, in particularly skilled writers, such as Shakespeare or Marx, or in anybody, as a kind of universal potential. However, he does help to clarify a number of interesting issues about the way texts actually convey meaning. In essence, he is arguing that it is impossible to control meaning when one writes, that the very terms one uses contain hints of other meanings, which are different from the ones that one intends. Derrida calls these 'ghosts', which 'haunt' the most tightly controlled writing.

A couple of specific arguments might help here. We know, for example, that for structuralist linguistics a sign actually consists of two components united together: the signifier (a word, gesture or picture) and the signified (the concept to be alluded to by the sign). We know that, for most signs, the connection between signifier and signified is arbitrary, that is, there is no necessary correspondence between them. The word for feline pet animals in English happens to be 'cat', but there is no particular reason for this, and literally any other word would do, as happens in other languages, of course. It just so happens that in

English the word 'cat' is connected to the signified 'feline pet animal'. To cite a famous discussion in Barthes (1973), it is the concept (actually of 'dog' in his case) that is signified, rather than any specific individual.

I read and noted this well-known argument, as have many students since, without ever really thinking about it. How come these two components actually are united? Why should they be united if they refer to different terms? Derrida wants to argue that the two components are not actually immediately united in the sign, that there is a relation of difference between them. There must be, if any connection between them is arbitrary. It simply looks as if they are immediately united, because we tend to use them as if they were. What we are actually doing, however, is to suppress the difference between them. In our attempts immediately to suppress this difference, we are also concealing a certain deferring, a process whereby meanings are postponed, so to speak. Derrida combines the two senses of differing and deferring by using the French term *différance*.

Some actual signifying work is being done, in other words, when one uses signs. The facility with which we immediately use them conceals this work, and so does a common conception of the way in which consciousness works to produce immediate connections between things. The argument is pursued in a particularly abstract yet fruitful way against Husserl and phenomenology, which we have discussed earlier (Chapter 4). To recap briefly, phenomenologists argue that consciousness itself makes meaning out of phenomena. Derrida argues against this, first, by asserting that even pure thinking as developed in phenomenological reflection requires language. Husserl thought that there was some primary form of language with which consciousness talks to itself, but Derrida carefully argues that any linguistic terms must contain a reference to other people, however disguised. Kamuf (1991) cites the use of a term such as 'jealousy': this clearly implies a relation to other people, of whom one is jealous, for example, and makes no sense without such a relation.

Another illusion to be dispelled is provided by our experience of speech. When we speak, especially if we are speaking rapidly and fluently, we seem to be immediately using signs to convey what we are trying to mean. In such immediacy, *différance* seems to disappear. Further, it is common to see speech as a kind of original form of signifying, with writing as some kind of secondary and derivative activity. Derrida wants to say that it is exactly the opposite. It is not that writing actually precedes speaking chronologically, but more that writing gets closer to the processes that human beings actually use when they try to signify.

I hope that the argument is still clear, although I have expressed it naïvely, of course. What all this is leading to is a powerful critical technique commonly known as 'deconstruction'. This term has been used to describe a wide variety of critical practices, in fact, which arise whenever one wishes to begin to unpick arguments and see what they are based on, what assumptions they contain, how they use evidence, and so on. But it assumes far more philosophical weight and import bearing in mind the points we have just made. We can now look at writing as an activity that suppresses difference in some cases, and tries to manage it in others. Our task as deconstructors is to try to restore what it is that has been suppressed, and demonstrate what has been managed.

I have included, as an online reading guide, a very brief illustration of some of the superficial aspects of the technique performed by Derrida himself on Marx (Derrida 1994). This may be a misleading example in many ways, I suspect, but it seemed right for this book. In that reading guide I apologise for omitting much of the poetry and playfulness of the original, but I hope that enough remains to get some idea of what deconstruction looks like. In the first place, fixed readings of Marx are denied. There is no single authoritative reading of Marx, because Marx did not write that way. We all know that there are several major interpretations of the works, such as Althusserian, gramscian, Hegelian, liberal, even Christian versions.

You can also get some idea of Marx's specific writing technique by trying a piece of it for yourself. You might be surprised, at first, to find that much of it is not rigorous, objective academic prose at all, but contains scandalous personal attacks, sarcastic asides, rather elitist references to works in Greek and Latin, and some really evasive metaphors, especially at crucial moments. Derrida suggests that we should abandon any attempt to impose one fixed reading on this rather curious collection of pieces, some of them intended for publication, others mere notes made in the margins of library books. Instead, we should celebrate diversity in difference.

Secondly, there is a great deal of admiration for Marx's writing techniques (to revert to normal language, for a moment, and work with the existence of Marx as a concrete individual). Marx deploys these metaphors, analogies and other literary tricks very skilfully, precisely to let readers see the connections between his work and the work of others. These connections are implicit in the words and utterances themselves. To take one example, Marx's reference to communism as 'the spectre that is haunting Europe' (in the *Communist Manifesto*) is very suggestive for Derrida, enabling him to pursue an investigation of ghosts and spectres in general, and specifically in Shakespeare's *Hamlet*, to make knowing references to his own use of the 'ghost' metaphor, to reawaken the presence of ghostly meanings as a rebuke to orthodox ontology trying to fix meaning (via a rather good pun – advocating 'hauntology'), and so on. Derrida uses some of the characteristics of 'ghosts' and their social role to offer a commentary on Marx, one that restores the importance of the discussion of fetishism (Althusserians had urged us long ago to abandon this discussion regarding it as a sign of Marx's immaturity). After this very accomplished and amusing tour, Derrida's own rather banal and tame conclusion – that we can remain true to the 'spirit' of Marx while rejecting all the inconvenient and unpleasant bits – does not seem quite so bad.

However, we have seen the kind of difficulties that Derrida himself also gets into when attempting to answer the question about the social or political significance of deconstruction like this. Fraser (1989; whom we have discussed earlier, in Chapter 8, and see the online reading guide to this work) spells out the contorted and eventually rather tragic fate of a series of seminars and discussion groups trying to derive a politics from this powerful critical technique. I hope the main points will be pretty obvious by now, but perhaps I should risk repeating them one more time.

Deconstruction as an abstract critical technique can clearly be applied to anything, any text, any political tract, to *Mein Kampf* as easily as to *Capital*. Derrida can be confident in predicting that each of these texts will contain suppressed differences, as we know. Every piece of writing must, otherwise no writer could make sense at all. Some texts may be constructed more clumsily than others, and some with a much more strategic intent than others, but deconstruction does not operate with explicit criteria such as clumsiness or strategic intent, but with something much more abstract and general. Fraser tells us that some participants wanted marxism to be somehow exempt from deconstructionist critique, or to allow marxism to serve as a master text controlling deconstruction and pointing it at ideologies. Yet other participants saw this as an unwarranted act of conformity, and thought that dictatorship or 'terrorism' (in the rather genteel and scholastic sense of permitting no academic dissent) might be a consequence. Fraser herself thought that deconstruction might be an excellent scholastic technique, but that it had the effect of deferring any actual political engagement, even over the future of the very Centre where the discussions were being held.

We seem to be caught on the horns of this unpleasant dilemma again. With all the debates we have had, in this chapter and the previous one, one route leads us towards a more and more sophisticated understanding of language, but the other wants to hold back from the abstract and rather scholastic implications, and retain a right to comment upon the political and social world. One path leads to the celebration of difference and relativism, but the other concerns itself with offering a more concrete critical commentary on particular variants of speech or discourse, undertaken in the name of some genuine universal emancipatory interest. In Habermas's terms, full, unrestrained reflection leads towards scholasticism and an inability to do anything other than play academic games (which intellectuals like and tend to see as important), whereas imposing a block on this reflection in the name of political activity steers us back towards the real world, but at the expense of making intellectuals and what they do seem pretty marginal and parasitic. To paraphrase a neat and incisive remark, by Gellner (1968), do we want to analyse the word or the world?

# References

Adlam, D. (1979) 'The Case Against Capitalist Patriarchy', *m/f*, Vol. 3.

Adorno, T. (1973) *Negative Dialectics*, London: Routledge and Kegan Paul.

Adorno, T. (1976) 'Introduction', in T. Adorno, H. Albert, R. Dahrendorf, J. Habermas, H. Pilot and K. Popper, *The Positivist Dispute in German Sociology*, London: Heinemann.

Adorno, T. et al. (1976) *The Positivist Dispute in German Sociology*, London: Heinemann.

Alexander, J. (ed.) (1988) *Durkheimian Sociology: Cultural Studies*, Cambridge: Cambridge University Press.

Althusser, L. (1977) 'Ideology and Ideological State Apparatuses (Notes Towards an Investigation)', in L. Althusser, *Lenin and Philosophy and Other Essays*, London: New Left Books.

Ang, I. (1985) *Watching Dallas: Soap Opera and the Melodramatic Imagination*, London: Methuen.

Arato, A. and Gebhardt, E. (eds) (1978) *The Essential Frankfurt School Reader*, Oxford: Basil Blackwell.

Atkinson, J. and Heritage, J. (eds) (1984) *Structures of Social Action: Studies in Conversation Analysis*, Cambridge: Cambridge University Press.

Atkinson, P. (1985) *Language, Structure and Reproduction: An Introduction to the Sociology of Basil Bernstein*, London: Methuen.

Ball, J. and Goodson, I. (eds) (1985) *Teachers' Lives and Careers*, Barcombe: Falmer Press.

Barbalet, J. (1982) 'Social Closure in Class Analysis: A Critique of Parkin', *Sociology*, Vol. 16, No. 5: 484–97.

Barnes, D., Britton, J. and Rosen, H. (1971) *Language, the Learner and the School*, Harmondsworth: Penguin.

Barthes, R. (1973) *Mythologies*, London: Paladin.

Barthes, R. (1977) *Image–Music–Text*, London: Fontana/Collins.

Baudrillard, J. (1983) *Simulations*, London: Semiotext(e).

Baudrillard, J. and Lotringer, S. (1987) *Forget Foucault and Forget Baudrillard*, New York: Semiotext(e).

Beck, U. (2000) *The Brave New World of Work*, Cambridge: Polity.

Becker, H. (1963) *Outsiders*, New York: Free Press.

Becker, H., Geer, B., Hughes, E. and Strauss, A. (1961) *Boys in White: Student Culture in Medical School*, Chicago: University of Chicago Press.

Becker, H., Geer, B. and Hughes, E. (1995) [1968] *Making the Grade: The Academic Side of College Life*, with a new introduction by Howard S. Becker, New Brunswick, NJ: Transaction Publishers.

Benhabib, S. (1984) 'Epistemologies of Postmodernism: A Rejoinder to Jean-François Lyotard', *New German Critique*, Fall: 103–26.

Bennett, T. (1980) 'Popular Culture: A Teaching Object', *Screen Education*, Vol. 34: 17–30.

Bennett, T. and Woollacott, J. (1987) *Bond and Beyond: The Political Career of a Popular Hero*, London: Macmillan Education.

Bennett, T., Boyd-Bowman, S., Mercer, C. and Woollacott, J. (eds) (1981) *Popular Television and Film*, London: BFI Publishing/Open University Press.

Bentham, J. (1983) [1803] 'Essay on Nomenclature and Classification', in *Chrestomathia: The Collected Works of Jeremy Bentham*, ed. M. Smith and W. Burston, Oxford: Clarendon Press.

Benton, T. (1977) *Philosophical Foundations of the Three Sociologies*, London: Routledge and Kegan Paul.

Benton, T. (1981) 'Realism and Social Science', *Radical Philosophy*, Vol.27.

Berger, P. and Luckmann, T. (1967) *The Social Construction of Reality*, Harmondsworth: Penguin.

Bernstein, R. (ed.) (1984) *Habermas and Modernity*, Cambridge: Polity Press.

Blumer, H. (1976 [1969]) The Methodological Position of Symbolic Interactionism', in M. Hammersley and P. Woods (eds), *The Process of Schooling: A Sociological Reader*, London: Routledge and Kegan Paul.

Bottero, W. and Prandy, K. (2001) 'Interaction and Social Space: Social Distance Measures of Stratification', unpublished paper given at the BSA Annual Conference, Manchester.

Bottomore, T. and Nisbet, R. (eds) (1991) *A History of Sociological Analysis*, London: Macmillan.

Bourdieu, P. (1977) *Outline of a Theory of Practice*, Cambridge: Cambridge University Press.

Bourdieu, P. (1986) *Distinction: A Social Critique of the Judgement of Taste*, London: Routledge.

Bourdieu, P. (1988) *Homo Academicus*, Cambridge: Polity Press.

Bourdieu, P. (1993) *Sociology in Question*, London: Sage Publications.

Bourdieu, P, Accardo, A., Balzas, G., Beaud, S., Bonvin, F., Bourdieu, E., Bourgois, P., Broccholichi, S., Champagne, P., Christin, R., Faguer, J-P., Garcia, S., Lenoir, R., Œvrard, F., Pialoux, M., Pinto, L., Podalydès, D., Sayad, A., Soulié, C. and Wacquant, L. (1999) *The Weight of the World, Social Suffering in Contemporary Society*, Cambridge: Polity Press.

Bourdieu, P. (2000) *Pascalian Meditations*, Cambridge: Polity Press.

Bowles, S. and Gintis, H. (1976) *Schooling in Capitalist America*, London: Routledge and Kegan Paul.

Bowles, S. and Gintis, H. (2002 ) 'Schooling in Capitalist America Revisited', *Sociology of Education*, Vol. 75, No. 2: 1–18.

Brake, M. (ed.) (1982) *Human Sexual Relations: A Reader*, Harmondsworth: Penguin.

Braverman, H. (1974) *Labour and Monopoly Capital: The Degradation of Work in the Twentieth Century*, New York: Monthly Review Press.

Breines, W. and Cerullo, M. (1976), in *Telos*, Vol. 28.

Brice-Heath, S. (1986) 'Questioning at Home and School: A Comparative Study', in M. Hammersley (ed.) *Case Studies in Classroom Research*, Milton Keynes: Open University Press.

Brown, S. (ed.) (1979) *Philosophical Disputes in the Social Sciences*, Brighton: Harvester Press.

Bryant, C. and Jary, D. (eds) (1991) *Giddens' Theory of Structuration: A Critical Appreciation*, London: Routledge.

Bryman, A. (1995) *Disney and His Worlds*, London: Routledge.

Buchanan, I. (2000) *Michel de Certeau, Cultural Theorist*, London: Sage Publications.

Byrne, E. and McQuillan, M. (1999) *Deconstructing Disney*, London: Pluto Press.

Carr, W., and Kemmis, S. (1986) *Becoming Critical*, Lewes: Falmer Press.

Centre for Contemporary Cultural Studies (CCCS) (1978) *On Ideology*, London: Hutchinson.

Centre for Contemporary Cultural Studies (CCCS) (1982) *The Empire Strikes Back: Race and Racism in 1970s Britain*, London: Hutchinson.

Clark, B. (1960) *The Open Door College: A Case Study*, London: McGraw-Hill.

Clarke, J. and Critcher, C. (1985) *The Devil Makes Work . . . Leisure in Capitalist Britain*, London: Macmillan.

Clough, P. (1992) *The End(s) of Ethnography: From Realism to Social Criticism*, London: Sage Publications.

Colletti, L. (1975) 'Introduction', in New Left Review (eds), *Marx: Early Writings*, London: Penguin.

Collins, R. (1994) *Four Sociological Traditions*, Oxford: Oxford University Press.

Connerton, P. (ed.) (1976) *Critical Sociology*, Harmondsworth: Penguin.

Coward, R. (1977) 'Class, Culture and the Social Formation', *Screen*, Vol. 18, No. 1.

Craib, I. (1992) *Modern Social Theory: From Parsons to Habermas*, 2nd edn, Hemel Hempstead: Harvester Wheatsheaf.

Crook, S. (1991) *Modernist Radicalism and Its Aftermath*, London: Routledge.

Crook, S., Pakulski, J. and Waters, M. (1992) *Postmodernization: Change in Modern Society*, London: Sage Publications.

Crosland, A. (1980) [1965] *The Future of Socialism*, London: Jonathan Cape.

Culler, J. (1976) *Structuralist Poetics*, London: Routledge and Kegan Paul.

Dahrendorf, R. (1959) *Class and Class Conflict in Industrial Society*, London: Routledge and Kegan Paul.

Davis, K. and Moore, W. (1967) ' Some Principles of Stratification', in R. Bendix and S. Lipset (eds), *Class, Status and Power*, 2nd edn, London: Routledge and Kegan Paul.

de Certeau, M. (1988) *The Practice of Everyday Life*, Berkeley: University of California Press.

Derrida, J. (1994) *Specters of Marx*, London: Routledge.

Dews, P. (ed.) (1992) *Autonomy and Solidarity: Interviews with Jürgen Habermas*, London: Verso.

Downes, D. and Rock, P. (eds) (1979) *Deviant Interpretations: Problems in Criminological Theory*, Oxford: Oxford University Press.

Downes, D. and Rock, P. (1988) *Understanding Deviance*, 2nd edn, Oxford: Clarendon Press.

Dreyfus, H. and Rabinow, P. (1982) *Michel Foucault: Beyond Structuralism and Hermeneutics*, Brighton: Harvester Press.

Dunning, E. (1990) 'Sociological Reflections on Sport, Violence and Civilization', *International Review for the Sociology of Sport*, Vol. 25, No. 1: 65–83.

Dunning, E., Murphy, P. and Williams, J. (1986) 'Spectator Violence at Football Matches: Towards a Sociological Explanation', *British Journal of Sociology*, Vol. 37, No. 2: 221–44.

Durkheim, E. (1951) [1897] *Suicide. A Study in Sociology*, Glencoe, Ill.: Free Press.

Durkheim, E. (1964) *The Rules of Sociological Method*, 2nd edn, London: Collier-Macmillan.

Eco, U. (1982) 'The Role of the Reader', in B. Waites, T. Bennett and G. Martin (eds), *Popular Culture, Past and Present*, London: Croom Helm/Open University Press.

Eco, U. (1987) *Travels in Hyperreality*, London: Picador.

Elias, N. (1978) *The Civilising Process, Volume 1: The History of Manners*, Oxford: Basil Blackwell.

Entwistle, N. and Ramsden, P. (1983) *Understanding Student Learning*, London: Croom Helm.

Fay, B. (1975) *Social Theory and Political Practice*, London: Allen and Unwin.

Fisher, B. and Strauss, A. (1991) 'Interactionism', in T. Bottomore and R. Nisbet (eds), *A History of Sociological Analysis*, London: Macmillan.

Fiske, J. (1989) *Reading the Popular*, London: Unwin Hyman.

Fletcher, R. (1966) *The Family and Marriage in Modern Britain*, Harmondsworth: Pelican Books.

Foucault, M. (1974) *The Archaeology of Knowledge*, London: Tavistock Publications.

Foucault, M. (1977) *Discipline and Punish: The Birth of the Prison*, London: Peregrine Books.

Fraser, N. (1989) *Unruly Practices: Power, Discourse and Gender in Contemporary Social Theory*, Cambridge: Polity Press.

Gane, M. (ed.) (1992) *The Radical Sociology of Durkheim and Mauss*, London: Routledge.

Garfinkel, H. (1967) *Studies in Ethnomethodology*, Englewood Cliffs, NJ: Prentice Hall.

Gee, H. (2000) *Deep Time: Cladistics, the Revolution in Evolution*, London: Fourth Estate.

Gellner, E. (1968) *Words and Things*, Harmondsworth: Penguin.

Giddens, A. (1974) *The Class Structure of the Advanced Societies*, London: Hutchinson University Press.

Giddens, A. (1976) *New Rules of Sociological Method*, London: Hutchinson University Press.

Giddens, A. (1979) *Central Problems in Social Theory: Action, Structure and Contradiction in Social Analysis*, London: Macmillan.

Giddens, A. (1982) *Profiles and Critiques in Social Theory*, London: Macmillan.

Giddens, A. (1984) *The Constitution of Society*, Cambridge: Polity Press.

Giddens, A. (1991) *Modernity and Self-Identity: Self and Society in the Late Modern Age*, Cambridge: Polity Press.

Giddens, A. (1996) *In Defence of Sociology: Essays, Interpretations and Rejoinders*, Cambridge: Polity Press.

Giddens, A. (1998) *The Third Way: The Renewal of Social Democracy*, Cambridge: Polity Press.

Giddens, A. and Held, D. (eds) (1982) *Classes, Power, and Conflict: Classical and Contemporary Debates*, London: Macmillan.

Giddens, A. and Turner, J. (eds) (1987) *Social Theory Today*, Cambridge: Polity Press.

Gintis, H. and Bowles, S. (1980) 'Contradiction and Reproduction in Educational Theory', in L. Barton (ed.), *School, Ideology and the Curriculum*, Barcombe: Falmer Press.

Giroux, H. (1992) *Border Crossings: Cultural Workers and the Politics of Education*, New York: Routledge.

Gledhill, C. (ed.) (1987) *Home Is Where the Heart Is*, London: BFI Publishing.

Goffman, E. (1968) *Asylums: Essays on the Social Situation of Mental Patients and Other Inmates*, London: Pelican.

Goffman, E. (1969) *The Presentation of Self in Everyday Life*, Harmondsworth: Penguin.

Goldthorpe, J., Llewellyn, C. and Payne, C. (1980) *Social Mobility and Class Structure in Modern Britain*, Oxford: Clarendon Press.

Gould, S. (1990) *Wonderful Life: The Burgess Shale and the Nature of History*, London: Hutchinson Radius.

Gouldner, A. (1971) *The Coming Crisis of Western Sociology*, London: Heinemann Educational Books.

Gouldner, A. (1979) *The Future of Intellectuals and the Rise of a New Class*, London: Macmillan.

Habermas, J. (1972) 'A Postscript to Knowledge and Human Interests', *Philosophy of the Social Sciences*, September; also in *Knowledge and Human Interests*, 2nd edn, London: Heinemann.

Habermas, J. (1976) *Legitimation Crisis*, London: Heinemann Educational Books.

Habermas, J. (1981) 'Modernity versus Postmodernity', *New German Critique*, Vol. 22: 3–14.

Habermas, J. (1984) *The Theory of Communicative Action, Volume 1: Reason and the Rationalisation of Society*, London: Heinemann.

Hall, D. (1994) *Richard Rorty: Prophet and Poet of the New Pragmatism*, New York: SUNY Press.

Hall, S. (1977) 'Culture, the Media and the "Ideology-Effect"', in J. Curran, M. Gurevitch and J. Wollacott (eds), *Mass Communication and Society*, London: Edward Arnold/Open University Press.

Hall, S. and Jacques, M. (eds) (1983) *The Politics of Thatcherism*, London: Lawrence and Wishart/*Marxism Today*.

Hall, S. and Jefferson, T. (eds) (1976) *Resistance Through Rituals*, London: Hutchinson.

Hall, S., Critcher, C., Jefferson, T., Clarke, J. and Roberts, B. (1978) *Policing the Crisis: Mugging, the State and Law and Order*, London: Macmillan.

Hall, S., Hobson, D., Lowe, A. and Willis, P (eds) (1980) *Culture, Media and Language*, London: Hutchinson.

Halsey, A., Heath, A. and Ridge, J. (1980) *Origins and Destinations: Family, Class and Education in Modern Britain*, Oxford: Clarendon Press.

Hammersley, M. (ed.) (1986) *Case Studies in Classroom Research*, Milton Keynes: Open University Press.

Hammersley, M. and Woods, P. (eds) (1976) *The Process of Schooling: A Sociological Reader*, London: Routledge and Kegan Paul.

Haraszti, M. (1977) *A Worker in a Worker's State*, London: Pelican Books.

Haraway, D. (1991) 'A Cyborg Manifesto: Science, Technology, and Socialist-Feminism in the Late Twentieth Century', in D. Haraway *Simians, Cyborgs and Women: The Reinvention of Nature*, New York: Routledge.

Hargreaves, J. (1986) *Sport, Power and Culture*, Cambridge: Polity Press.

Harris, D. (1987) *Openness and Closure in Distance Education*, Barcombe: Falmer Press.

Harris, D. (1992) *From Class Struggle to the Politics of Pleasure: The Effects of Gramscianism on Cultural Studies*, London: Routledge.

Harris, D. (1993) '"Effective teaching" and "study skills": the return of the technical fix?', in T. Evans and D. Murphy (eds) *Research in Distance Education*, Vol. 3, Geelong: Deakin University Press.

Harris, D. (1996) *A Society of Signs?*, London: Routledge.

Harris, D. (2002) *Dave Harris (and Colleagues): Essays, Papers and Courses*, [online] http://www.arasite.org/

Hebdige, D. (1988) *Hiding in the Light*, London: Comedia/Routledge.

Henderson, E. and Nathenson, M. (eds) (1984) *Independent Learning in Higher Education*, Englewood Cliffs NJ: Educational Technology Publications Inc.

Hindess, B. (1977) *Philosophy and Methodology of the Social Sciences*, Hassocks: Harvester Press.

Honneth, A. (1985) 'An Aversion Against the Universal: A Commentary on Lyotard's *Postmodern Condition*', *Theory, Culture and Society*, Vol. 2, No.3: 147–56.

Hopper, E. (1971) 'Notes on stratification, education and mobility in industrial societies', in E. Hopper (ed.), *Readings in the Theory of Educational Systems*, London: Hutchinson University Library.

Hopper, E. (1981) *Social Mobility: A Study of Social Control and Insatiability*, Oxford: Basil Blackwell.

Horkheimer, M. and Adorno, T. (1979) [1944] *Dialectic of Enlightenment*, London: Verso.

Horowitz, I. (ed.) (1967) *Power, Politics and People: The Collected Essays of C. Wright Mills*, Oxford: Oxford University Press.

Husserl, E. (1973) [1950] *Cartesian Meditations: An Introduction to Phenomenology*, The Hague: Martinus Nijhoff.

Humm, M. (ed.) (1992) *Feminisms: A Reader*, Hemel Hempstead: Harvester Wheatsheaf.

Hutton, W. (1995) *The State We're In*, London: Jonathan Cape.

Jameson, F. (1991) *Postmodernism, or the Cultural Logic of Late Capitalism*, London: Verso.

Johnson, R. (1981) 'Really Useful Knowledge: Radical Education and Working-Class Culture 1790–1848', in R. Dale, G. Esland, R. Ferguson and M. MacDonald (eds), *Politics, Patriarchy and Practice: Education and the State*, Vol. 2, Basingstoke: Falmer/Open University Press.

Kamuf, P. (ed.) (1991) *A Derrida Reader: Between the Blinds*, New York and London: Harvester Wheatsheaf.

Kuhn, T. (1962) *The Structure of Scientific Revolutions*, Chicago: University of Chicago Press.

Lakatos, I. (1979) 'Falsification and the Methodology of Scientific Research Programmes', in I. Lakatos and F. Musgrave (eds), *Criticism and the Growth of Knowledge*, Cambridge: Cambridge University Press.

Lash, S. (1990) *The Sociology of Postmodernism*, London: Routledge.

Lawn, M. and Ozga, J. (1988) 'The Educational Worker? A Reassessment of Teachers', in J. Ozga. (ed.), *Schoolwork Approaches to the Labour Process of Teaching*, Milton Keynes: Open University Press.

Leach, E. (1969) *Genesis as Myth and Other Essays*, London: Cape Editions.

Leach, E. (1970) *Lévi-Strauss*, London: Fontana Modern Masters.

Lechte, J. (1994) *Fifty Key Contemporary Thinkers: From Structuralism to Postmodernity*, London: Routledge.

Lévi-Strauss, C. (1977) [1944–57] *Structural Anthropology*, Vol. 1, London: Peregrine Books.

Lockwood, D. (1992) *Solidarity and Schism: 'The Problem of Disorder' in Durkheimian and Marxist Sociology*, Oxford: Clarendon Press.

Lomax, H. and Casey, N. (1998) 'Recording Social Life: Reflexivity and Video Methodology', *Sociological Research Online*, Vol. 3, No. 2 [online] http://www.socresonline.org.uk/socresonline/3/2/1.html

Lukes, S. (1975) *Émile Durkheim, His Life and Work: A Historical and Critical Study*, Harmondsworth: Penguin.

Lyotard, J. F. (1984) *The Postmodern Condition: A Report on Knowledge*, Manchester: Manchester University Press.

McCarthy, T. (1984) *The Critical Theory of Jürgen Habermas*, Cambridge: Polity Press.

Macey, D. (1980) 'Review Article: Jacques Lacan', *Ideology and Consciousness*, Vol. 4: 113–128.

McLellan, D. (1973) *Karl Marx: His Life and Thought*, London: Macmillan.

Manis, J. and Meltzer, B. (eds) (1972) *Symbolic Interaction: A Reader in Social Psychology*, 2nd edn, Boston: Allyn and Bacon, Inc.

Manning, P. (1989) 'Ritual Talk', *Sociology*, Vol. 23, No. 3: 365–85.

Marcuse, H. (1968) *One-Dimensional Man*, London: Sphere Books.

Marcuse, H. (1972) *Negations*, Harmondsworth: Penguin.

Marin, L. (1977) 'Disneyland: A Degenerative Utopia', *Glyph*, Vol. 1, No. 1: 50–66.

Marx, K. (1968) [1888] 'Theses on Feuerbach', in K. Marx and F. Engels, *Selected Works*, London: Lawrence and Wishart.

Marx, K. (1977a) [1843] 'On the Jewish Question', in K. Marx and F. Engels, *Collected Works*, Vol. 3, London: Lawrence and Wishart.

Marx, K. (1977b) [1857–61] *Grundrisse*, London: Pelican Books.

Marx, K. (1977c) [1861–3] 'Theories of Surplus Value: Revenue and Its Sources', in K. Marx and F. Engels, *Collected Works*, Vol. 32, London: Lawrence and Wishart.

Marx, K. (1977d) [1867] *Capital*, Vol. 1, London: Lawrence and Wishart.

Marx, K. and Engels, F. (1970) [1845–6] *The German Ideology, students' edition*, London: Lawrence and Wishart.

Marx, K. and Engels, F. (1977) [1848] 'Manifesto of the Communist Party', in K. Marx and F. Engels, *Collected Works*, Vol. 6, London: Lawrence and Wishart.

May, T. (1996) *Situating Social Theory*, Buckingham: Open University Press.

Mennell, S. (1985) *All Manners of Food*, Oxford: Basil Blackwell.

Mennell, S. (1992) *Norbert Elias: An Introduction*, Oxford: Basil Blackwell.

Merck, M. (1987) 'Difference and its Discontents', *Screen*, Vol. 28, No. 1: 1–9.

Merton, R. (1968) *Social Theory and Social Structure*, New York: Free Press.

Morgan, A. (1993) *Improving Your Students' Learning: Reflections on the Experience of Study*, London: Kogan Page.

Mulvey, L. (1975) 'Visual Pleasure and Narrative Cinema', *Screen*, Vol. 16, No. 3.

Mulvey, L. (1999) [1981] 'Afterthoughts on *Visual Pleasure and Narrative Cinema* Inspired by King Vidor's *Duel in the Sun* (1946)', in S. Thornham (ed), *Feminist Film Theory: A Reader*, Edinburgh: Edinburgh University Press: 121–9.

Murphy, R. (1986) 'Weberian Closure Theory', *British Journal of Sociology*, Vol. 37, No. 1.

Nava, M. (1991) 'Consumerism Reconsidered: Buying and Power', *Cultural Studies*, Vol. 5, No. 2: 157–74.

Nichols, T. (ed.) (1980) *Capital and Labour: A Marxist Primer*, Glasgow: Fontana Paperbacks.

Nicholson, L. (ed.) (1990) *Feminism/Post-modernism*, New York: Routledge.

Norris, C. (1992) *Uncritical Theory: Postmodernism, Intellectuals and the Gulf War*, London: Lawrence and Wishart.

Offe, C. (1984) *Contradictions of the Welfare State*, London: Hutchinson.

Open University (1982) *Popular Culture (U203)*, Milton Keynes: Open University Press.

Open University (1988) *Educational Organizations and Professionals (E814)*, Milton Keynes: Open University Press.

Pakulski, J. and Waters, M. (1996) 'The Reshaping and Dissolution of Class in Advanced Society', *Theory and Society*, Vol. 25, No. 5: 667–91.

Parkin, F. (1979) *Marxism and Class Theory: A Bourgeois Critique*, London: Tavistock Publications.

Parsons, T. (1961) 'The School as a Social System', in A. Halsey, J. Floud and R. Anderson, (eds), *Education, Economy and Society*, Glencoe, Ill: Free Press.

Pask, G. (1976) 'Styles and Strategies of Learning', *British Journal of Educational Psychology*, Vol. 46: 128–48.

Pinch, T. and Clark, C. (1986) 'The Hard Sell: "Patter Merchanting" and the Strategic (Re-) Production and Local Management of Economic Reasoning in the Sales Routines of Market Pitchers', *Sociology*, Vol. 20: 169–91.

Plant, S. (1992) *The Most Radical Gesture: The Situationist International in a Postmodern Age*, London: Routledge.

Plummer, G. (2000) *Failing Working-Class Girls*, Stoke on Trent: Trentham Books Limited.

Poulantzas, N. (1975) *Classes in Contemporary Capitalism*, London: New Left Books.

Ramazanoğlu, C. (ed.) (1993) *Up Against Foucault: Explorations of Some Tensions between Foucault and Feminism*, London: Routledge.

Ramsden, P. (ed.) (1988) *Improving Learning: New Perspectives*, London: Kogan Page.

Rex, J. (1961) *Key Problems of Sociological Theory*, London: Routledge and Kegan Paul.

Rex, J. (1970) *Race Relations in Sociological Theory*, London: Weidenfeld and Nicolson.

Ritzer, G. (1993) *The McDonaldization of Society*, Thousand Oaks, CA: Pine Forge.

Ritzer, G. (1994) *Sociological Beginnings: On the Origins of Key Ideas in Sociology*, New York: McGraw-Hill.

Ritzer, G. (1996) *Sociological Theory*, 4th edn, Singapore: McGraw-Hill.

Ritzer, G. (2001) *Explorations in Social Theory: From Metatheorizing to Rationalization*, London: Sage Publications Ltd.

Rocher, G. (1974) *Talcott Parsons and American Sociology*, Ontario: Nelson.

Rojek, C. (1986) 'Problems of Involvement and Detachment in the Writings of Norbert Elias', *British Journal of Sociology*, Vol. 37, No.4: 584–96.

Sayer, D. (1991) *Capitalism and Modernity: An Excursus on Marx and Weber*, London: Routledge.

Schütz, A. (1972) *The Phenomenology of the Social World*, London: Heinemann Educational Books.

Scott, K. (1998) 'Girls Need Modems! Cyberculture and Women's Ezines', Master's

Research Paper, Women's Studies, York University, submitted 30 January, [online] www.library.wisc.edu/libraries/WomensStudies/mags.htm, accessed 15 January 2002.

Sivanandan, A. (1990) *Communities of Resistance: Writings on Black Struggles for Socialism*, London: Verso.

Smart, B. (1993) *Postmodernity*, London: Routledge.

Soros, G. (1997) 'The Novelty of the Finance Market', *Guardian*, 18 January.

Stacey, J. (1987) 'Desperately Seeking Difference', *Screen*, Vol. 28, No. 1: 48–61.

Sztompka, P. (1986) *Robert K. Merton: An Intellectual Profile*, London: Macmillan.

Taylor, I., Walton, P. and Young J. (eds) (1975) *Critical Criminology*, London: Routledge and Kegan Paul.

Thompson, G. and Held, D. (eds) (1982) *Habermas: Critical Debates*, London: Macmillan.

Turkle, S. (1995) *Life on the Screen: Identity in the Age of the Internet*. New York: Simon and Schuster.

Turner , B. (1981) *For Weber: Essays on the Sociology of Fate*, London: Routledge and Kegan Paul.

Turner, B. (1992) 'Weber, Giddens and Modernity', *Theory, Culture and Society*, Vol. 9, No. 2: 141–75.

Turner, B. (ed.) (1996) *The Blackwell Companion to Social Theory*, Oxford: Basil Blackwell.

Van Krieken, R. (1999) 'The Barbarism of Civilisation: Cultural Genocide and the "Stolen Generation"', *British Journal of Sociology*, Vol. 50, No. 2: 297–315.

Walby, S. (1990) *Theorizing Patriarchy*, Oxford: Basil Blackwell.

Walker, M. (1997) *Guardian Weekend*, 7 December.

Waters, M. (1994) *Modern Sociological Theory*, London: Sage Publications Ltd.

Westoby, A. (ed.) (1988) *Culture and Power in Educational Organizations*, Milton Keynes: Open University Press.

Williams, C. (1994) 'After the Classic, the Classical and Ideology: The Differences of Realism', *Screen*, Vol. 35, No. 3: 275–92.

Williamson, D. (1987) 'Language and Sexual Difference', *Screen*, Vol. 28: 10–25.

Willis, P. (1977) *Learning to Labour: How Working Class Kids Get Working Class Jobs*, Farnborough: Saxon House.

Willis, P. (1978) *Profane Cultures*, London: Routledge and Kegan Paul.

Winch, P. (1958) *The Idea of a Social Science and Its Relation to Philosophy*, London: Routledge and Kegan Paul.

Women's Study Group (1978) *Women Take Issue*, London: Hutchinson.

Woods, P. and Hammersley, M. (eds) (1993) *Gender and Ethnicity in Schools: Ethnographic Accounts*, London and New York: Routledge/Open University.

Young, M. (ed.) (1971) *Knowledge and Control: New directions in the Sociology of Knowledge*, London: Collier Macmillan.

# Index

423x25